THE SETTLEMENT OF THE AMERICAS

A New Prehistory

THOMAS D. DILLEHAY

BASIC
BOOKS

A Member of the Perseus Books Group

Copyright © 2000 by Thomas D. Dillehay

Published by Basic Books,
A Member of the Perseus Books Group

A CIP catalog record for this book is available from the Library of Congress.
ISBN 0-465-07668-8

Designed by Rachel Hegarty

FIRST EDITION

00 01 02 03 / 10 9 8 7 6 5 4 3 2 1

CONTENTS

FIGURES AND PHOTOS

ACKNOWLEDGMENTS

I could not have written this volume without the extremely generous support of many colleagues in Latin America. Since 1976, when I first began archaeological research at the Monte Verde site in Chile, I have traveled extensively throughout Latin America. Much of this travel has related to residency in several countries to field research, visiting professorships at national universities, to participation in professional meetings, and to invited lectures. As a result, I have had the opportunity to discuss the late Pleistocene archaeological record with regional experts, to visit many early sites in most Latin American countries, and to inspect firsthand the archaeological collections from these sites. I am most grateful to Gerado Ardila, Gonzalo Correal, Carlos López, Thomas van der Hammen, and others in Colombia; Erika Wagner and Arturo Jaimes in Venezuela; Ernesto Salazar, Olaf Holmes, Presley Norton, Patricia Netherly, and Matilde Temme in Ecuador; Jesus Briceño, Cesar Galvez, Augusto Cardich, Peter Kaulicke, Thomas Lynch, John Rick, Ramiro Matos, and Roger Ravines in Peru; Julio Montané, Calogero Santoro, Lautaro Núñez, Mario Pino, Juan Varela, Rubén Stehberg, Donald Jackson, Carlos Ocampo, Pilar Rivas, Mauricio Massone, Afredo Prieto, Américo Gordon, Fransisco Mena, and Mateo Martinic in Chile; Alberto Rex González, Gustavo Politis, Hugo Nami, Hugo Yaccabacio, Augusto Cardich, Luis Borrero, Juan Schobinger, and Nora Flegenheimer in Argentina; Tomás Valenzuela in Paraguay; José López, José Iriarte, and Arturo Toscano in Uruguay; Niède Guidón, Maria Beltrão, and Renato Kipnis in Brazil; and Richard Cooke in Panama.

I am grateful for discussions about the peopling of the Americas with all of the above colleagues, as well as with Alan Bryan, Ruth Gruhn, Michael Collins, David Meltzer, Dennis Stanford, Peter Kaulicke, Robson Bonnichsen, C. Vance Haynes, Donald Grayson, Thomas Lynch, James Richardson, John Rick, Claude Chauchat, Danièlle Lavallée, and many others.

I am much indebted to William Frucht of Basic Books for inviting me to write this book. He made numerous valuable suggestions that clarified my thoughts and improved the text. I thank David Toole for copyediting the manuscript. I also thank David Meltzer, Jack Rossen, James Dixon, Gerardo Ardila, Renato Kipnis, Patricia Netherly, Santiago Giraldo, Luis Borrero, Debra Crooks, and Vera Markgraf for reading and commenting on various chapters. Professor Dana Nelson deserves special mention for her unrelenting support, for inspiring me, and for providing valuable editorial comments. I also thank the numerous colleagues who provided me with unpublished and published radiocarbon dates from various sites. The radiocarbon table that makes up the appendix is not intended as a complete listing of all dates from late Pleistocene sites because a few colleagues never responded.

Also helpful throughout the past twenty-eight years of my travels through Latin America and my research on the first South Americans were my graduate student research assistants, including Jack Rossen, John Warner, Cecelia Manosa, José Iriarte, John Calabrese, and Jeffrey Stvan. Jeffrey Stvan, in particular, was very patient and cooperative in researching site locations and in producing the maps. I thank Dennis Stanford for Photo IB.

This study is in effect part of a wider and ongoing effort to contribute to our understanding of the peopling of the Americas, an endeavor that would have been much harder without the support of several institutions. I thank the Fulbright Commission, the National Science Foundation, and the National Geographic Society for funding various aspects of my research. I also am grateful to several academic and research institutions for similar support: the University of Kentucky; University of Illinois at Champaign–Urbana; Cambridge University; University of Chicago; Smithsonian Institution; Universidad Nacional de Los Andes, Bogotá, Colombia; Universidad Nacional de San Marcos, Lima, Peru; Universidad de Chile, Santiago; Universidad Pontifícia Católica, Santiago and Temuco; Universidad Austral de Chile, Valdivia; Universidad de Catamarca, Argentina; and the Universidad Nacional de Uruguay, Montevideo.

PREFACE

For most of the last 3 million years, people lived exclusively in the Old World. No evidence of humans—such as *Homo erectus* and Neanderthals—has ever been found in the New World. About 50,000 years ago, however, people began to immigrate into new and distant environments, including Australia and, later, the Americas. What were these people like, how did they get to the Americas, and what did they do once they arrived?

Many books have been written about the archaeology of the first North Americans and the processes that led to their arrival and dispersion throughout the Americas. No such book exists for South America. Yet, the early archaeological history of South America is different from that of North America and requires separate attention. Careful examination of the Pleistocene archaeology of South America gives us an entirely new picture of the settlement of the Americas.

The Southern Hemisphere supplies some of the earliest sites in the Americas, sites that exhibit the persistence of Pleistocene megafauna into the early Holocene. In fact, most of the important new early sites have been found in South America, and more are being discovered at an unprecedented rate. During the 1970s and 1980s, sites in Colombia, Chile, Brazil, and Argentina yielded so many important finds that it will take years to give them the thorough analysis that is now devoted to such collections. But it is not simply the number of South American finds that is significant and exciting but also the nature of the artifacts and their age. Archaeologists have found not only spearpoints for hunting but simpler stone and bone tools for gathering plants and shellfish. It is now apparent that humans were in the Americas much earlier than we previously thought and that for much of that time the first Americans were not just big-game hunters but plant-food gatherers as well. We are also realizing that the first immigrants probably came from several different places in the Old World and that their genetic heritage and physical appearance were much more diverse than we thought.

Because many South American archaeologists did not see the North American Clovis theory as applicable to the Southern Hemisphere, they developed different and exciting ideas about the peopling of the Americas that are largely unknown in the English-speaking world. Theories in archaeology are often constructed from little data, and constantly we run the risk of overinterpretation and, therefore, biased conclusions. This weakness of the discipline sometimes causes important discoveries to be ignored. Such, for many years, has been the fate of several South American sites that contained evidence of non-Clovis cultures. Only in recent years have North American archaeologists looked seriously beyond North America to study the origins of the first Americans.

I became involved in the study of the first Americans in 1976, after a student at the Southern University of Chile, where I was teaching and doing archaeological research, discovered a large mastodon tooth and other bones at the archaeological site of Monte Verde and brought them to the university museum. They turned out to have curious markings on their surface that might have been natural scratches produced by animals trampling old bones or cutmarks made by humans when they removed the meat. In 1977, in an at-

tempt to determine the origin of the marks, I conducted limited excavations at the site. We studied its geological context and searched
for convincing evidence of human activity. The excavation was successful: We found mastodon bones with probable cutmarks, clay-
lined hearths that contained charcoal and burned plant foods, and
genuine human-made stone tools—all buried in the same thin geological layer under a muddy bog. Because of the mastodon bones,
I thought Monte Verde probably dated in the late Ice Age, sometime between 11,000 and 10,000 years ago.

My colleagues and I were startled, however, when radiocarbon
tests on the bone, charcoal from firepits, and wooden artifacts consistently yielded dates of more than 12,000 years ago. These dates
were simply impossible. As a graduate student, I had been trained
to believe (and never seriously question) that the first culture in
the New World was the Clovis culture, that these people had come
to North America no earlier than 11,200 years ago and to South
America perhaps 11,000 to 10,500 years ago. How could people
have reached Monte Verde in southern Chile some 1,300 years
earlier? The site chronology must be wrong, or the site must have
been disturbed by erosion or flooding that left artifacts of different ages mixed together. Besides, there were none of the massive
spear points that distinguished the Clovis culture.

Here was an intriguing mystery. Over the next ten years, I di-
rected a research team of more than eighty professionals who col-
lectively excavated a wide variety of wooden, bone, and stone
tools, as well as scraps of animal hide and chunks of meat, human
footprints, hearths, and thousands of fragments of edible and
medicinal plants, all patterned in and around the remains of
wooden hut foundations in Monte Verde. Additional radiocarbon
dates and excavations proved conclusively that the site was a valid

human locality, and that it was at least 12,500 years old. Monte Verde forced me and my colleagues to revise what we thought we knew about early South American cultures and about the peopling of the Americas.

For nearly seventy years, since those characteristic spear points were first discovered near Clovis, New Mexico, in 1932, our knowledge had revolved around the Clovis people. Their culture is best known for its kill sites, where the bone remains of extinct large animals are found alongside stone spearpoints skillfully chipped on both sides to give a leaf-shaped, fluted appearance (Photo I.A). These spearpoints are distributed throughout much of the Northern Hemisphere and into Central America, and perhaps even farther south, giving the impression of a highly uniform, big-game hunting culture that diffused rapidly throughout the Americas. In fact, among many North American archaeologists for more than half a century, Clovis technology became the icon of the migration of early American culture—the first great American invention, the Ice Age equivalent of the spread of Coca-Cola or baseball caps.

Because Clovis represented one of the most deeply entrenched archaeological theories in the New World, we knew we would have a difficult time explaining the age and type of artifacts at Monte Verde before stringent Clovis loyalists who had spent their entire careers defending the theory against one pre-Clovis candidate after another. Our excavations were slow and tedious. The research team spent ten years excavating and ten years analyzing and publishing the vast amount of archaeological material retrieved from the site.[1] The evidence was clear: People lived at Monte Verde around 12,500 years ago, and they practiced a generalized hunting and gathering lifeway, not just big-game hunting. The archaeological remains of this age not only included stone tools, bones of extinct animals, and firepits

Fluted Clovis point. (Courtesy of William S. Webb Museum of Anthropology, University of Kentucky.)

5 cm

but also well preserved perishable materials such as wooden tools, plant foods, and pieces of animal hide and meat. The site had been preserved by an overlying wet peat lens that protected the artifacts from decay by forming an airtight seal over them. The spatial layout of these remains suggested the remnants of a long tent, formed by foundation timbers and a pole frame covered by hides. The artifacts and firepits were scattered on the buried ground in and around the structure. The artifact assemblage is what we would expect of a well-preserved late Pleistocene hunter and gatherer campsite.

In spite of the clarity of the evidence, during our twenty years of excavation and analysis many archaeologists were reluctant to accept the age of the site and the broader implications of the artifacts we found there, since Monte Verde contradicted not only the Clovis model but also more general assumptions about late Pleistocene archaeology in the New World. Die-hard proponents of the Clovis-first model criticized the site, claiming that the radiocarbon dates must be wrong because they predate the 11,200-year-old Clovis culture. They argued further that the mixed artifact assemblage, unlike anything found to date in the Northern Hemisphere, must have been formed by floods washing out and commingling materials from several younger sites located upstream from Monte Verde, and that when we excavated the site in the late 1970s and 1980s, we failed to detect the alleged disturbed cultural deposits. Some people have also cast doubts on the integrity of Monte Verde by arguing that the long, complex interdisciplinary study of the information retrieved from the site was not done properly.

Unfortunately, none of the Monte Verde critics have had experience in designing long-term, interdisciplinary field research at wet, early archaeological sites. They are unaware of the kinds of excavation difficulties (such as on-site conservation of recovered organic remains) and of the types of materials associated with wet sites that often make it necessary to shift excavation and analytical strategies. Instead, they are accustomed to finding stones and, if they are lucky, bones in dry sites and interpreting them as the remains of specialized big-game hunters. These critics have a long history of rejecting any site that counters the Clovis-first model. In their haste to defend the Clovis model, they fantasize floods and other natural events to explain the association of the different cultural traits often found at non-Clovis sites, or, worse, they invent mistakes in the analysis of these sites to give cause for dismissing them. What all this boils down to is the politics of science and the replacement of one paradigm by another.

In 1997, a special group of archaeologists, including many who were initially skeptical of the findings and the radiocarbon dates,

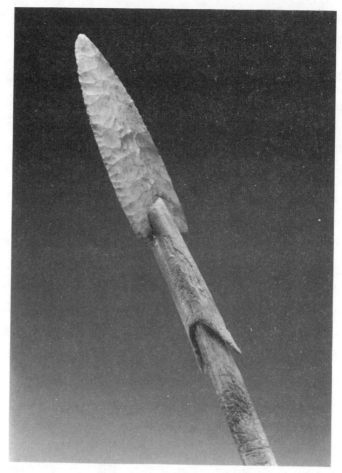

Clovis point with the flute socketed in the bone foreshaft of a spear. (Courtesy of Dennis Stanford, Department of Anthropology, National Museum of Natural History, Smithsonian Institution.)

viewed the site and human artifacts and decided that Monte Verde is a legitimate pre-Clovis site. Since this inspection, other sites that seem to date from pre-Clovis times have been taken more seriously, including Meadowcroft Shelter in Pennsylvania, the Cactus Hill site in Virginia, the Topper and other sites in South

Carolina, the Piedra Museo site in Argentina, and several sites in eastern Brazil. These and other potential pre-Clovis sites in eastern Brazil have effectively convinced the scientific community of a pre-Clovis occupation in the Americas. As a result of these fresh finds and new ideas, a more realistic view of the first human settlement of the Americas is beginning to emerge.

Parts of this book were written for the two-volume work on Monte Verde that I wrote a few years ago, but in the end I left this material out because I wanted those books to focus mainly on the site itself. While I was working on the Monte Verde findings and on other research projects in South America, I traveled extensively throughout the Americas, especially Latin America, visiting early sites, studying artifact collections, talking with colleagues about the peopling of the New World. This book is in part the result of those travels and conversations. Unlike the two-volume work on Monte Verde itself, my aim here is to tell the story not only of the peopling process but also of the difficulties of studying the early archaeological record, though clearly what I have to say is not the final word on either topic.

I have learned over the past twenty-eight years that the integrity or intactness of the archaeological record is extremely important. Equally important is the way we archaeologists read or misread, observe or fail to observe, the record as a result of biases ingrained in our thinking. My own feelings about these biases will become clear as I discuss controversies in the archaeology of the first Americans. I do not wish to leave the impression that the discipline is overwhelmed with difficulties. Searching for the first humans on any continent is a difficult but exciting and rewarding task.

I have written with specialists as well as interested students and laypersons in mind. Because this is the first book in any language on the recent archaeological findings of the first South Americans, I have tried to avoid technical terms, and when I use them, I explain them, where possible, on their first appearance. For the layperson and student not familiar with the technicalities of archaeology, I have provided a glossary. I have also included a table of the radiocarbon dates from most sites discussed in the text.

The traditions and theories of the discipline have influenced the way we do late Pleistocene archaeology, which is to say that they have established the way we archaeologists construct our conflicting interpretations of the past. Of course, these interpretations are based on archaeological evidence, and I will present as much of this evidence as possible. Readers who feel that this evidence is often too fragmentary to warrant the interpretations that are based upon it will be absolutely right. In part this gap between the evidence and the interpretation is simply the result of a book of this nature; I cannot mention every scrap of evidence that has been discovered and discuss its fullest implications. But even if I could, one would realize that interpretations do not always follow from the data of a specific archaeological site. Our interpretations are drawn both from single sites dated to a specific time and from broad geographical regions and an equally broad chronological expanse. In the end, the focus is upon the history of human migration throughout the entire Western Hemisphere. I will thus tell the story of the first South Americans as a continuous narrative of the cultural developments of a single people. After the first human population entered the New World, hundreds of local and regional migrations of small, splintering populations surely took place over several millennia, but for the most part it is the broader movements across both North and South America that are important.

CHAPTER ONE

Setting the Stage

Whence have they come? Have they remained in the same state since the creation of the world? What could have tempted, or what change compelled, a tribe of men to leave the fine regions of the north . . . to enter on one of the most inhospitable countries within the limits of the globe? Such and many other reflections must occupy the mind of every one who views one of these poor savages.

—CHARLES DARWIN, ON THE PEOPLE OF TIERRA DEL FUEGO,
The Voyage of the Beagle

SOMETIME AFTER THE EMERGENCE OF *Homo sapiens* in the Old World, the forebears of Native Americans entered the previously uninhabited New World, eventually making their way southward to the cold, barren landscape of Tierra del Fuego—one of the last places on earth reached by prehistoric humans. When did this happen? What kind of people were they, and where did they come from? For decades, archaeologists felt sure they knew the answers: The first Americans were skilled hunters and toolmakers who arrived from northeast Asia around 11,200 B.P., moved rapidly through the Western Hemisphere, and within a few centuries had traversed the New World, while driving to extinction such big-game animals as ground sloths, mammoths, mastodons, camels, and native horses.[1] These migrating big-game hunters are known in scientific circles as the Clovis people, and the archaeological signatures they left behind are called the Clovis culture.

Epochal archaeological findings have recently overturned many aspects of this account, which is known as the Clovis theory. We now know that people were in the Americas long before 11,200 B.P., that they probably came several times from several parts of Asia, and they were not just big-game hunters. They had well-designed wood, bone, and stone technologies with which they exploited a wide range of foods, including plants, small game, and marine animals. Many of these new discoveries have taken place in South America. The first South Americans were clearly very different than their North American counterparts. Their culture was not uniform like Clovis; it was made up of a wide variety of regionally distinct cultures that predate Clovis times.

This book recounts the story of new scientific discoveries, conclusions, and controversies about the first Americans, with special emphasis given to the important South American archaeological evidence that recently has changed so many of our ideas. Particularly in the last twenty years, excavations in South America have raised exciting new ideas and questions about the first Native Americans. Much of this excitement revolves around several new conclusions spurred by the acceptance of the Monte Verde site.[2] These are:

1. People were in South America by at least 12,500 years ago, implying that they must have been in North America by at least 15,000 to 20,000 years ago, if we accept migration into the Americas by way of land.

2. There were multiple early migrations into the Americas, probably from different points within Asia and possibly elsewhere.

3. Although late Pleistocene South American cultures are historically related to North American ones, they are also distinct, characterized by different technologies and generalized hunting and gathering lifeways.

4. Much cultural diversity existed throughout the Americas, but especially in South America, by 11,000 years ago. By that time the Americans had been in this hemisphere for some thousands of years, regional populations had grown geographically isolated, and they had rapidly and efficiently adapted to diverse environments.

5. There is some (though scant) evidence from human skeleton and genetic comparisons that regional populations were physically more different from one another than we once believed, suggesting not only early cultural but biological diversity. Both the cultural and biological records indicate that the first Americans were much more sophisticated and varied than we scientists had previously thought.

These conclusions add up to an entirely fresh view of the settlement of the New World—a world that archaeology has increasingly made a vital part of our common heritage. The story of this heritage begins with the question of when and where the first Americans found their way into this hemisphere.

THE DATING GAME AND CLOVIS CLONES

The appearance of Ice Age people in the Americas has always been a mystery. At the turn of the twentieth century, Archbishop

Usher's date of 4,004 B.C. for the creation of the earth was still largely accepted, and Native Americans were believed to have descended from either Egyptians, Phoenicians, Greeks, Romans, Chinese, Japanese, Welsh, Irish, or from the ten lost tribes of Israel, or to have sailed to the Americas in historic times from the lost continents of Atlantis or Mu. We now know that the Native Americans are much older than any of these people or places, and we know that they probably migrated into the Americas from Asia. What we do not know is exactly when this migration occurred.

Indeed the question of when people first entered the Americas has produced much scholarly argument, in part because much more is at stake than a date.[3] The date of entry has an important impact on our understanding of who the first Americans were, how they came to America, and how they adapted so efficiently to many different environments.

Since the findings of butchered mammoths at the Clovis site in New Mexico in the 1930s, most archaeologists have been convinced that the first Americans were nomadic hunters who moved rapidly to search for big game. The idea is that people equipped with the efficient Clovis spearpoints wandered from Siberia into Alaska, tracking animal herds as they moved across the open tundra of the Bering Strait (which was exposed by lowered sea levels). This initial migration probably took place sometime in the late Pleistocene (or Ice Age), which ended in different regions between 14,000 and 11,000 B.P. Eventually, the first Americans pursued other game southward until they reached temperate climates in the continental United States, and then they pushed even farther south to Tierra del Fuego. So goes the theory.

Under close inspection, however, the big-game Clovis theory has many problems. For instance, several recent excavations in various parts of the Americas show that early hunters also consumed less glamorous foods, such as turtles and other small game, aquatic plants, snails, insects, shellfish, and tubers. Also, evidence for the large numbers of herd animals needed to support the Clovis lifestyle is absent from many parts of the Americas, especially the forested regions of the eastern United States and Central America, as well as vast areas of South America. This lack of evidence does not mean that Clovis people were not hunters, but if they hunted in the forest, it would have taken more work.

Further, Clovis was a short-lived culture.[4] All radiocarbon dates from Clovis sites in North America cluster tightly between 11,200 and 10,800 B.P. This tight span forces us to ask how humans could have reached the southern tip of South America by 11,000 B.P. How could people have populated an entire hemisphere in just 300 to 500 years—the time between the arrival in Beringia and the appearance of human-made artifacts in Tierra del Fuego? With the possible exception of the Arctic, there is no analogue anywhere in human history or prehistory for such rapid movement across such a vast and unknown region. Also, there are no clear archaeological traces of the Clovis culture in Alaska and Siberia. Where, then, did this culture originate? Were Clovis points perhaps invented in the lower forty-eight states? If so, then the Clovis theory does not even explain the peopling of North America. How, then, can it explain the first settlement of South America?

Still other lines of evidence have brought the Clovis theory into question. Linguists argue that modern North and South American indigenous languages probably evolved from a single ancestral tongue. But they also note that the languages of the north and the south differ greatly from one another and that it is hard to imagine how these differences could have evolved in just a few centuries. Led by Johanna Nichols, several historical linguists now claim that only a span of more than 30,000 years can explain the antiquity and diversity of New World languages as well as the differences between the languages of North America and South America.[5] Similarly, the mitochondrial DNA of many present-day Native Americans differs so much from group to group that a single, relatively recent ancestral group seems unlikely. Many molecular anthropologists believe that the genetic diversity of New World peoples requires a human presence lasting more than 25,000 years. Others argue for a single arrival no earlier than 15,000 years ago.[6]

So the consensus from many sources is that the Clovis model does not explain the peopling of the Americas. Although scholars are still far from broad agreement about the inadequacies of the Clovis theory or about an alternative to it, the broad strokes of a new picture of American origins are emerging. The evidence supporting this new picture comes from early sites all over the Americas but especially from sites in South America, including Monte Verde in Chile, Taima-Taima in Venezuela, Tequendama in Colombia, the Itaparica Phase sites in Brazil, and several coastal sites in northern Chile and southern Peru.[7]

South America is very different archaeologically from North America because no single culture dominated the continent the way the Clovis culture, with its representative spearpoints, dominated North America. The first South Americans were not Clovis clones. In South America, the earliest technologies consisted of different kinds of stone tools, including a wide variety of spearpoints, unifacial tools made of flakes, and sling stones. Furthermore, many areas in South America witnessed the development of broad hunter and gatherer diets before 11,000 B.P., a pattern usually thought to be associated with later Holocene or early Archaic cultures dated after 10,000 B.P.[8] And big-game hunting was simply one of many different economic practices; it never achieved the importance it did in North America.

All of the South American sites mentioned above testify to varied patterns of technology and subsistence in different environments, including big-game hunting in grassy plains and savannas, generalized foraging in forests and parklands between at least 12,500 and 10,500 B.P., and active plant manipulation in some areas of South America by 10,000 B.P. (suggested by the presence of domesticates possibly as early as 9,000 to 8,000 B.P.).

Until recently, most specialists thought that it was only with the decline and extinction of large mammals at the end of the Pleistocene period and with the later increase of human populations that material cultures and subsistence patterns became more generalized. These changes were supposed to have occurred around 10,000 to 9,000 B.P., or at the beginning of the Holocene period. This time of generalized adaptation is called the Archaic period by American archaeologists, for whom the name denotes both a chronology and a way of life. Although the divide between the late Pleistocene and early Holocene period is essentially climatic (the retreat of those ice sheets), it is also conceived as a cultural watershed where the "Paleoindian lifeway"—specialized big-game hunting—gave way to the more generalized early Archaic hunting and gathering lifeway. Under the influence of this model, most work on the first inhabitants of South America has emphasized big-game hunting. Yet the evidence of many South American sites indicates that people in most areas of the continent combined what were probably sporadic large mammal kills with reliance on smaller game and plant resources.

Clearly the developmental sequence from big-game hunting in the late Pleistocene to diverse hunting and gathering in the early Holocene was not universal throughout South America, nor even throughout North America. A generalized, broad-spectrum economy existed at Monte Verde around 12,500 B.P. and in other areas by at least 11,000 B.P., although it differed from the classic and later Archaic period in that some people still hunted the soon-to-be-extinct big animals.[9] This hunting, however, was only one activity among others. Specialized big-game hunting is evident only at a small handful of sites in South America.

Thus it is incorrect to refer to all early South American people as Paleoindians, a term best reserved for some North American groups. Yet because some early South Americans were hunting big animals that were not yet extinct, it is also incorrect to call them early Archaic people, a term more appropriately reserved for later cultures of the Holocene period. To avoid an overemphasis on the Paleoindian and Archaic lifestyles, I will call the South American late Pleistocene the proto-Archaic period, a term that reflects the time's highly diverse hunting and gathering economies and technologies.

This widespread cultural diversity evident in the archaeological record of South America probably had something to do with the relative lack of glaciers on the continent. Unlike North America, South American glaciers were confined to patchy high areas of the Andean mountains and to high latitudes near the southern tip of the continent. Immigrants coming to South America sometime before 13,000 years ago could have moved freely across the entire continent, and they probably settled early in many lush, temperate environments, a settlement pattern that spawned different hunter and gatherer adaptations and different regional cultures.

Between 12,500 and 10,500 B.P., South America saw many of the cultural developments typical of the late Pleistocene period elsewhere. People began to exploit coastal resources with a more sophisticated marine technology, concentrate their settlements in river valleys and deltas, and selectively use certain plants and animals. Later changes (between 10,500 and 9,000 B.P.) included most of those commonly considered typical of early Archaic economies (Mesolithic in the Old World)—more habitation sites, more use of plant foods that required care, more intensive exploitation of coastal resources, greater technological diversity, and the appearance of ritual practices and rock paintings.[10] The first pulses of civilization in the form of permanently occupied sites, the appearance of architecture and art, and the use of plant and animal domesticates, may have occurred within just a few millennia after people first arrived in South America. As the last continent occupied by humans but one of the first sites of prehistoric civilization, South America offers an important study of rapid cultural changes. And once humans moved into the interior river corridors and coastal fringes of the continent, between 11,000 and 10,000 B.P., this development was rapid indeed.

What caused these sudden changes? Were they related to climatic shifts, internal developments within regional populations, the imitation of neighbors, or the arrival of new people on the scene? Or was the cause perhaps a combination of these factors, along with the exploitation of different foods and other resources in more lush environments? Or does the answer lie in the growing cultural experience, cognitive skill, social capacity, and constantly changing lifestyle of a population that had made a rapid migration down the entire length of the Western Hemisphere? The answers to these questions are crucial to our understanding of the first chapter of human history in the Americas and to the entire history of humankind.

THE COGNITIVE EXPLOSION

The story of human movement into the Americas begins in the Old World. Although people have been moving from place to place for more than 2 million years, modern *Homo sapiens,* beginning around 100,000 years ago, were the first to explore large territories and adapt to all continents. This experience itself must have had a profound impact on modern humans and the divergence and variety of regional cultures they developed. Having changed more during the period shortly after 40,000 B.P. than during the previous several million years, and after spreading throughout the Old World, people eventually brought their remarkable innovations into Australia and the Americas, where, in late Pleistocene times, they produced a wide variety of cultural patterns and regional histories. Of the many different histories made by our human ancestors, those made by the people migrating into the Americas, especially South America, represent the least known. They were the last people on earth to successfully colonize a continent.

Although anatomically modern humans lived in Africa and the Near East more than 100,000 years ago, it was not until roughly 40,000 B.P. that there occurred a sudden explosion of new kinds of stone and bone tools, artwork, and elaborate burials.[11] This transformation of anatomically modern humans into behaviorally modern people, seems to have happened simultaneously in Africa,

Asia, and Europe. It is the most dramatic advance in human evolution since hominids began to walk on two legs more than 3.5 million years ago.

Forty thousand years ago, our ancestors occupied much of the Old World, including the cold tundras of Pleistocene Europe and Asia. The human brain was of modern size. These people used primitive tools, but these tools had persisted essentially without change for tens of thousands of years. People showed concern for their fellow humans by burying the dead and taking care of the handicapped and injured. Then long patterns of development that had begun 2 million years earlier began to flower, bringing language and communication, ritual and ideology, social organization, art and design, settlement and technology. Tools and methods began to vary from region to region and became rapidly more sophisticated. More implements were made from a greater variety of raw material than ever before. Bows, boats, buttons, fishhooks, lamps, needles, nets, spear-throwers, and many other items appear in the archaeological record for the first time. The dog was domesticated as a hunting companion and occasional source of food. With the dawning awareness of art and image-making, caves and artifacts were decorated with paintings, carvings, and engravings. Sites from this period are larger and more common than those from previous periods, suggesting larger social groups, more economic activity, and perhaps rapid population growth. From almost any perspective, this period represents a dramatic change in human behavior.

The conquest of new territory accelerated sharply at the same time. Having spread to North Africa and the Near East by at least 100,000 B.P., anatomically modern people advanced slowly across Europe and Asia until they reached China, Japan, and Australia around 40,000 B.P. In some areas the newcomers replaced, and in others interbred with, other humans such as the robustly built Neanderthals. At 40,000 B.P. the movement into uninhabited landscapes accelerated. These people explored new continents and brought with them the basic cultural foundations of early American culture.

The causes of this remarkable migration and cultural explosion are a mystery. Some anthropologists suggest that a change in the brains of modern humans improved their linguistic ability, which led to more sophisticated cultures. Others emphasize the rapid change in people's social and economic organization, perhaps caused by some fundamental behavioral change.[12] Either way, demographic changes and possibly food shortages compelled some humans around the world to abandon one way of life for another, and so to invent new technologies and lifestyles.

Still other researchers argue that the crucial element may have been the human species' extreme sociability, which created an environment conducive to sophisticated tools, language, and artwork. Evidence of the extensive social relations among early *Homo sapiens* in Europe, for instance, is everywhere. Starting around 40,000 B.P., our ancestors left behind the remains of large campsites, suggesting that they occasionally gathered in large groups, possibly for ceremonial purposes. Richard Klein and others believe that the huge leap in the sophistication of hunting techniques and fishing technologies reveals the beginning of intense cooperation among group members.[13] Discoveries of shell, bone, and flint hundreds of miles from their original sources indicate that modern humans had vast networks for exchanging goods.

Cognitive skills, belief systems, and art probably played key roles in the development of a complex network of groups after people initially moved into new environments. Their learning capacity was obviously crucial to the way they adapted to new environments and developed new cultural patterns. But the belief systems of groups were probably equally important. These systems probably preserved some degree of community, an acceptance of the social system, and hence a general social solidarity, particularly in times of duress. Communal beliefs may also have functioned to store and transmit ancient knowledge as groups split up and entered new worlds.

CULTURAL DIVERSITY AND HISTORY

Biologists consider diversity within populations an essential feature of biological adaptability. In the case of *Homo sapiens*, the same point can be made for cultural diversity. Like genetic variability, cultural variability or diversity provides the raw materials from which a population can adapt swiftly to changed circumstances. Anthropologists know that any population, regardless of its size, contains a great deal of intracultural diversity, permitting divergent ideas and inventions to come to the fore to meet the requirements of new situations.

Yet when studying the first regional cultures of South America, archaeologists have focused mainly on the similarities rather than the differences between cultures. We have viewed the first South Americans much as we did the first North Americans—as an unchanging people in a changing land. Only recently have we become more interested in explaining cultural differences and cultural histories.

Perhaps the simplest view of cultural diversity is that each regional group has its own history, resulting from its immediate environment and pressures. The environment includes, of course, the climate, the resources used by people, and the culture of a specific group and its neighbors. Cultural diversity, as manifested by different archaeological records, is thus connected with both environmental and cultural change and adaptation.

The change in thinking forced on us by Monte Verde and other sites is much deeper than the simple matter of when people first set foot in the New World. We must view the settlement of the Americas as an integral part of a worldwide human social and cognitive explosion that first took off some 40,000 years ago and continues to this day. And within that broad movement early American prehistory is not a story of a single monolithic culture sweeping from pole to pole but rather of an intricate, constantly shifting pattern of diverse local cultures, each with its unique history and lifeways.

It is mainly archaeology, I believe, that can enlighten us about these histories. Genetic, linguistic, and biological studies also have much to teach us about the histories of human migration and biological and cultural diversity. Still, the ultimate key to understanding these histories lies in the archaeological record—in the record of how humans once used the environment and the resources of small places. The sum of the similarities and differences among these archaeological sites and the histories we glean from them is the only means to a truer picture of the broad continental and hemispheric prehistory of the Americas. Most crucial to our understanding, then, is an appreciation of the nature of the archaeological record, its preservation in different settings, and the way archaeologists approach the study of the past.

CHAPTER TWO

Debating the Archaeology of the First Americans

F OR A CENTURY OR MORE, new and controversial archaeological findings have continually challenged our thinking
about the first Americans and have created a long-standing debate, as emotionally charged as the century-long argument over
the antiquity of humans in the Old World. For most of the past
century, archaeologists thought that all early sites in the Americas
were Clovis, dating no earlier than about 11,200 years ago. If a site
appeared to be earlier than Clovis and did not contain Clovis
points, a debate ensued about misidentification of evidence from
the site. As a result, the evidence from all pre-Clovis candidates
was considered unconvincing and was dismissed.[1] Recently, however, the debate has taken a new turn because of a small number
of sites excavated in the 1970s and 1980s, including Meadowcroft
Rockshelter in Pennsylvania, probably the Cactus Hill site in Virginia and the Topper site in South Carolina, and several sites in
eastern Brazil, Taima-Taima in Venezuela, Tibitó in Colombia,
and Monte Verde in Chile. All of these sites yielded more convincing pre-11,000-year dates and evidence suggestive of a gener-

alized (non-big-game) hunter and gatherer lifeway. In other words, these sites contained not only more convincing radiocarbon dates, human-made artifacts, and reliable stratigraphic association but also evidence of early cultures that pre-dated Clovis.

The South American sites were especially important in challenging the assumptions of the Clovis theory and raising passions on both sides. Unlike some earlier discoveries, these sites were excavated by professional archaeologists and thus were taken more seriously than others. Nonetheless, they stirred much debate due to their early dates, to the kinds of artifacts they contained, and to the way they were interpreted by their excavators. All doubts and controversies began with early radiocarbon dates. Pre-11,200-year sites without Clovis points simply raise problems for their excavators.

Specific reasons exist for these problems, ranging from conceptual and epistemological differences in research approaches to the ambiguous nature of the archaeological record. The destructive nature of archaeological research is also a source of the problems: Site excavation simply destroys much of our evidence, making it very difficult or impossible to verify and duplicate the exact context in which artifacts were found and their relation to other buried objects (especially in early sites, where traces of human activity are often meager). Although these legitimate difficulties underlie much of the controversy over the peopling of the Americas, the excavations in the 1970s and 1980s often led us into more and different kinds of trouble.

Much of the argument over the early sites was about the validity of the archaeological evidence as it was presented by the excavators and about the criteria the proponents of the Clovis theory used to judge the validity of these sites. The Clovis advocates claimed that most pre-11,200 B.P. localities contained highly questionable evidence of human activity and thus were unreliable records. They thought these sites represented nothing more than disturbed geological deposits containing jumbled archaeological and natural materials. Radiocarbon dates, human artifacts, and their geological association in these sites were all rejected. This stance enjoyed the firm support of history. Since the 1960s many supposed pre-Clovis localities had been found to contain disturbed deposits and had produced questionable radiocarbon dates and artifacts. This history led many archaeologists, including myself, to take a cynical attitude toward any claim of early settlement, especially in South America, where sites are isolated from mainstream research in North America and are thus out of the sight, so to speak, of Clovis proponents.

Some pre-Clovis advocates countered that Clovis advocates far too often rejected sites without proper scientific evidence of disproof. One pre-Clovis proponent, Alan Bryan of the University of Alberta, extended the criticism even further, charging that many Clovis supporters were obsessed with the rapid spread of the big-game-hunting model in American archaeology, and that in advocating it so passionately they practiced a form of archaeological imperialism.[2] Bryan believed that many North American archaeologists held an irrational reverence for Clovis as the first great American culture and for its fluted points as the first great invention, and so arbitrarily rejected any alternative interpretation of the first human settlement of the New World. Clovis proponents, he said, were too narrow-minded, adhered too strictly to the Clovis model, and did not understand the early record in South America.

There is no doubt that just as some zealous archaeologists can go overboard in the field, in the laboratory, and in their interpretations, critics can be overzealous as well, uncritically applying the

Clovis theory to all early archaeological sites in the Americas or dismissing a site because it produced pre-11,200-year dates without Clovis points. Like other scientists, archaeologists live in academic communities. They think and work within a shared and presupposed picture—a theory or paradigm—and, generally, do not question established theories. Indeed, membership in the research community is often defined by loyalty to the reigning theory, and much of the bickering over the Clovis occupation in the Americas was really about individual scientists' unwillingness or inability to accept data that undermined the reigning theory.

Unfortunately, much of the dispute over the entry date of the first Americans and the validity of early archaeological evidence has served to trivialize our methods of scientific proof, criticism, and debate and has led us away from more interesting and more important questions of archaeological study: How does the archaeological record of a site come into being? What human or natural processes form it? How do archaeologists conduct fieldwork and interpret sites?

Until recently, in the absence of an interdisciplinary approach to such questions, archaeologists have had a free hand to create stories about the past. What we thought we knew about the past has strongly influenced (or biased) how we went about our work. We now know more clearly than we used to that unless we ask the right questions, have an open mind, and have clear ideas, it is difficult for us to know how to approach or interpret the early archaeological record. The rest of this chapter is concerned with what can go (and has gone) wrong with archaeological study: how the integrity of the record can be compromised; how our expectations, biases, and previous conclusions may lead us astray; and how archaeologists spent decades steeped in controversy.

THE INTEGRITY OF THE ARCHAEOLOGICAL RECORD

What do we expect to obtain from studying an archaeological site? First, in order to reconstruct the economic, technological, and settlement history of a regional population, we must have a basic understanding of the pattern of habitation and activity a site represents. Second, we must understand the local environment: the type and frequency of foods and other resources it makes available. The benefits and constraints of each environment help us understand why people settle in certain places but rapidly pass through or avoid others. Third, we must study the geology and geomorphology of an area in order to predict where and why sites are located within it and to explain the preservation and integrity of the archaeological deposits they contain. This last point is crucial for evaluating the age, context, and association of remains. The issue of whether all of the archaeological remains in a site are culturally related and of the same age has been the greatest cause of controversy in the study of early sites.

We can divide these three tasks into the study of the cultural and geological formation of sites.

The Cultural View

From a cultural standpoint, an archaeological site is the preserved remains of artifacts and other items produced by people's activities in a specific locality. A site consists of all the material remains that a human group (or sequence of groups) produced over a period of time in one place: a single flake, a small hearth, distinct clusters of hearths and stone, bone or wooden tools, or a large and complex settlement with permanent structures. Because all artifacts, features, and burials in a site were deposited in the same place, they should be related to each other in a meaningful way that reflects the cultural system of which they were once a part.

A site may have been occupied at different times by different cultural systems. Each distinct occupation leaves behind its own archaeological deposit or signature. Whereas some groups may have stayed in a defined territory year-round, others may have divided up during certain seasons of the year or separated into different work groups that left material remains at different places. Still other groups may have moved many times and carried out different activities—such as butchering animals, collecting berries, or quarrying for stone raw materials to make tools—in different places. Only by combining all the different types of sites produced by a mobile group can we gain a complete picture of its adaptations and lifestyles.

This complete picture of a group's activities, adaptations, and lifestyles is called its "settlement-subsistence pattern"—a pattern of organized human behavior that developed in response to such things as available food, environmental factors, site location on the landscape, and the presence of other groups. Archaeologists piece this pattern together by comparing various sites with one another and also by studying the internal organization of a site—the kinds of materials found there and how they are arranged spatially. Indeed, it is through the close study of a site's internal organization that archaeologists discover the various activities that characterized the culture of the people who once used the site.

One of the challenges of establishing a settlement-subsistence pattern for a particular group of ancient people, and thus of drawing conclusions about an ancient culture, is that all of the evidence has been subjected to the vicissitudes of nature. Like a detective searching for undisturbed clues at a crime scene, archaeologists are always concerned with the possible disturbance of the archaeological evidence by natural forces, which bring us to the topic of the geological record.

The Geological View

Although sites are cultural entities, they are usually buried in the sediments of caves, river terraces, or other physical places and thus are geological deposits as well.[3] In effect, sites are created by people but preserved by natural agencies. Because sites are part of the geological record, we must be concerned with the long-term impact of natural forces on their physical integrity. These forces make the evidence less straightforward than it may first appear. Although archaeological evidence of early humans may be associated with materials that have old radiocarbon dates or with the bone remains of extinct animals, this association may not indicate that the human materials and, say, the bone fragments, were originally deposited together. The association may be due to natural mixing from flooding, below-ground animal and root activity, or other natural forces.

There also is no reason for an archaeologist or geologist to presume that all the stone, bone, and plant materials found in the same stratigraphic layer at an archaeological site refer to the same human event, because several cultural and natural forces could have mixed the deposits of old and young events. Stones and bones regarded as artifacts by their excavators are therefore sometimes viewed with skepticism by other archaeologists, and the chronological placement of the site may be in dispute. Over the past forty years, many pre-Clovis (and Clovis) claims have suffered this fate.

Until the 1930s, it was routine for field archaeologists, some of whom had proper training, to read their own site stratigraphy (buried layers of sediment deposited in chronological order, with the oldest being the deepest and the youngest being the closest to the surface). But as geologists became increasingly interested in early archaeological sites, the so-called intact stratigraphic layers became subject to careful examination; many sites once considered highly important proved worthless. The geologists were particularly interested in caves and rockshelters, which can be subject to a great deal of disturbance.

Geology gives us a more realistic understanding of the impact of changing environments on the preservation and visibility of archaeological sites. For example, in many areas of the world, soil tends to form fairly rapidly on all but the steepest slopes, engulfing artifacts and obscuring them from view without necessarily burying them deeply. In some deserts, where erosion is predominant, artifacts may be exposed indefinitely on the surface. In other settings, such as river terraces, a little more downcutting of a stream, lateral stream erosion, or deflation, and many of the presently preserved archaeological sites would be destroyed. The corollary of erosion—aggradation, or the deposition of silt and gravel—produces the opposite effect, and in valleys and plains, sites and artifacts can become buried relatively quickly, perhaps to be washed out and reburied by later floods. Natural forces may even create an apparent site where no human settlement ever existed. Stones, bones, and other cultural materials may be carried downstream by a river and deposited in dense accumulations that, to the casual eye, give every appearance of having come about through human activity. These and many other events can destroy, preserve, or distort the archaeological record, particularly of early sites that have been subjected to longer exposure to environmental changes.

Once established, sites can be differentially preserved. They are disturbed or destroyed when sediment is redeposited or removed through transport, differential burial, selective preservation, and other natural actions. They also may be modified by cultural intervention. For instance, some human groups may have returned to a site to scavenge raw stone material, or reoccupied the site and mixed new artifacts with previous ones. The old and new artifacts are later buried together and appear to represent the same human event.

An archaeological site can thus be a highly complex and incomplete reflection of a living site. Furthermore, the sample of sites found by archaeologists may not represent all types of sites most frequently utilized by hunters and gatherers but only those most easily preserved and most visible both geologically and archaeologically. These problems are not insurmountable, but they do challenge archaeologists to work to develop reliable information about the past.

Investigators have sometimes been misled into believing that the bones or stones scattered on a buried ancient surface represented an original living floor, when in fact the "floor" was simply the product of natural forces. Forces in nature that create what appear to be human artifacts also sometimes mislead archaeologists. At the Calico site in California, for instance, Ruth Simpson and Louis Leakey recovered a collection of flakes from deep shafts in cement-hard alluvial fill. Many of these flakes, they claimed, were very early tools. The site was visited in 1970 by a large group of geologists and archaeologists, several of whom agreed that some flakes indeed looked like those made by ancient people. But, there were no valid artifacts, no charcoal from human-induced fires, no particular concentrations of flakes indicative of human activity areas, and no convincing evidence of hearths or other structures. The geological evidence also was much disputed; geologists working at the site estimated ages of several million years, prompting Leakey to propose a very early human presence in the New World. The site visitors concluded that the flakes at Calico were made by ancient alluvial fans that broke the rocks.

Another location that appeared at first glance to be a valid site is on Santa Rosa Island, off the coast of California. Here, in 1978, Ranier Berger found burned and unburned mammoth bones in deeply buried sediments associated with radiocarbon dates ranging from 20,000 to over 35,000 B.P. No artifacts were found in association with the bones. Although some archaeologists have claimed that humans are responsible for the burned bones, there is no convincing evidence of human involvement with the fire or even of a human presence that long ago. This is a case of no human artifacts and thus of no association between the bones and alleged human activity.

Numerous examples of disturbed sites and disputable artifact collections can be found throughout the Americas. At many localities, either the finds turned out to be surface deposits or the claimed association or age assignment dissolved in the face of rigorous reexamination. As a result, researchers have become very cautious in accepting sites as valid.

The late Pleistocene archaeological record, in particular, can be filled with frustration for archaeologists. We can clearly see the potential difficulties of our evidence, and we are frequently overwhelmed by the task of making better sense out of it. Our best hope is for new evidence, from old or new sites, collected and interpreted with an awareness of these problems.

TYPES AND STEREOTYPES

Even the best techniques and unlimited site visits cannot resolve all our problems, however, because we also are often hampered by biases built into the way we classify and interpret sites. Many of the questions we ask in archaeology, questions that govern our entire approach to the discipline, are determined by paradigms or theories that have conceptual weaknesses. Most of us, for example, have adopted a typological approach for our basic interpretative framework; that is, artifacts are given a cultural identity and are ordered chronologically based upon the presence of groups of similar features, such as the fluted trait on long spearpoints of the Clovis type or the short stems and broad shoulders on other types.

Using a typological approach, archaeologists arrange excavated materials in large chronological blocks, which are then organized in an evolutionary sequence, from which we try to depict ancestral technological relationships between the earlier and later materials. For instance, the Clovis points between roughly 11,200 and 10,800 B.P. are followed temporally and stratigraphically by Folsom, Cumberland, Dalton points, and by other variants, which come from layers dated roughly 10,500 to 9,500 B.P. These points in turn give way to regional variations in terminal Pleistocene times and the early Archaic period. We say that these later points in a sense grew out of, or are refinements of, the earlier, in the same sense that a Lexus is a refinement of a Model T.

Archaeologists employing these spearpoints to study the chronology and movement of early human migration can be crudely divided into splitters and lumpers. Splitters recognize a new distinct style with each new find; lumpers, while taking into account individual variation, tend to group slightly differing points under a single point type. For instance, all lance heads with waisted or eared stems and any sign of fluting are considered to be Clovis or Clovis variants. On the other hand, those with waisted stems but without fluting, such as the Goshen point of the northern Great Plains, may be classified as a different point type. Splitting produces more variation in the archaeological record, and lumping more similarity. Once an archaeological record is filled out, we usually see more contact and continuity between regions than the splitters envisioned, and the single-point classification of the lumpers appears strained. Many Clovis proponents are lumpers. I think I am somewhere in the middle, leaning toward being a splitter.

This typological thinking is common to archaeologists around the world. Names are simply a convenient way of reducing the infinitely graded variation of the real world to a finite verbal approximation. For all its merit, the weakness of this approach is that once archaeologists recognize a category by name, they tend to invest it with a kind of sanctity that emphasizes its distinction from the rest of reality. This weakness has been especially evident among American archaeologists, who have adopted what we might call a type-society approach, whereby particular types of artifacts, such as Clovis points and the bone remains of big-game animals, are associated with a particular human population or society. Among many American archaeologists, the Clovis artifacts came to symbolize a uniform culture so completely that other possibilities were ignored. In other words, the Clovis theory became a stereotype.

As I pointed out in Chapter 1, until very recently few specialists considered the possibility that the early prehistory of South America might be different from that of North America. In part this oversight is the legacy of typological thinking and of the way it influenced migration theory in American archaeology. Thus archaeologists working under the influence of these biases assumed that any sudden appearance of a new trait in the archaeological record, such as the Clovis flute, usually signified rapid migration of people from one place to another. Other ideas of continuity or change, such as innovation and diffusion of point styles, were thought to be too slow to explain the sudden appearance of new traits. All fluted point types resembling the Clovis form were thus uncritically lumped together to create a hemisphere-long migratory population. As a result of this thinking, we often ignored other important cultural attributes in the archaeological record, such as the development and spread of early unifacial industries, grooved bola stones, and a wide variety of unfluted, stemmed projectile points in South America. Arguments for long-distance migration must be founded on something more rigorous than a simple reference to the appearance of a single, possibly foreign trait. A narrow focus on a single trait or small group of traits conceals many other cultural adaptations.

For the study of the first Americans, the type-society approach is not entirely satisfactory. It can misrepresent and underestimate cultural diversity by assuming that all Ice Age groups could organize their social and economic practices in only certain ways—for all times and places. There is usually little concern for how these practices fit specific environmental contexts. This approach also creates false continuities that give rise to needless mysteries, such as the mystery concerning the apparent existence of big-game hunters in all parts of the Americas between 11,200 and 10,000 years ago. When not obscured by the narrow lens of the type-society approach, the archaeological record from early sites demonstrates that there is no simple sequence of pure economic types from the legendary big-game hunters of the late Pleistocene period to the broad-spectrum hunters and gatherers at the end of this period and into the early Archaic.

BIASES IN INTERPRETING EARLY RECORDS

Many false notions about the peopling of the Americas have been accepted as working truth and form a major part of the theoretical framework of American archaeologists, researchers, students, and professors. Neither contrary facts nor recent research have been able to weaken them. Constant repetition in innumerable books and articles gives these dogmas a life independent of the evidence. The ease and rapidity with which such ideas as the myth of the Clovis big-game hunter came to influence the interpretation of the first Americans suggest the degree to which these ideas accorded with the spirit of the time. Let us review three common images of the first Americans and try to challenge them by suggesting why they have persisted and how they have influenced our thinking.

Bias 1: Man the Mighty Hunter

Until recently, most models of human evolution in general, and of the development of technology in particular, were centered on the "Man the Hunter" theory. The traditional view is summarized nicely by Kathleen Gordon, a biological anthropologist:

> For several decades now, long enough to have influenced generations
> of students, the most familiar picture of early man has been that of
> the hunter, whose very instincts, social behavior, and mating patterns
> were all honed by the stringent demands of a predatory existence.
> This preoccupation with hunting as the "master behavior pattern of
> the human species" . . . has been fueled by many factors: the indis-

putable evidence of large-scale big-game hunting in Upper Paleolithic Europe; the visible archaeological record, with its emphasis
on stone "weapons" and animal bone fragments; and also (perhaps
somewhat subliminally) the high value accorded meat and hunting
as a leisure activity in Western society.[4]

Gordon's comment is surely applicable to the Americas. In recent years, archaeologists have questioned the apparent dominance
of big-game hunting in Clovis populations, suggesting that it primarily reflects archaeological visibility and preservation rather than
actual dietary preference. They note that most modern human
hunters and gatherers eat a wide range of (predominately vegetable) foods; that the range of foods preserved at very early human
sites at least occasionally suggests a similar broad spectrum of exploitation; that the items (such as plants) usually considered late
additions to the first Americans' diet are archaeologically fragile
and may simply have been removed from the early record by differential preservation; and that on the coastlines, where much of a
broad spectrum diet also is expected, early sites have now largely
been destroyed by rising sea levels since the end of the Pleistocene.

Another reason for the bias that the first Americans were specialized hunters is that much of our thinking in recent years has
been spurred by a theory in ecology called "optimal foraging theory." This theory states that groups prefer a limited diet, which
they expand only in response to a population increase, a decrease
of prey (from an improvement in food-getting technologies), a decline in high-ranked resources, a degradation of the environment,
or all of the above. This theory also presumes that large game animals such as mammoths and giant ground sloths were the early
American's preferred foods. Some proponents of this theory argue

that small game, avifauna, shellfish, and plant foods are taken only when large game animals are unavailable or too costly to procure.

This line of thinking is predicated entirely on assumptions about the pressure that growing human populations put on food supplies. Many archaeologists have argued that the emergence of hunters and gatherers worldwide in the late Pleistocene period was caused by an increase in human numbers and a corresponding pressure on resources—and not by technological or social progress or even, primarily, by an adjustment to changing climates. A major proponent of this notion is Mark Cohen, who thinks that changes in human subsistence are the result of necessity rather than choice. Simply put, the idea is that hunting and meat consumption are preferred over most plant foods. But since meat can be hard to come by, especially in arid areas, and may cost considerable energy to procure, a decrease in its availability will force hunters to turn toward less attractive vegetable foods.

Aside from the lack of hard evidence anywhere in the world to demonstrate population pressure among early hunters and gatherers, there are other problems with this approach. For example, neither scavengers nor hunters were always successful. They often returned empty-handed. As a result, in nearly all the hunter and gatherer societies that we know of from the historical record, hunters supplied only part (usually less than half) of the group's food. It was the gatherer's responsibility to ensure a dependable supply of fruit, seeds, nuts, and other vegetable materials, together with the smaller items of animal food such as eggs, snails, and small game. In addition to the vital function of leveling out the ups and downs in the food supply, such things as nuts and grains, unlike quickly rotting meat, kept a long time and could be rationed out in small quantities as needed. Of course, like game and fish, gathered foodstuffs were usually more abundant in some seasons than in others, and people had to know when and where to find them. But in some areas, this task may have been easier, and certainly less dangerous, than hunting because plants were easier to gather. One did not have to outwit a potato.

Furthermore, tools for plant gathering can be much cruder than those for hunting and fishing. Fruits can be picked by hand or knocked down with a hooked pole. Roots, tubers, small animals, and insects and their larvae can be gotten with a simple digging stick. Nuts and acorns can be picked off the trees or shaken to the ground; seeds can be beaten into containers, and shellfish pried from rocks with sticks.

The hunting hypothesis is also problematic because it limits the scope of human ingenuity to the activity of killing large animals. In fact, gathering supplies of small foods requires considerable foresight, much more than we might have thought. As an entirely new approach to the extraction of resources, it is one of the most important developments in early human history and one of our entirely original behaviors. The novel use of leaves, bark, or skin to make containers and of digging sticks to reach roots and bulbs are technological advances every bit as important as the use of fluted points for killing animals. But because such technology is less elaborate and preserves much less frequently, it is less important to archaeologists. The whole question of gathering and its technology has been neglected largely because perishable tools leave little trace in the archaeological record. But ignoring them leaves us with only half the archaeological picture. The importance of gathering in widening the resource base of the first Americans cannot be exaggerated. Perhaps it is in the context of gathering plants that both technological and social information began to play a greater role in the development of early societies, laying the foundations for settling into lush environments.

In South American archaeology, a corollary of the big-game hunting myth is that the first inhabitants were highly selective in their choice of environments to exploit, preferring relatively open, game-rich areas like the savannas and grasslands of Brazil and Argentina or the puna and altiplano grasslands of the high Andes in Peru, Bolivia, and Chile.[5] This single-environment view is another reason we think in terms of population pressure on resources. Not until people had killed and eaten the last animal in open terrain did they then, regrettably, turn to eating plants in vegetated areas.

In fact, the archaeological evidence suggests that 10,000 to 12,500 years ago the human population in South America was probably less than a few thousand. Some areas were surely more heavily inhabited than others, but overall it is unlikely that the population outgrew the food supply. Furthermore, most of the high Andes above 14,000 meters in elevation were inhospitable, and harsh winters or dry, blistering summers made places like the savannas at least seasonally unlivable. Thus, contrary to the single-environment view, the most densely populated areas were probably wetlands along the coasts and open forests in major riverine systems, where a broad-spectrum economy would have been the basis of subsistence.

Bias 2: The Primacy of the Projectile Point

Within the Pleistocene period we are accustomed to think of uniform cultural patterns of bifacial industries (technologies made by chipping both sides of a stone tool to produce a sharp edge on a spearpoint or knife) like the Clovis culture in North America and

Magdelenian and Solutrean cultures in Europe. Some stone tool industries of late Pleistocene South America were based on bifacial traditions, but often these traditions coexisted with unifacial industries that had different characteristics, which appear to have been the result of an independent tradition (see Chapter 4). Unifacial tools include choppers and flake tools made for the most part of pebbles or roughly tabular blocks. Unifacial assemblages rarely contain bifacial tools. Unifacial tools are associated with the cultures of hunting people, fishermen, herders, and people gathering and manipulating some plants, and they are found widely throughout the continent. In some areas the bifacial and unifacial traditions overlapped and blended; in other areas they were separate.

Bias 3: From Present Tense to Past Tense

The final bias is that the late Pleistocene period must be judged in light of modern hunter and gatherer groups. This impulse, to start with the known and proceed to the unknown, is only natural, and the application of ethnographic observations to earlier archaeology has been with us in one form or another since the nineteenth century.[6] But how relevant are our observations of modern hunter and gatherer societies in helping us interpret the vastly different societies of the late Ice Age? After all, the first Americans were moving into entirely unknown territory that had no other human occupants and that stretched the length of two continents. There is no historical or modern analog for this migration. And most modern hunters and gatherers have great knowledge of their landscapes, are in contact with neighbors who practice pastoralism or horticulture, and migrate only short distances.

To raise questions about the limits of applying ethnographic observations to archaeological study is not to suggest that the archaeologist should divorce herself from ethnography, for we need a comparative knowledge base. The observation of present-day hunters and gatherers has helped archaeologists infer such things as the factors accounting for concentrations of bones from some parts of animal bodies but not others, how artifact styles change from place to place, and why groups abandon sites and select a locality somewhere else. Analogy also gives us a better understanding of how material objects might have functioned in early hunter and gatherer societies and how, where, and why these were left behind. By comparing present-day hunters and gatherers with the groups connected to archaeological sites, we also gain knowledge of material indicators such as burial practices and the layout of campsites. This knowledge could enable archaeologists to identify early local and regional cultures.

Archaeological analogy is also used to relate certain archaeological ideas from other regions to the South American past. For example, the southern continents of South America and Australia were both colonized very late in Pleistocene times, and there may be lessons to learn from similarities and differences between them. General explanations applied to the initial entry and dispersion of people into other continents should be applicable to South America as well.

THE DEBATE OVER EARLY SOUTH AMERICA

Not long ago, when most of today's senior scientists received their training, it seemed intuitively obvious that the South American archaeological record should be a clone of the North American record. The presence of a single cultural trait, the alleged fluted points first excavated by Junius Bird in Fell's Cave in the 1930s that later demonstrated the presence of Ice Age humans in Patagonia, initially seemed to corroborate that thinking.[7] But more recent evidence from sites all over the continent has shown that, contrary to our intuition, the South American record has been grossly misrepresented.

Some of these misrepresentations originated in the works of Bird and of Tom Lynch, previously at Cornell University but now at the Brazos County Museum in east Texas. With their uncritical acceptance of the North American fluted point culture and its extended representation in South America, these two men, in their time the leading experts on the peopling of the continent, set much of the tone for our understanding of early South American cultures. In several dialogues with Alex Kreiger of the University of Washington (a pre-Clovis advocate) in the 1960s (and with some contemporary archaeologists in the 1980s and 1990s), Bird and Lynch clearly emerged as the more forceful and convincing investigators.[8] And because of their ability to convince people of their views, Bird and Lynch have been copied uncritically, to the point that most of their ideas are repeated verbatim in the writings of others. By the time my generation began doing field work in the 1970s, archaeologists were conditioned to view all sites with radiocarbon dates prior to 11,000 B.P. as suspect and to see most first South Americans as big-game hunters.

Although Bird and Lynch are responsible for spreading the view that South American archaeology simply mimics the North American discoveries of Clovis, the dogma of a very late peopling of the New World and the suspicion of any data from South

America that indicates otherwise actually dates back to the turn of the twentieth century. It received its strongest impetus from Alês Hrdlička, who in 1911 was commissioned by the Smithsonian Institution to reassess all claims that human beings had been in the Americas deep into the Pleistocene period.[9] One of the first serious claims for an early human presence in the Americas was that of the Dutch naturalist Peter Wilhelm Lund, who in 1842 reported an association between human bones and extinct animal bones in a cave near the town of Lagoa Santa in Brazil. Hrdlička also had to contend with such finds as the "early man" of Nebraska and Florentino Ameghino's announcement that he had found human cultural remains in Argentina that were from the Miocene period. Hrdlička found no good scientific evidence to support any claims of early hominids in the New World. A dominant, forceful individual, Hrdlička played a crucial part in establishing a deeply rooted resistance among archaeologists to any effort to push back the antiquity of human arrival in the Americas.

In the 1930s, when Bird excavated several important sites in Tierra del Fuego, he initially thought the oldest deposits in Fell's Cave and Palli Aike Cave dated back no farther than 5,500 B.P. But in the 1950s, radiocarbon tests and additional excavations proved that people lived in the extreme south as early as 11,000 to 10,800 B.P. Bird's finds in the deepest levels of Fell's Cave were particularly important because the animal bones of extinct species, human skeletons, and stemmed Fishtail points (tapered bifacial spearpoints in the form of a leaf, with shoulders and a stem, which may have a flute) were sealed off by fallen rocks. This find proved that the association between extinct animals and human artifacts was not due to the later intrusion of the human materials. Since Bird's campaign in southernmost Chile, excavations at sites in Argentina, Peru, and elsewhere have brought forth cultural materials of comparable age.[10]

In the late 1950s archaeologists had good reasons to be critical of the Clovis model. Within the confines of the Clovis theory, Bird's early dates for the deeper levels of Fell's Cave meant that people had to have migrated on a direct linear path, and extremely quickly, down the entire length of the western hemisphere, arriving at the tip of South America just 200 to 500 years after they entered the New World. In the 1960s and 1970s, Kreiger and Bryan raised questions about this rapid migration, as well as about other aspects of the Clovis model. But the Clovis proponents had an answer: Paul Martin's blitzkrieg hypothesis, a model of big-game hunting, rapid movement throughout the hemisphere, and the extinction of large mammals at the end of the Pleistocene due to human overkill.[11]

Martin, an ecologist at the University of Arizona, noted that the extinction of several species of large mammals in North America—such as the woolly mammoth, giant ground sloth, and American camel—coincided with the dates the Clovis theory gave for the first entry of humans into the region at the end of the Ice Age. He believed that in 1,000 years or less, given the right environmental conditions, a small group of hunters moving into Beringia could have spread across the New World in a wave and wiped out game animals in a hunting "blitzkrieg." This model has been used by archaeologists to account for the jet-like movement of humans throughout the New World.

Despite the ready acceptance of Martin's model by some Clovis supporters, there remained many archaeologists who saw problems with this model and who believed, on the basis of intuition and logic, that there must be earlier sites in both North and South

America. There was no consensus about just how early these sites might be, but the prediction (which had no scientific basis) was that the most ancient stone tools would be technologically simple and that big-game hunting, with its kill sites and fluted points, represented a later, more specialized development. According to this view, instead of big-game hunters, the first Americans were probably small bands of foragers and scavengers who ate whatever plant and animal foods the local environment offered. To support this alternative account, archaeologists cited discoveries throughout the New World of sites with rudimentary chipped stone tools, no spearpoints or pressure flaking (a method of making stone tools by applying pressure from a wood or stone object, such as an antler, to push flakes from the edge of a core), and no fossil bones of large extinct animals.

The first archaeologist to articulate this position was Kreiger. In the 1960s, he and others interpreted the widespread presence of choppers, percussion- (as opposed to pressure-) flaked tools, and pebble tools (stone artifacts made from deliberately chipped river pebbles and small cobbles) as a horizon—a pre-projectile point phase—found throughout most of the Americas. On typological grounds, he equated this horizon with the Early and Middle Paleolithic of Europe, which was also characterized by choppers and flaked tools. Percussion-flaked tools are large and crude, and many resemble the sharpened cores and pebbles of earlier South Asia traditions. They are never associated with projectile points, finely chipped knives, or other specialized tools. Kreiger thought this pre-projectile-point stage, not Clovis, represented the true first American culture.

In support of his argument, Kreiger cited numerous candidate sites scattered through the Americas. Although most of the collections consisted entirely of stone materials, some included fragments of large bones of large animals. Generally these collections were recovered from surface sites or limited excavations from river terraces or lake beaches. They also had no valid archaeological context. Often the specimens were heavily varnished by water and wind wear, giving the appearance of being very old.

Kreiger's argument gained few followers and numerous skeptics, with Bird at their lead. Why were these sites rejected by skeptics? The skeptics correctly pointed out that crude does not necessarily mean old, that natural agents can remove flakes from pebbles to produce pseudotools, and that none of the proposed early sites were reliably dated. In short, the sites Kreiger used to support his argument met few of the minimum criteria archaeologists insist on for an artifact complex to be accepted. Kreiger's materials were not buried in undisturbed geological stratigraphy; they were not associated with extinct mammal species; they lacked diagnostic and unquestionably human-made artifacts; and they could not be dated by reliable radiocarbon tests or other means. Some of the pebble tool sites Kreiger and others put forth in the 1960s and 1970s may indeed be exceedingly old, valid human sites, but none of them have yet presented any indisputable evidence.

In the end, Bird's view prevailed over Kreiger's, but the victory was won by papering over some real contradictions. For instance, when several new stone tool technologies were discovered in South America in the 1970s, Bird could never articulate a clear evolutionary pattern among them or convincingly relate them to his own study of early cultures in Tierra del Fuego. Yet he continued to uncritically advocate the Clovis migrationist approach. Lynch, on the other hand, also in the 1970s, produced a compelling synthesis of the late Pleistocene period in South America, based on a good compilation of evidence from sites in most areas of the continent.[12] Still, he clearly favored the Clovis model and strongly questioned all possible pre-Clovis sites. In recent years, Lynch has carried this view even further, claiming that people did not reach South America any earlier than 10,500 B.P. Of course Bird and Lynch represent the extreme, yet in denying that there might have been independent developments in South America, these two hyper-migrationists were only voicing a view shared by a growing number of North American archaeologists.

Curiously, the opposition to pre-Clovis sites has often been strongest among those who have made prior mistakes in the field. In 1972, for example, Lynch and Kenneth Kennedy published a report on human skeletal remains from Guitarrero Cave in northern Peru, which they thought were radiocarbon dated to approximately 10,500 B.P., based on a stratigraphic association with charcoal in the cave's deeper levels.[13] A later radiocarbon analysis showed the bones were much younger. Gary Vescelius's subsequent evaluation of the cave's stratigraphy showed heavy disturbance of the cultural deposits.[14] Lynch also excavated other sites in the highlands, including Chobshi Cave in Ecuador and Quishqui Puncu in Peru, and he studied surface materials in the Punta Negra area of northern Chile, in each case expecting an early human presence but finding only disturbed cultural deposits. As a result of his own experiences with disturbed sites and the criticisms he endured for his own mistakes, Lynch became an avid and influential critic of almost all early sites, claiming that they contained disturbed stratigraphy and mixed deposits or that they produced unreliable radiocarbon dates and artifacts that only appeared to be of human origin. Many people believe his criticisms, which were sometimes justified, would have carried more credibility if he had actually visited all the sites he questioned, studied their artifacts and contexts, and interviewed their excavators.

Some North American archaeologists are still influenced by Lynch, at least to the extent of believing that early humans arrived in South America no earlier than 11,000 to 10,500 B.P. Yet hyper-rapid migration has had little appeal for a younger generation of archaeologists as an explanation of early prehistory in South America. By the mid-1980s, the archaeological record was sufficiently well known that cultures in North and South America were recognized to be stylistically distinct, and many were thought to have developed independently from the Clovis culture. The migrationist milieu implicitly assumed a limited human capacity for innovation. The idea was that any basic discoveries (such as fluting) were unlikely to have been invented twice and hence must have spread from one area to another. Thus, almost all cultural change in the archaeological record was attributed to the migration (and later diffusion) of ideas from one group to another or to migrations that had led to the replacement of one people and their culture by another. The new generation of archaeologists places no such limits on the power of human ingenuity.

Since the 1970s, Bryan has taken up Kreiger's cause and, by pointing out the weaknesses of the Clovis model, has led the charge against imposing Clovis onto the South American record.[15] Indeed, no one in recent years has articulated the pre-Clovis position any better than Bryan. Like Kreiger, Bryan believes that early foragers were equipped with a "simple basic technology, composed of flakes and simple core tools which could be used to make useful objects from fiber, wood, sinew, skin, and bone" and that this technology contained few standardized tools.

Bryan supports his position by noting that the earliest stone tool technologies in Australia do not contain projectile points but only simple flaked tools that date as far back as 30,000 years.

More importantly, Bryan has continually stressed to archaeologists the differences and nuances within the South American record itself and has urged them not to accept Bird's and Lynch's ideas uncritically. Although Bryan has made a tight argument conceptually for a pre-Clovis culture characterized by a unifacial stone tool technology and a generalized hunting and gathering lifeway in the Americas, he has never nailed it down empirically by finding an early site with these features. He has yet to break the Clovis time barrier. He and Ruth Gruhn, also of the University of Alberta, have perhaps come close in their excavations of the Taima-Taima site in Venezuela, the Wilson Butte Cave in Idaho, and other sites scattered throughout the Americas. Bryan and Gruhn continue to work at several sites in both North America and South America. Yet by their own admission, almost every locality they have excavated has had disturbed deposits, questionable artifacts, or unreliable radiocarbon dates.

As David Meltzer of Southern Methodist University has argued, all that has ever been needed to nail down the pre-Clovis argument is a single finding of undeniably human-made tools (or other proof of human activity) in an undisturbed, well-dated geological deposit from before 11,200 B.P., the earliest reliable Clovis dates. Over the past three decades, numerous archaeological sites in both North and South America have been offered as candidates, but most scholars are now convinced that the Monte Verde site in Chile is the first site to break the "Clovis barrier".[16]

During the last two decades, the study of American prehistory has moved into a new phase. The majority of archaeologists working on the late Pleistocene period in past generations were concerned with artifact typology and technology, its development through time, and the sequential and regional relationships of assemblages of stone artifacts. Recently the emphasis has shifted toward finding out as much as possible about the relationship between early humans and their environments. Archaeologists now see artifacts as only one aspect, although an important one, of any past culture. To gain a well-rounded picture of the cultural, biological, and physical environment and the way it was utilized by people and preserved by nature, we must study other categories of evidence, including all animal, plant, and other organic remains in associated cultural or geological deposits. For archaeologists working in South America, this new emphasis leads to a fundamental question: How did major climatic and environmental changes alter the continent's many regions during the late Pleistocene?

CHAPTER THREE

Early Humans in Past Environments

BEFORE STUDYING THE FIRST ENTRY OF HUMANS into South America, it is wise to glance at the environment in which their history unfolds. The environment should not, of course, be emphasized unduly: Although people's natural world is important, it is not so important that it overshadows their history. Physiography and climate can force people to change their mode of life, but even so these factors remain external to the history of a people.

How, then, can paleoecology, the study of the past environment, help archaeologists understand human history in late Pleistocene times? How does the environment account for differences we see in regional archaeological records? How do archaeologists perceive the role of humans in a changing and previously uninhabited landscape? The answers to these questions depend on how specific resources conditioned early human occupation in different geographic settings.

Paleoecology helps us reconstruct the geography of the past. From this reconstruction we learn about the most likely areas of initial human entry into the continent; the type and distribution of settlements in different landscapes; the kinds of plants, animals, and stone types available; how people exploited their environments; and what natural conditions may have disturbed various protected sites. We can then begin to reconstruct the human past through the study of what archaeologists call "site structure"—the spatial distribution of artifacts, features, and food remains in sites. The interplay between site structure and past geography helps us understand the regional character of different cultures. A crucial aspect of this understanding is the realization that the South America of the late Pleistocene was a very different place from the South America of today, and not in only the obvious ways. Assumptions drawn from today's environment may not be applicable to those of 12,000 to 10,000 years ago.

SOUTH AMERICAN LANDSCAPES

What main features of the landscape influenced people's movements and adaptations in late Pleistocene and early Holocene times? The most noteworthy physiographic feature in South America is the rugged Andean mountain wall running up the entire length of the continent's western side. An extension of the North American Rockies, the Andes rise out of the Caribbean and form a long extended parapet from Colombia to southern Chile. In fact these mountains are not a single range but are formed by several ranges—in various places, the almost unbroken western rib is flanked by two, three, or four lesser ranges to the east. Between these ranges are the highland valleys and plateaus that have played a large part in South American life both before and after the

Spanish Conquest. In addition to the Andes, there are two older mountain masses, the Eastern Highlands of Brazil and the Guinea Highlands. The former highlands rise a short distance from the Atlantic Ocean south of the equator. The low Guinea Highlands adjoin the Caribbean sea.

In addition to mountains and highlands, the most noteworthy feature of South American geography is the tropical forest that covers a large part of the eastern flat country, except in the south, where the Pampa of Argentina and Uruguay comprises thousands of square kilometers of grassland and steppe (Figure 3.1).

The river systems of South America also influenced its early human history. Many river systems were not completely formed until 11,000 to 8,000 B.P., when the massive ice sheets in the Andes had melted and the resulting flooding had ended. The largest such systems, the Orinoco, Amazon, and Parana, drain almost half the continent and lie mainly under warm, humid or sub-humid climates. The Amazon, with its numerous tributaries, occupies the central jungle plain. Navigable for hundreds of miles inland even today, it affords the only practical means of penetrating into the heart of the continent. The smaller Orinoco system flows into the Caribbean and drains the great interior plains, or llanos, of Venezuela. Finally, the Río de La Plata system of the southeast is made up of the Parana, Paraguay, and Uruguay rivers and their lesser western tributaries. The navigability of these river systems influenced both settlement patterns and the cultural cohesion of peoples in each region.

In the northwest, Colombia's Río Magdelena and Río Cauca provide entrances to the interior of that area. But the west coast rivers of Ecuador, Peru, and Chile, descending in rapids from mountains that crowd close to the sea, are short, swift, and hardly

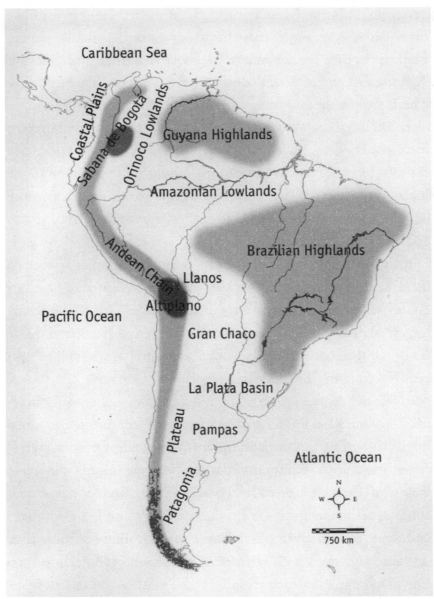

Caribbean Sea

Coastal Plains

Sabana de Bogota

Orinoco Lowlands

Guyana Highlands

Amazonian Lowlands

Andean Chain

Brazilian Highlands

Llanos

Altiplano

Pacific Ocean

Gran Chaco

La Plata Basin

Plateau

Pampas

Atlantic Ocean

Patagonia

N
W · E
S

750 km

FIGURE 3.1   Major Physiographic Areas Mentioned in the Text

navigable. Still, though many are useless for transportation, these rivers provide access to many different environments stretching from the narrow coastal plain to the adjacent mountains.

Some sections of South America have large or numerous lakes. The large Andean lakes—including Lake Titicaca on the Altiplano between the Peruvian and Bolivian border, the highest lake in the world— were formed in late glacial times. Also present in the late Pleistocene were thousands of small lagoons that developed in wetter periods. Although many of these are now dry, they left visible depressions on the landscape, especially in the Patagonian lowlands of southern Argentina and Chile.

Altitude plays a very important role in the climates of considerable areas of the continent. Even though a large proportion of South America lies within the tropics, much of this tropical territory has a temperate or even cold climate. The high intermontane plateaus and sierras of the Andes and the highland areas in eastern Brazil are tropical but often cold.

In the higher altitudes of the Andes, climates are classified vertically into zones. All the basic elements of weather and climate (temperature, humidity, pressure, and winds) are modified by increasing elevation, with temperature the overriding factor. Three main zones are usually recognized: the *tierra caliente* (hot country), *tierra templada* (template country), and *tierra fría* (cold country).

The tierra caliente, usually lying below 1,000 meters, is in effect a vertical extension of the hot conditions of the equatorial lowlands. The tierra templada has a mild climate. This zone normally lies between 1,000 and 2,000 meters in elevation but in some regions extends to nearly 3,000 meters. Above the temperate lands is the tierra fría, which begins at approximately 3,000 meters—this is the zone in which frost occurs. Seasonal variations in these zones vary according to changes in temperature and precipitation. The upper limit of the tierra fría is 3,500 meters in equatorial latitudes and somewhat lower farther from the equator. Above the tierra fría, the alpine pastures known as *paramos* extend from about 3,500 meters to the snow line, at approximately 5,000 meters. The snow-capped peaks of the Andes are in a climate of perpetual frost.

The extreme differences in altitude in South America are reflected in human biological adaptation. For instance, the geneticist Paul Baker has found evidence of genetic adaptations among indigenous peoples in Peru living at elevations between 2,600 and 5,500 meters, an area characterized by both a high birth rate and a high death rate; the latter rate is especially high among childbearing women, both during pregnancy and after they give birth. Birth weights are low, but placenta weights are high in order to supply the fetus with sufficient oxygen. The natives also have high blood flow to extremities during exposure to cold, and in the adult males, maximum oxygen consumption is high. Historically, both the Spanish and blacks, by contrast, have had problems adapting to high altitudes. The Spanish, for instance, suffered low birth rates and frequent miscarriages, abortions, and infant deaths.

From the point of view of early human settlement, the cool uplands and mountain slopes provided comfortable environments for people in latitudes that, at lower elevations, were persistently hot and humid.

GLACIATION AND DEGLACIATION

Although it is easy to think of rivers, lakes, and forests as permanent features, the world that greeted the first people in South

America was fundamentally different from what we see today.[1] The landscape and drainage patterns of both the Andes and the Amazon basin have changed radically since the beginning of human settlement. The picture of the past that paleoecology has given us is that of a mosaic landscape under constant change, supporting ever shifting mixtures of vegetation and animals. Thus many questions of early South American prehistory are basically environmental ones.

Together with paleoecologists, archaeologists are trying to correlate climate events with human movement to explain early human migrations into new areas and to understand why and how people adapted to local circumstances. Yet with the exception of Chalmers Clapperton, too few brave paleoecologists and archaeologists have tried to integrate the various aspects of the paleoenvironment into a continental overview that might be of use to those interested in the first human occupation of South America. Perhaps the archaeologists' battles over this topic have scared people away, or perhaps too little attention has been paid to developing research methodologies that are conducive to scenario building.

Rushing in where few others have feared to tread, I will attempt in this section and the next one to describe the general patterns of late Pleistocene climate and vegetation that are of interest to early human settlement. This task involves, first, associating archaeological records (mainly represented by stone tool industries and site locations) with climatic episodes represented in the geological record and, second, trying to work the paleoecology of different regions as far as the evidence will allow. Let us take a closer look at the older landscapes, beginning around 18,000 B.P., when glacial maximum conditions existed and drastic changes were occurring around the world.

The Pleistocene period as a whole (1.9 million to 11,000 years ago) was a time of highly variable global climate characterized by long-term glacial ice advances (glacial periods) alternating with short-term retreats (interglacials). There were also some irregular but well-defined episodes of somewhat milder climate occurring during glacial periods; these episodes are called interstadials. Ice cores recently drilled in central Greenland tell us of extreme climatic instability during both interglacial and glacial periods, with climatic changes beginning abruptly and lasting in some cases only decades or centuries. Glacial ages are generally very cold, but we do not know exactly how cold. Although there is much regional difference, we can generalize and say that glacial periods were about 7°C colder than interstadial periods and 12–13°C colder than our present interglacial.

In the New World, the Late Glacial Stage began between 19,000 and 14,000 B.P. and ended between 11,000 and 10,000 B.P. In general, the climate of a full-glacial period is extreme but not highly variable; a late glacial climate, on the other hand, is highly variable. Regional patterns vary considerably. For instance, in northern North America, Holocene (post-glacial) environments began only around 10,000 years ago, whereas in South America they were forming by 13,000 years ago in some areas. One of the most important differences between the two continents is the limited range of ice sheets in South America.

Except in the highest Andean mountains and in the extreme southern latitudes near Tierra del Fuego, ice sheets were far less extensive than in North America. This placed fewer restrictions on the movement of people. During the last glacial maximum around 18,000 B.P. only the high Andes above 3,000 meters would have been uninhabitable, although any human populations in the lowlands to the east and west would have been isolated from each other, except where unglaciated land routes existed across the Andes.

Even within South America itself, climate changes were not uniform.[2] We can get a sense of the variation within South America itself by reviewing the major glacial periods as they affected the continent from north to south.

Using a variety of techniques, Jean-Claude Thouret and his colleagues have identified a sequence of six glacial advances and retreats in the central cordillera of Colombia. The cold periods occurred before 48,000 B.P., between 48,000 and 33,000 B.P., between 28,000 and 21,000 B.P., and from 16,000 to 14,000, 13,000 to 12,400, and 11,000 to 10,000 B.P. Glaciers in this region apparently reached their greatest extent when the climate was cold and moist, but shrank considerably after 21,000 B.P. because of greatly reduced rainfall. The dryness and cold lowered the upper forest limit to perhaps 1,800 meters, in contrast to its modern altitude of 4,000 meters.

Slightly to the east in Venezuela, as Valenti Rull and others have suggested, the tropical lowlands, now covered by dense forest, were arid or semi-arid during the Late Glacial Period.[3] After 13,000 B.P., the climate of eastern Venezuela fluctuated between colder and warmer periods, while the adjacent tropical lowlands grew warmer and drier. Between 12,500 and 11,400 B.P., there is evidence of a brief colder climate, indicated by a lowering of snow lines in the northern Andes. Pollen and glacial records suggest that just as this cold spell was ending in Venezuela, the regions to the south in Ecuador and northern Peru were cooling down.

In Ecuador, Clapperton studied two late glacial advances in the eastern cordillera.[4] These advances were similar in age to those in northern Peru, suggesting that a warming trend affected a wide area of the northern and central Andes south of the Equator, in the regions between 4,000 and 4,500 meters. Radiocarbon dating of organic material associated with the first advance indicates that a large ice cap began to shrink about 13,200 B.P. and that the area probably became ice free before 11,900 B.P. A smaller ice cap formed again, starting around 11,000 B.P., and advanced over the paramo vegetation of Ecuador before disappearing by 10,000 B.P.

Many high, subtropical desert basins in the Andes of southern Peru, northern Chile, and western Bolivia, whose floors consist of dried, salt-encrusted playas, contained freshwater lakes in late glacial times. The nature of the Ice Age climate in these regions of the Andes has generated considerable debate among geologists. Whereas some maintain that expansion of the lakes came from an increase in rainfall, others believe that it reflects a decrease in rainfall accompanied by a decrease in evaporation that resulted from lower temperatures. Regardless of the specific causes, the lakes represent important environmental changes.

Sediment records from high altitude lakes at 5,000 meters in Peru and Chile also show glaciers retreating rapidly between 10,700 and 9,700 B.P. In Bolivia, the records from Lake Titicaca are the most informative. The water level of the lake reached its maximum between 13,000 and 12,000 B.P. and a subsequent wet event occurred between 12,000 and 9,500 B.P.[5] Deglaciation produced large quantities of meltwater, most of which quickly found its way to the ocean. During full-glacial times, glaciers carried heavy loads of sediment to their margins, creating moraines. These sediments were then reworked and deposited as outwash by swollen braided rivers.

Retreating glaciers, in contrast, formed terraces, as streams cut downward into existing landscapes. Meltwater at the margins of the retreating ice was trapped by ice dams, which then gave way, producing enormous floods. The best evidence of these today can be found along the western slopes of the Andes in Peru and, especially, Chile, where impounded meltwater formed glacial lakes. When these lakes were suddenly released, they washed away surface sediments along with any archaeological remains that were in their path.

In the present-day fjords of southern Chile, the ice sheets extended beyond the present coastline, in many places all the way to the full-glacial shoreline. Relatively few stretches of ice-free coast are believed to have existed along the extreme southwest shore; nevertheless, unglaciated refuges may have been scattered between broad ice sheets, permitting people to move along the shoreline. Along most of the coast, the exact form of the glacial margin is not known, for the data lie largely submerged on the continental shelf. The massive glaciers of southern Chile, some fronting the ocean today, would have presented formidable barriers to people's movement.

Even farther south, in the far southern Andes of Chile, a late glacial advance ended by 14,000 to 13,000 B.P.[6] There also is evidence of a glacial readvance in Peru and southern Chile at 15,000 B.P., a warmer climate between 13,000 and 12,500 B.P., and another glacial readvance between 12,500 and 10,000 B.P. In southern Patagonia, there is evidence of a rapid withdrawal of glaciers around 16,500 B.P. The Patagonian ice fields had withdrawn by 13,000 B.P., when they reached their present-day borders.[7]

In sum, the evidence suggests that most parts of South America, albeit at different times and in different extremes, experienced a full-glacial climate that was drier than the present climate, with the exception of portions of the high Andes and in high latitude areas of the southern cone, where evidence of swollen lakes and a lower tree line indicates a wetter Ice Age climate.

It is important to bear in mind that many high altitude areas remained snow-covered and inhospitable even after deglaciation. Extensive glaciers still covered some areas of the Andes in 11,000 B.P. and remained until 10,600 B.P. in Ecuador and Peru. This means that several caves and rockshelters above 3,500 meters probably were not very hospitable until around 11,000 B.P. because some time would be needed for soils, plants, and animals to become established.

In other words, the end of the Ice Age was not the end of environmental change. Ice sheets remained in many areas of the high altitudes and the lower latitudes of the continent. World sea levels continued to rise, although at a steadily diminishing rate, and would not stabilize until 5,000 B.P. Extensive areas of land were literally rising due to the removal of the great glacial weight. And rainfall patterns continued to shift. In some areas, the large-scale migrations of plants and animals set in motion at deglaciation continued into the early Holocene period. Late Pleistocene people lived through a series of complex, rapid, and often highly localized environmental changes.

VEGETATION AND TEMPERATURE

We have had moderate success in reconstructing the vegetation patterns of glaciation and deglaciation, mainly by examining pollen records contained in bog and lake sediments. Plant species displaced by changing climate and spreading ice sheets persisted throughout the glacial age in various refuges in more temperate latitudes; some were probably located on the exposed continental shelves of the Pacific side of the continent.

The retreat of the ice sheets exposed vast areas for recolonization. At the same time, changing climates brought about changes in vegetation communities. In the Andes, vegetation movements frequently involved shifts in elevation. Species that once occupied highlands and that had moved downward into desert basins during glacial times reinvaded the higher elevations as glaciers retreated. Elsewhere, studies of pollen show that different tree types migrated at differing rates and in different directions from their widely separated refuges of full-glacial times. As various species moved around and combined in different locations, they created changing mosaics of vegetation communities. This redistribution of plants and animals probably took place a little more slowly than either the recession of glaciers or the changes in climate.

The large tropical rain forest of the eastern lowlands of South America currently occupies about 5,000,000 square kilometers; about 80 percent of that area is located in Brazil. The Amazon ecosystem houses more living species than any other region on earth. Today, for example, some 80,000 vascular plant species can be identified, and as many as 30 million animal species may exist. But this may not have been true in the past.

There are two divergent views concerning the Ice Age environment of the eastern lowland tropics.[8] The first is that the tropical rain forest has been a relatively permanent feature over the past million years. The second view holds that global climate change associated with the advance and retreat of glaciers brought about large-scale changes in the rain forest, as the forest shrank during the aridity of the Ice Age and then grew as the result of interglacial moisture. Indeed, in the last two decades, this periodic expansion and contraction has been the most frequent explanation for Amazonia's great mosaic of tropical forests, savannas, and parklands. During glacial periods, Amazonia had a much drier climate, resulting in the spread of savannas and driving the forest to scattered refuges. Then during interglacial periods, the forest expanded and the savanna was reduced to refuges. In time, this oscillation between one kind of refuge and the other created the current mosaic.

Scattered paleoecological evidence supports these shrinking and expanding zones of mosaic vegetation patterns. For example, pollen data from southwestern Amazonia indicate that savannas replaced rain forests during dry periods between 41,000 and 19,000 B.P. And in the western Chaco, to the immediate south of the Amazon Basin, depositions of windblown sand and loess suggest that what is now rain forest was desert from 19,000 to 13,000 B.P. Other studies have shown that central Brazil was humid between 32,000 and 21,000 B.P., arid between 17,000 and 11,000 B.P., and humid again from 10,000 B.P. onward. In the eastern lowlands of Brazil, the evergreen forests of glacial times began to change after 13,500 B.P. as deciduous species appeared in rapid succession. The result of this process was a succession of ephemeral forest communities that continually changed as new plant species arrived. By 10,000 B.P., the plant composition was somewhat similar to what it is today.

Farther south, vegetation and climate data show that the central Pampa grassland in Argentina was a dry steppe before 10,500 years ago, and the southwestern pampa was dry woodland. At about 10,000 B.P., the vegetation became more characteristic of ponds, swamps, and floodplains, telling of a wetter climate.

The desert coastal plains of western Peru and Chile also appear to have differed greatly from today. Paleoecological evidence shows wetter conditions between 14,000 and 10,000 B.P., with mountain forest in the foothills near what is now coastal desert but was then, at least in northern Peru, grassland.

Fossil beetle evidence from the southern Chilean lake region suggests that the mean summer temperature of the glacial climate was 4–5°C lower than today.[9] The beetle fauna after 19,000 B.P. was composed of species of wet moorland habitats. By 14,000 B.P., arboreal species were replacing species of open habitats, reflecting the shift to a warmer climate. By 12,500 B.P., the transition was complete, and fossil beetle assemblages consisted entirely of rain forest species.

What does all this patterning mean? It implies three things. First, most of the paleoenvironmental data across the continent suggest that the mixed environments of the late Pleistocene have few modern analogs. Today, deciduous and tropical forests are often cleanly separated; they may not always have been so during the late Pleistocene. Savanna and parkland, now clearly distinct zones, may not have been mutually exclusive. Conditions may have been similar to an ecotone, where mixtures from adjacent zones co-exist. We must admit to ourselves that some of the first Americans were probably adapted to closely juxtaposed or highly mixed environments, not always to specific zones such as desert or savanna. As we become better able to sort out past diets through reconstruction of paleoenvironments and recovered food remains, we may be able to measure the length and intensity of occupation and the way people organized themselves to exploit different foods.

Second, despite these mixed and rapidly changing landscapes, I suspect that some late Ice Age environments, such as the grassland plains of Argentina and parts of the arid coastal plains of Peru and northern Chile, remained fairly stable. People who may have moved into these areas after about 13,000 B.P. would not have been subjected to the kinds of drastic temperature and vegetation shifts typical of the Andes, the extreme southern reaches of the continent, and possibly the Amazon Basin. It seems that the most common outcome of environmental change in the Andes, the Amazon Basin, and south was not just mixing of species but a re-arrangement of ecosystems. That is, whole biotic associations—such as woodlands, with all their associated organisms—were simply relocated. For most human groups, particularly hunters, adjusting to this process amounts to following suites of resources over time.

Third, if we hold aside animal extinction, the Ice Age ended in South America not between 11,000 and 10,000 B.P. (as most archaeologists believe) but between 14,000 and 12,000 B.P. And in some areas this transition had minimal environmental effects. Clearly, the variety of environmental niches increased after 11,000 B.P., when the retreat of the glaciers created new resources and water sources, as well as rising sea levels, and thus promoted movement of both animals and people, especially toward the southern grasslands. But the glaciers directly impacted only about 20 percent of the continent, and for several thousand years prior to 11,000 B.P., there were numerous niches on the continent that humans could have inhabited.

REACHING SOUTH AMERICA BY LAND

Where did the first Americans come from? For long periods of time during the latest glaciation (called the Wisconsin stage), northeastern Asia was linked to Alaska by a land connection that was fully 2,000 kilometers wide from north to south. Exposure of this broad plain, known as Beringia, resulted from a lowering of worldwide sea levels by as much as 130 meters due to the volume of water locked up on land in the massive ice sheets that blanketed much of the higher latitudes. Beringia itself, however, remained an ice-free refuge, a dry plain covered with mosses, lichens, and sedges. Despite its treeless and barren appearance, Beringia's rich tundra supported huge herds of grazing animals, as well as the hunters who preyed on them.[10]

Beringia remained open for long periods. Geologists have determined that except for short spans, the passageway between the continents existed as dry land between 27,000 and 10,000 B.P., and for other extended periods even before that time. It probably was during one of these episodes that the Americas received their first inhabitants.

Access to the New World south of Alaska was more difficult. At times of maximum glaciation, the two great North American ice sheets (Cordillera in the west and Laurentian in the east) sometimes joined as one. It was once thought that during milder periods, people and animals could enter the south through an ice-free corridor along the eastern flank of the Canadian Rockies, where the edges of the ice sheets melted back from one another. Geologists now think that the corridor was impassable due to cold, wet conditions, even in so-called warm times or interstadials. It is more likely that people moved along the Pacific coastlines from Asia to North America and eventually South America.

As for South America, the only reasonable direction from which people could have initially entered the continent was in the north, presumably through the Panamanian Isthmus. Immediately upon entering the continent, they would have encountered a wide variety of environments, ranging from mangrove swamps, savannas, parklands, and tropical forests, to coastal estuaries in Colombia. These environments provided an abundance of rich game and plant resources, giving the settlers an incentive to adopt a proto-Archaic lifeway of varied hunting and gathering. As they moved south along the Colombian and Ecuadorian coastline, they would have encountered more mangrove swamps and more east-to-west descending river valleys until they reached the Guayaquil Basin, which back then was much smaller due to a lowered sea level. The environment was also drier, with more open grassland, than it is today. This area is particularly interesting because the wide coastal plain adjoins the narrowest and lowest section of the Andean mountains, providing direct access to the Amazon basin to the east. In fact, this may have been one of the primary routes of entry into the eastern lowlands of South America. Further south, the Andes widen and are much higher, reaching their maximum elevation in central Argentina and Chile at about 7,000 meters.

If the migrants had instead taken the eastern coastline, along the Caribbean coast into Venezuela, they would have encountered similar tropical environments and more desert. It probably is no coincidence that some of the earliest known pottery in the Americas is found in the coastal tropics near San Jacinto, Colombia.[11] I suspect that the diverse lowland and highland environments in northern Colombia and Venezuela and in many areas of the present-day Amazon basin led people to adopt or intensify an early proto-Archaic lifeway right from the outset. I say *intensify* because the proto-Archaic lifeway was probably developed somewhere in Central America and then brought into South America.

Alternatively, the foothills of the northern Andes may also have been a main route into South America.[12] Thomas Lynch believes that the first people in South America stuck to the same lands that had supported their North American ancestors: the savannas, open parklands, and woodlands of the tropics, and the high altitude paramo, puna, and altiplano areas where camelids were located. If the first South Americans entered first into the highlands, they probably followed the deltas of the lower intermontane valleys near the Caribbean coast of Colombia into the higher Magdalena, Cauca, and Sinu valleys, which stretch southward along the crest of the Andes. Their progress would not have been affected by extensive ice sheets unless they tried to move to higher elevations, which is unlikely. The incentive to continue along the highland crest was probably minimal until 13,000 to 11,000 B.P., by which time only patchy glaciers remained above 4,500 meters in Ecuador and Peru. During this period, more game animals probably started moving into higher elevations, and caves became available for human habitation. Thus we find human cultural remains in the basal deposits of caves dated between 10,800 and 10,000 B.P. in Ecuador and Peru. Any movement southward of Bolivia into Chile and Argentina would have been blocked by permanent glaciers until 13,000 B.P. Tierra del Fuego could have been reached only by the Patagonian plains and the canals of southern Chile. The present evidence suggests that people arrived in Tierra del Fuego by 11,000 B.P.

In spite of the possible route that took the first inhabitants into the Andes, the earliest sites in South America are located in the lowlands along both sides of the continent, which suggests that the first human populations moved along the Pacific and Atlantic coasts. As these populations dispersed southward, higher zones may still have presented impenetrable barriers to migration and human contact. The resulting geographic and genetic isolation would have caused some difference between eastern and western cultures, as they diverged farther and farther from their common source. Much of this cultural diversity can also be attributed to frequent movement into different environments and to isolated, local adaptations.

During the terminal Pleistocene, when glaciers receded and aridity increased, more people could have passed between the eastern and western parts of the continent. This might have led to more contact with people looking for more humid environments and resources. Such movement and contact would explain the first widespread horizon trait—the Fishtail point dated to between 11,000 B.P. and 10,200 B.P.

REACHING SOUTH AMERICA
BY SEA OR SEASHORE

Over the past generation, geologists have recognized that Earth's surface is a system of moving plates and that the collisions of these plates are largely responsible for the rise of mountain ranges and their associated geological turmoil. The Pacific coast of South America is the site of one such collision, and the interpretation of the South American coastal evidence is complicated by the rapid uplift of the Andes and its impact on archaeological visibility. Earthquakes and volcanoes undoubtedly altered landforms and shorelines and changed the course of rivers. The relationship of late Pleistocene cultures to such tectonic activity is highly complex. We know few specifics. At present all that can be said is that these changes must have had profound and far reaching effects, not only upon the mountain regions but upon the whole continent—and particularly upon the piedmont regions adjacent to the mountains, including the desert coastal plains of Peru and northern Chile, and upon coastal areas submerged by rising sea levels.

The global drop in sea level at the last glacial maximum is generally estimated to have been between 100 and 150 meters. Portions of the continental shelf were exposed as ocean shorelines shifted seaward, with the width of exposed land depending on the geometry of the shelf. Because the shelf along the Pacific side of South America is narrow, the shoreline generally shifted by less than 50 kilometers, whereas along the Atlantic and Gulf coasts, where the shelf is wide and gently sloped, the shoreline moved by 100 kilometers or more. Plant and animal remains recovered from the sea floor off eastern Argentina give evidence of an Ice Age biota that once lived on land.

We know that people could have migrated southward along old shorelines. But could they have reached the Americas by boat across the Atlantic or Pacific in late Ice Age times? We currently have no archaeological evidence to suggest that this ever happened. We can consider the possibility by looking to Australia, which was colonized in late Pleistocene times, evidently by sea. Australia was the last continent initially inhabited by boat people, sometime before 40,000 B.P., but the voyage from Southeast Asia to Australia is much shorter than that between the Americas and the distant shores of Asia or Europe.

Although there is no archaeological evidence for the existence of boats in the late Pleistocene period, the presence of people in southern Australia by at least 40,000 years ago clearly suggests that people somewhere in Southeast Asia must have invented some sort of watercraft. Recent archaeological evidence from outer Micronesia also indicates people were there by 30,000 B.P.

This presence requires a boat capable of sailing at least 400 kilometers of open sea. Was it a raft of tied bamboo and reeds, used for offshore fishing? Did they paddle a dugout canoe of the kind used today by modern Melanesians? Why did they travel to Australia? Did they set sail purposely, and if so, why? What was their motive? Or did they accidentally cross the ocean? Could they have made their way to the Americas by boat? We do not have answers to these questions.

Traversing the wide Pacific would have been a very difficult task. Thor Heyerdahl's voyage in the balsa-log Kon-tiki, across the Pacific from Peru in 1947, showed that drift voyages from east to west were possible. But a greater challenge faced the first Pacific colonists, who we know came from Indonesia. The islands of Polynesia were deserted until about 3,000 to 2,000 B.P. When the outrigger canoe was developed sometime before 3,000 B.P., people began to migrate eastward to the islands. Most archaeologists believe that an accidental or deliberate drift voyage to the Americas was very unlikely.

A popular alternative to both a Bering land bridge crossing and an ocean crossing has the first Americans traveling by rafts or canoes from Asia along the northwest coast as early as 20,000 to 15,000 B.P. Based on Charles Fairbank's geological work in Alaska, we now know that from 20,000 to 18,000 B.P., when the ocean level was at least 120 meters below its current surface, river gradients were greater than those of today.[13] Further, braided rivers meandered across preexisting coastal plains, and deltas formed shorelines near the present-day shelves. Many late Pleistocene alluvial plains, deltas, and coastal wetlands, now submerged along the entire Pacific coastline, probably served as environments for early hunters and gatherers. These environments were rich with resources: reliable water, abundant aquatic food sources, ease of travel and exchange. It is likely that the earliest people moving into the Americas from Siberia traversed these older shorelines, possibly in canoes or rafts, and then moved southward along the Pacific shelf and, later, perhaps along the Caribbean and Atlantic shelves as well.

Knut Fladmark and Ruth Gruhn also believe that these shelves may have been characterized by biologically rich coastal habitats capable of sustaining travelers.[14] This idea is gaining some support in light of new geological findings that suggest that glacier-free northern coastlines (from islands off Japan to Beringia and south through the Aleutians) were more extensive in 13,000 B.P. than previously believed. Moving fast and exploiting ice-free shores or islands for game animals and seafood, early boat travelers could have reached South America by 15,000 B.P. or earlier. But archaeologists looking for proof of such movement face difficult problems, including the possibility that post-glacial sea rise and coastal erosion may have covered or destroyed many sites.

Gruhn also believes that the first Americans may not have been big-game hunters. She suggests that coastal hunters migrating from Asia could have moved along the shoreline during warm periods around 50,000, 35,000, and 22,000 B.P., when temperatures in Beringia were probably more temperate than they are today. As they moved south, these coastal travelers could have fished and hunted sea mammals and migratory wildfowl. Gruhn believes that for ease of travel and for the abundance of plentiful food, the coastlines were much more appealing to the first Americans than were the interior environments. Both she and Fladmark suggest that even glacier coastlines in the far north would have provided refuges for travelers moving southward. When they reached

Panama, Gruhn thinks that some groups continued along the Pacific side to Chile. Others crossed Panama to the Caribbean and Atlantic coasts and eventually reached Argentina and Tierra del Fuego. And some groups may have headed into the interior of Colombia and Venezuela.

There is no secure archaeological record to confirm Gruhn's hypothesis. Instead, she relies mainly on linguistic patterns to make the case that the first Americans entered the continents on the Pacific side. Linguistic data suggest that the longer people have lived in an area, the more diverse their language becomes. In the New World, the area with the greatest diversity in native languages is along the Pacific Coast, from Puget Sound south. But linguistic data does not give us sufficient grounds to accept or reject the coastal migration hypothesis. It will take solid archaeological data to prove the hypothesis. Our only hope is to find early sites on offshore islands or sites that we can trace back to the inland counterparts of coastal migrants.

There is also recent consideration of an Atlantic crossing. Several archaeologists, including Dennis Stanford and Bruce Bradley, have found strong similarities between certain stone and bone industries of the Clovis culture and of the Solutrean culture of Spain and southern France (dated between 24,000 and 16,000 years ago). Stanford and Bradley suggest that late Pleistocene Spaniards or Frenchmen could have reached the eastern shores of Canada and the United States. Much like their Pacific counterparts, these people also could have migrated by boat along the edges of ice sheets extending from northwest Europe to the Atlantic side of North America. Although the North Atlantic was perhaps a more inhospitable environment than the Pacific, the possibility of such a crossing requires attention.

Rapid movement of the first immigrants exclusively along a coastline is not entirely appealing to me for three reasons. First, if we look at the earliest record of human migration in the Old World, we see very slow movement from region to region. Many areas of the Old World were inhabited hundreds of thousands of years after the first out-migration from Africa (although older coastal sites may be submerged). If coastal routes were so appealing and feasible to early humans, and if these routes led to rapid migration, then why are there no cases of this kind of migration documented in Europe?

Second, some archaeologists believe that the first Americans were sophisticated adventurers seeking new lands and new travel experiences. But if we have learned anything about more sophisticated cultures, it is that through time they tend to settle down rather than to become more nomadic. What, then, is the motivation for rapid coastal movement?

Third, as groups moved along the coast they probably encountered hundreds of hospitable deltas and river valleys that must have promised a wide variety of lush environments farther inland. If we adhere briefly to the adventure theory, I would think that the lure of the interior would at least occasionally have been more compelling than the monotony of the coasts. The fact is, people probably moved very slowly in some areas and quickly in others, depending on local resources, water supply, and many other variables. And the possibility of a coastal route says nothing about whether, at any time or place along the coast, they moved farther into the interior of North America. They may, for instance, have passed through open corridors not yet known to geologists.

Unfortunately, most of the crucial archaeological evidence that would confirm or disprove the coastal scenario now probably lies under the oceans. As the climate warmed slowly toward the end of the Ice Age, huge volumes of water locked up in northern glaciers melted, refilling the ocean basins. The rising seas inundated not only the Bering land bridge but also most of the Ice Age coastline of the Americas, so it is nearly impossible with our current technology to establish exactly when the first coastal communities developed along the Pacific rim. Archaeologists' only options are to look for sites inland or on offshore islands, and to search bays and shorelines for early sites that have been uplifted by tectonic activity. Such sites have recently been found in uplifted areas of southern Peru and northern Chile (see Chapter 4), but because they are no older than inland sites scattered across the continent, they tell us little about the date and path of human entry.

I suspect that as more archaeological sites become available, we will find evidence of multiple migrations into the Americas, along both the coastline and the interior. With new geological data demonstrating that most of the northern Pacific Ocean was deglaciated between 14,000 and 12,000 B.P. and that the southern coast of Beringia would have been passable at this time, we can imagine a coastal migration into the New World that had a rather limited impact on the interior of North America. The people who came over from Siberia may have continued down the coast to South America, bypassing much of the northern hemisphere. Other groups may have moved into the interior of the lower forty-eight states and never migrated farther south. Some groups may have been less effective than others in hunting game, or they may have exploited resources such as seafood and plants more intensively. Different migrations and different subsistence patterns could have led to improved technologies, increased population density, new cognitive skills, and a high degree of social organization. This kind of movement would also explain many of the early dates in the southern hemisphere and the lack of early dates in the North American interior, as well as why we find major technological and economic differences in the two continents' archaeological records.

THE EXTINCTION OF MAMMALS

By the end of the Pleistocene, some thirty-five species of large land mammals, nearly half the total number, were extinct in South America. The giant ground sloth, giant armadillo, native American horse, camel, bear, mastodon, paleo-llama, saber-toothed tiger, all much larger than their modern counterparts, became extinct by 10,000 B.P., although there is scant evidence from southern Argentina suggesting that the sloth may have survived until 8,000 B.P.

What caused this sudden demise of so many animals? Scientists, archaeologists, paleontologists, climatologists, and others have debated this question for decades. Two major causes have been proposed: climate change and hunting overkill by humans. In this debate, each side puts forward facts and conjectures that appear to contradict those of the other side. For example, proponents of Paul Martin's overkill model, which I described briefly in Chapter 2, argue that similar climatic changes during earlier interglacials failed to kill off many species such as the mastodon that were adapted to a broad range of environments.[15] Why should the most recent of many similar warmings be uniquely deadly? Supporters of the overkill model also note that the widespread appearance around 11,200 B.P. of hunters with Clovis points in North America and of analogous hunters with Fishtail points in South America coincides closely with several extinctions. These points have been found in association with the bone remains of extinct mastodon, horse, paleo-llama, camel, and sloth, suggesting that late Pleistocene hunters killed or scavenged these animals in at least some habitats. Furthermore, overkill supporters point to analogous extinctions in other parts of the world—for instance in Australia and New Zealand—that were coincident with human arrival.

Archaeologists who doubt the overkill hypothesis point out that certain extinct species are never found at kill sites. For instance, there is no direct evidence of human predation on bears and saber-toothed tigers, though perhaps humans were killing off the tiger's prey. Or maybe the mastodons were doing something that degraded the bear's or tiger's habitat. In other words, this argument may underestimate the ecological dependency between different species. On the other hand, other nonmammalian species also suffered extinction at the end of the Pleistocene, and there is little reason to suspect human intervention in the extinction of all these species.

Critics of the overkill hypothesis also note that the presence of butchering tools and the bone remains of large animals at some sites may indicate that people scavenged the kills of saber-toothed tigers and other large predators or fortuitously came across a natural death located by a water hole. Archaeologists used to think that any association between projectile points and the bone remains of large game meant a hunting event. In recent years, however, due to more sophisticated techniques in archaeology and the observation of modern-day hunters on the plains of Africa, we have come to realize that early humans probably took portions of animals from predator kill localities, which means that people may not have played the major role in extinction we once thought. The projectile points left behind at sites may have been utilized for butchering and not for killing animals.

New evidence for increasing aridity at the end of the Ice Age also casts doubt on human hunters as the sole factor in the extinctions. This climatic change caused a shift in the distribution of small species that may have been devastating to large animals. Because they require more food and more space to live, large animals generally are more vulnerable to environmental changes. Because they are also less common than small animals, the loss of even a few individuals in an area could have serious consequences during mating season, leading the population into a slow downward spiral. This relationship between climatic change and the fate of large animals implies that relatively little hunting is required to achieve "overkill."

The work of Vera Markgraf supplies us with one example of the impact of environmental change on large animals. Markgraf has compared pollen records from various archaeological and geological sites in southern Patagonia and Tierra del Fuego with fossil dung of the late ground sloth.[16] She has found that between 11,000 and 10,000 B.P., the cold, species-poor grassland of this region became a warm, dry, species-rich shrubby grassland. Markgraf believes that this change coincides with the ground sloth's extinction. She also suggests that the influx of other species into the grasslands put undue stress on food resources of the sloths and hastened their disappearance. Hunting pressure may simply have been the final blow.

To explain why changes in climate might have contributed to the extinction of certain species in the late Pleistocene, given that some of those species had survived earlier interglacials, the proponents of the climatic change theory argue that seasonal differences in the late Pleistocene may not have been particularly pronounced. Winters may have been warmer and summers cooler than they are, for example, in the present interglacial. As seasonal differences increased at the close of the Pleistocene, environmental changes probably would have been more dramatic. When combined with effective human predation, these climate-induced environmental changes may have been too much for many large animal species.

Other researchers working on the notion that climate change was the cause of extinction have argued that some species became extinct not at the close of the Pleistocene but several thousand years earlier, at the outset of deglaciation, before humans began to exploit them. However, given a pre-Clovis time of human arrival in the New World, the argument for an early disappearance of some species is not an argument against a human role in the extinction process. In fact, pre-Clovis sites add credence to the overkill hypothesis. If the loss of a few individual animals created an "extinction debt," then a slow attrition over many centuries—which is consistent with a hunter and gatherer lifeway—would have thinned populations sufficiently that they could not replace themselves. Or perhaps they were weakened enough so that they could not recover from the added stress of climate change or the invention of the deadlier Clovis point.

In the end, once more paleoecological and archaeological data are gathered, we will probably find that both climatic and human factors were involved in extinction. Because archaeologists have overemphasized dramatic big-game hunting among the first Americans, generally they have probably given too much credit to Martin's overkill hypothesis as the sole cause of extinction. The most spectacular and visible early North American sites to date have been large-animal kill locations—Clovis, Folsom, Plain-view—but the people who created them were probably exploiting a wide range of both plant and small-animal foods as well, and so were not, as Martin assumes, completely dependent on large ani-mals. The issue is also complicated by the fact that some species may have been extinct by the time humans came into the New World. Others, like the giant ground sloth of the southwestern United States, seem not to have been hunted at all, so to include them as victims of overkill requires discovering some (presently unknown) indirect effect. Thus, the human role in New World ex-tinctions remains unresolved.

FROM PLEISTOCENE TO HOLOCENE TIMES

The end of the Pleistocene and the onset of the Holocene, between 14,000 and 10,000 B.P. in most areas of South America, saw a brief return to full interglacial conditions in many places, with most glac-iers withdrawing inside their present limits. As I said at the start of this chapter, we must think of environmental change during this transition rather differently from the way we have been considering the changes of the late Pleistocene. For instance, during the transi-tion to the Holocene, most of the continent became drier. Inactive rivers have been recorded throughout the Pacific desert plains from northern Peru to central Chile, indicating a widespread drop in rainfall patterns. Due to aridity and the higher temperature, melt-ing glaciers in some regions caused rivers to build up plains and fill valleys, and subsequently to incise their channels. Fossil dunes seen along the eastern and northern edges of the continent from Venezuela to Brazil—a distance of approximately 1,600 kilometers-

—indicate desert conditions at this time. It is important to consider these and other changes in terms of their effects on the distribution and adaptation of regional human populations.

On the other hand, the effect of people on the environment at this time was probably marginal, affecting only particularly sensitive areas. When they first entered South America, some people were still largely at the mercy of their environment. Climate changes undoubtedly stimulated the more resourceful human groups to diversify their methods of extracting resources from many different environments, but human groups probably did not bring about visible changes in their surroundings until 11,000 to 10,000 B.P. By that time the environment began to show human fingerprints, as people, deliberately or not, altered their surroundings by such means as burning off forest and grassland, reducing certain species by excessive hunting, and protecting and increasing the number or range of other species.

With the establishment of a climate much like the present one at the beginning of the Holocene, some groups that had moved to new territories or adapted to changing conditions, and were thus conditioned to change, became able to exploit new opportunities. At this stage, there can be little doubt that people not only affected their environment but made increasingly conscious efforts to control it. Any assessment of environmental change from 13,000 to 10,000 B.P. must take this conscious manipulation of the environment into account. The control and movement of herds of camelids and other animals outside their natural territories; the building of huts and the establishment of settlements, with all that this entails in terms of the collection of fuel and fodder; the clearance of land (often, no doubt, by burning off trees, bushes, and coarse grass far beyond the area required); and the manipulation and eventual cultivation of selected plants—all these activities, and many others, and their collective secondary effects upon the countryside surely brought about far-reaching changes.

Cultural complexity among hunters and gatherers became more widespread after the Pleistocene, especially in wetland areas such as coastlines, bays, rivers, and estuaries, which offered abundant fish, shellfish, mammals, and aquatic plants. The advantage of aquatic resources was that they were both plentiful and predictable and thus may have provided the incentive for groups in these areas to adopt a sedentary lifeway. The full potential of these resources, however, was realized only in a few parts of the continent, especially in the tropical coastal lowlands of Colombia, Ecuador, and Venezuela, and in coastal Peru and Chile.

In sum, the transition from the Pleistocene to the Holocene was a time of changing environments and of people's strategies to survive within them. As I said at the start of the chapter, we cannot deny the important influence of the environment on people, yet the first Americans did not simply live at the mercy of the environment. Over time, they made decisions about how to best position themselves to take advantage of critical resources: food, water, raw materials for tool making—or even, in some cases, access to other humans. The results of these decisions—some of them—come down to us as archaeological sites.

LANDSCAPING CULTURES:
THE ARCHAEOLOGICAL SITE

Archaeologists today see humans and their environments as interacting systems whose parts mutually influence each other. The roots of this perspective can be found in ecology and in the geographer Carl Sauer's concept of the "cultural landscape," the domain of mutual interaction between people and their natural world. To archaeologists, the cultural landscape is a literal place—the archaeological site, a product of this interaction.

In simple terms, we can say that the environment is perceived and used by different societies and individuals in any number of ways. But it is in fact the complexity of the mutual interaction between society and environment that creates the cultural landscape. The concept most often used by archaeologists to explain this interaction is "culture ecology," in which society, environment, and technology play roughly equal roles in human adaptation to a particular environment; that is, a society creates and perpetuates a sustaining technology that in turn extracts resources from the environment for human use. Of course, the technology itself is created as a response to the environment, and its impact extends beyond the environment to the social and economic complexity of society itself. The notion of "culture ecology" is an attempt to conceptualize the complexities of the interactions between these three facets of human existence.

In Pleistocene archaeology, investigators have traditionally assumed that the environment was the strongest factor in the lives of the first Americans. Human activities thus gained shape as they either buffered or accentuated environmental conditions. For instance, according to the traditional model, hunter-gatherers were almost totally dependent on the availability of animal and plant foods. When these were depleted, people presumably moved to another locality with a plentiful supply, and the cycle started again. Thus this simple environmental determinism assumes that the environment dictates human outcomes, but in fact, the first Americans were not simply at the mercy of their environment.

We must keep in mind that hunter-gatherers have economic choices in any environment. They can adapt to changing circumstances, and rarely are they restricted to a single option. We must also remember that similar environments can host different choices and adaptations—and the choices people make will depend a lot on how they perceive their environment. Thus, human perception is an important mediator between culture and environment. With its emphasis on environmental determinism, traditional Pleistocene archaeology overlooked this mediating factor.

For many contemporary archaeologists, on the other hand, the most important world to study is the world of human perception, intention, and behavior. Goals, values, and perceived needs condition the way hunters and gatherers choose to interact with their environments. This means that when we interpret archaeological sites, we must think not only in terms of the different resources available across space but also in terms of how people's interaction with the environment was conditioned by their perception of such things as travel time, social relationships, seasonal changes in the availability of resources, and the accessibility of resources, given the available information and technology. A group such as the first settlers in South America would have had to anticipate future conditions that may or may not have resembled its past experiences in other environments. Whatever new constraints this group encountered, technology and a flexible social organization could probably—and ultimately, of course, did—overcome them. We can surmise that there must have been numerous ways people adapted and changed socially and culturally to fit new situations as they spread throughout the continent. This variety of adaptation is what produced the differences in regional archaeological records.

As archaeologists try to piece together the complex relationship between social organization, technology, and the environment in the lives of the first Americans, they must also consider the spatial proximity of various sites. The location and spacing of the first settlements in a newly inhabited environment probably influenced the location of later ones, as new campsites stayed in touch with old. As groups expanded into new areas, their motives, preferences, modes of thinking, and traditions were surely drawn from previous experiences and from their existing social and cultural context. If archaeologists can discover links between various sites, particularly sites in the same region, then they may be able to gain even more insight into the activities of the early inhabitants of the Americas.

In sum, environments help determine the location, duration, and intensity of early human settlement. But environments cannot be separated from culture. The seasonal availability of food, its distribution across the landscape, and the difficulty in obtaining and processing it influence a group's activities and economic decisions, but so, too, do the available technology and the group's perceptions of its needs, its goals, and so on. How a group chooses to exploit natural resources and interact with its surroundings is thus a complex affair.

Classifying Sites

Different kinds archaeological sites represent different settlement patterns and different relationships to changing landscapes and shifting economic activities. In South America, six categories of hunter-gatherer sites have been observed: long-term habitational or base camp sites; seasonal or short-term campsites; butchering stations; quarry sites; transitory stations; and localities that only appear to be sites. These classifications are based on ethnographic examples of modern hunters and gatherers, on evidence of the animals hunted and plants and other foods gathered, and on analyses of artifacts found in these sites.

LONG-TERM BASE CAMPS   Base camps are the largest type of site; most known camps are located in large, chambered caves and rockshelters that would have commanded a good view of passing game. Some are outdoors and may occupy up to 200 to 300 square meters. The camps are close to water, fuel, and sources of stone for making tools. Most toolmaking and food preparation took place at these base camps, resulting in a great density and diversity of refuse. Excavations at base camps have produced concentrations of chipping debris from the making of stone tools, identifiable bone remains, tools for making other tools, food-processing tools (including grinding stones), ornaments, and a wide range of other artifacts. Because tools were made mainly from local materials, they are diverse, with unifacial tools especially varied and abundant. Base camps have more hearths than other types of sites, and they can have clearly defined living floors. It appears that during late Pleistocene times, regular living sites were established on the banks of rivers, in the open, and in rockshelters. The similarity of sites and the diversity and density of tool forms suggest extended occupation or reoccupation.

SHORT-TERM CAMPSITES   The short-term campsite is composed of small sites, with tool kits containing a narrow range of small formal tools and expedient butchering and processing tools made from local materials. Artifacts are generally sparser, but tool forms are highly varied.

BUTCHERING STATIONS Most butchering stations were probably kill sites or small rockshelters and are seldom larger than 100 square meters. Hunters who had made a kill used these camps to butcher the animal before returning to the base camp. Artifacts at butchering stations include killing and butchering implements, but the grinding stones and other all-purpose tools found at base camps are usually lacking. Each used surface of a butchering station usually contains the remains of one or two animals, which may be from different species. Usually only selected parts of carcasses of large animals were brought back to the base camp or to short-term campsites.

TRANSITORY STATIONS Many locations may have served as lookouts for hunters searching for game, who passed the time by preparing new tools and weapons. These sites may have also been used for catching small animals and gathering plants during the appropriate seasons. They usually contain scattered chipping debris and occasionally stone tools.

QUARRIES There can be little doubt that quarry sites were located near sources of raw material for tools—good quality chert or quartzite, wood, shell, and bone. These sites probably served wide areas, but just how wide in each case is a matter for future research. In many cases their products must have traveled far beyond the territory of the single group occupying the site. Thus, the economic and organizational implications of quarry sites can be profound. The web of social and economic relations based on the use of quarry sites and the exchange of raw materials must have involved groups well beyond a single extended family.

These sites are characterized by stone tool debris, a variety of expedient tools, and a small quantity of curated tools. There are clear indications that tools were made at these sites. For instance, we find bifaces that were broken during manufacture and then modified for a different task. The same early tool forms that are found at the other types of sites are found on quarry sites. As evidenced by the presence of hearths and domestic refuse, it appears that some quarry sites may have been used for a variety of purposes besides obtaining raw material.

LOCALITIES THAT ONLY APPEAR TO BE SITES   Some localities may appear to be intact archaeological sites but are not. These include, for instance, small concentrations of artifacts with or without an apparent specific character; open sites in any of the above categories that were subsequently covered by deposition of sand, silt, loess, and so on, and that are now seen in geological section or in the process of exposure by erosion, flooding, or road cuts; redeposited material in geologically stratified deposits, either in river terraces or in buried strata; scatters of varying numbers of artifacts on old erosion surfaces; and isolated finds of single artifacts.

Locating Sites

Where are these various kinds of sites usually located? The movements of a small group of people entering an area for the first time, or shifting throughout an established territory, must have been immensely complex. Many different activities were carried out in different locations, as represented by these different sites. Some locations would have been base camps for long-term occupation; others would have been temporary campsites for short-term stays to procure a specific resource. The size and location of these campsites probably varied considerably, depending on the resource and the season.

As expected, most sites are located near water sources and, sometimes, near stone and other resources. Campsite location, therefore, must have been chosen primarily because of water availability, particularly in deserts, which left little latitude for considering other resources. Springs, ponds, and small lakes are common features in some arid environments. In wet areas, people probably looked for high and drier terrain and for a location near multiple resources.

People often lived in caves. Yet not all caves or rockshelters contain archaeological material, let alone late Pleistocene evidence. Assuming a cave was ever inhabited, there must have been an accumulation of sediment both before and after occupation for the evidence to be preserved. Not all caves contain sediments. Further, not all caves and rockshelters, especially in the high Andes, were occupied by early people or even existed in late Pleistocene times.

River terrace sites make up a large category of early sites in South America and are geologically the most complicated. Radiocarbon dates and recent geological studies have shown that many of our ideas about late Pleistocene and early Holocene terraces are much too simple. In past years, archaeologists have correlated terrace settlements over large areas, connecting different drainage basins into large imaginary networks of contemporaneous populations. Unfortunately, many of these long-range correlations are difficult to substantiate. Hydraulic forces and rates of sedimentation may differ markedly within small drainage basins or even along an individual stream. The number and age of terraces may vary between different streams that all drain into the same major river. Furthermore, many buried terrace surfaces with cultural evidence may be erosional features and mixed deposits rather than intact archaeological surfaces. Radiocarbon dates from a number of buried terrace sites in South America indicate that the ages of archaeological surfaces may vary considerably both vertically and horizontally, casting serious doubt on the validity of their cultural deposits.

Sites buried in ancient sand dunes are particularly subject to destruction by wind deflation. Surface artifacts in sand blowouts are common in many dune areas of Peru and Chile.

In sum, the places people lived, temporarily or more or less permanently, are the most obviously interesting, if the sites are intact, and have the greatest potential for yielding reliable cultural and environmental evidence. But we can get a more complete picture by considering all types of sites in a region, even if their chronological relationships at first are not clear. By surveying all the available evidence we can begin to work out how different kinds of sites relate to each other and to their environmental setting, and we can then interpret what archaeologists have found there.

Site types and their locations bring us to the question: How did the landscape and the structure of food resources influence the technology, economy, and social organization of the first Americans?

Landscapes and Adapting Lifestyles

Both globally and within South America, the plants and animals encountered by early humans influenced their group size, technological organization, and mobility patterns. For instance, the mosaic structure of forests, savannas, and parklands in the Amazon basin 12,000 years ago would have been ideally suited for what archaeologist Lewis Binford has called "residentially mobile foraging groups."[17] Both the more homogeneous forest cover in parts of Brazil and the grasslands of the high Andes—the Pampa and Patagonia—would have been conducive to residentially mobile adaptations, where people foraged over the landscape, readily moving on as food became locally exhausted. It is this continued relocation, especially during their initial entry, dispersion, and settlement, when groups were probably highly nomadic, that produced many of the numerous, ephemeral short-term sites we find today. The traces left by these foragers are dominated by what are called expedient assemblages—tools that were casually made, used, and then thrown away. (Diagnostic bifaces are rare or absent in such assemblages, as is the use of high quality stone material, unless it happens to outcrop locally.) Although foraging groups may have ranged over large areas, single moves tended to be fairly short, typically no greater than the distance to the nearest undepleted food supply.

Another strategy identified by Binford is that of "logistically organized collectors." Certain mosaic resource zones are best exploited by groups that radiate out short distances from central base camps or staging areas, staying at temporary camps as long as necessary to collect resources and then returning to the home base. This adaptation is also known more simply as a collector strategy. Although groups practicing collector strategies sometimes move their base camps, they usually do so only when local resources are exhausted to the point where the costs of moving are less than those of finding food. The archaeological record of collector groups includes base settlements and outlying camps. The latter sites commonly contain highly diagnostic tool kits, assemblages that reflect the specific goals of the collecting expeditions.

This may have been the strategy the first South Americans employed in forests and coastal areas where the resources were more varied and abundant than in open grasslands and savannas. Given the generally poor preservation of early archaeological records, however, it is often difficult to determine whether a site represents a collector or foraging strategy. One key is that the tools from early sites of collectors are both well-made and "throw-away" tools, versus the predominately expedient assemblages that characterize the sites of foragers. Many of the curated artifacts at the sites of collectors are bifaces that were carried from place to place, sharpened and reused as necessary until they were worn out. These tools were frequently made of high quality stone, which would have facilitated reworking and hence helped conserve raw material. (High quality stone keeps a sharper edge longer than poor quality material.) Collector populations moved over large areas from home bases that were centered on quarries or other desirable environmental features. Once resources in the home areas became depleted, people began to relocate the base settlement, which may have required a long-distance move.

The sorts of land settled by these various early groups reveal much about their relationships with nature. Although the archaeological record is biased both by our belief that the first Americans were hunters preferring open environments and by a lack of visibility in such heavily vegetated areas as the forested tropics, people eventually lived in nearly all South American environments. We once thought that wetlands, temperate forests, and savannas were probably preferred over other environments because they supported an abundance of aquatic and other resources or herds of grazing animals that provided a predictable food supply. Less-populated areas supposedly included the deserts, the rain forests, and the dense evergreen woods of the south—a substantial portion of the continent's surface. Wherever grazing animals were lacking, it was thought, less evidence of early humans would be found, but we now know that this is not necessarily so. Tropical forests in particular, which have been investigated less than more accessible environments, contain a wide variety of edible plants and are where many species most likely were domesticated, which would indicate that humans inhabited these areas.

Past environments and their relation to Pleistocene archaeology provide the skeleton for a new understanding of early South American prehistory. The most significant advances toward this understanding have been the discovery of new archaeological sites in previously unexplored areas and the confirmation of a pre-Clovis human presence on the continent. This skeleton is gradually being articulated and clothed with flesh as other aspects of the first South Americans come into focus.

CHAPTER FOUR

The Stone Tool Traditions

No MAJOR REGION OF SOUTH AMERICA is without Ice Age sites. In some places, such as the Eastern Highlands of Brazil, the Andean foothills on the north coast of Peru, and the steppes of southern Chile and Argentina (Figure 4.1), such sites can be found in profusion. (In other areas, such as the tropical forests of the Amazon Basin, sites are hard to find and little work has been done.) Wherever archaeologists have studied Ice Age lifestyles, they have found increasing regional and local diversity, both in stone tool technology and in other artifact types, as well as increasing adaptability. During deglaciation (between 14,000 and 11,000 B.P.), many human communities remained stable in the face of drastic increases in temperatures and aridity.

Unfortunately, lifestyles and adaptations are not what we excavate: We uncover chipped stone tools, animal bone fragments, and occasional evidence of plant foods and prehistoric features such as firepits or hearths. Where preservation of organic remains is good, the evidence indicates a far richer and more diverse culture with a more varied diet than has been recognized previously.

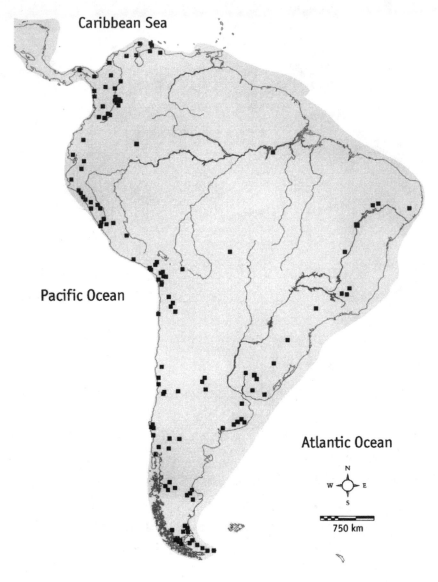

FIGURE 4.1   Distribution of Known Late Pleistocene Archaeological Sites in
South America

Since diet is an important part of a culture, archaeologists try to reconstruct the first South Americans' hunting and gathering practices. Plant remains, including seeds, nuts, and wood, can be recovered by a technique known as flotation. Archaeologists working at late Pleistocene sites, however, have seldom applied this technique to excavated deposits. Thus unless large plant specimens are preserved and cataloged at the time of excavation, plant remains usually go undetected, which biases the record greatly. Past lifeways can be interpreted only from the objects that are preserved by nature and then collected by archaeologists. Because nature usually does not preserve plant remains and because archaeologists only occasionally collect the remains that have been preserved, the objects that most readily enable archaeologists to reconstruct the diet and the lifeway of the first South Americans are stone tools and animal bones. Because stone tools, in particular, are ubiquitous at early sites, they are clearly worth our attention.

STONE TOOL TECHNOLOGIES

As in other parts of the world, the early stone tool industries of South America are classified into traditions based on their size, shape, and methods of manufacture. These traditions can be broadly divided into bifacial and unifacial industries. Stone tools are made by striking flakes from cobbles and chunks of stone raw material. Bifacial tools are made by chipping two adjacent faces of the stone to produce a sharp, workable edge for cutting, scraping, gouging, drilling, and so on. Making good bifaces is a delicate and often complex task. Even today, the modern flint knappers who have tried to rediscover these techniques have found it difficult to duplicate the precision of the ancient knappers. South America contains a wide variety of bifaces, including projectile points, heavier cutting and chopping artifacts, and parallel-sided blades.

Unifaces are made in the same way as bifaces but are worked or trimmed on only one face to produce a useable edge. Unifacial tools often are simpler and involve fewer manufacturing steps than bifaces, but they perform many of the same functions. Distinct unifacial industries are found in most regions of South America, with the major exception of the grasslands of Patagonia. Unifacial tools are also found in North America but only with bifacial industries. In South America, the two industries appear both separately and together.

Because the terminology used in South America to describe these two industries comes mainly from the North American Paleoindian period (which is associated with Clovis and later Ice Age cultures), assumptions about the age of South American stone tools are often based on their resemblance to similar tool forms in North America. Thus the terms imply a technological tie to North America and, by extension, a later time period for South American versions of a particular type.[1] The North American designations also enforce a rigid separation of tool types. In many regions of South America, for example, unifacial tools are included within a bifacial industry, and it is assumed that the same people made both types to fit different circumstances.[2] There also are regions such as parts of eastern Brazil and of the north coast of Peru, where only unifacial industries are found in sites. These industries are usually different from those associated with bifacial industries and can be readily distinguished by their simpler forms. Yet some archaeologists, steeped in North American stone tool technology, simply refuse to believe that unifacial sites exist. They prefer to think that the bifaces have not yet been found at these sites. Yet both the unifacial and bifacial industries have definite regional distributions in South America that distinguish them from their North American counterparts.

Furthermore, despite some rough similarities, the South American biface industry generally has few striking relationships to its northern counterparts. The distinction between the two continents is profound and complex. In North America, only bifacial technologies are seen as diagnostic of particular cultures and periods. Those technologies appear in clear stylistic and technological sequences that can be followed from the beginning of the Paleoindian period around 11,200 B.P. and from one elongated projectile point type to another (for example, from Clovis to such regional variants as Folsom, Plainview, Dalton, Cumberland). These common stratigraphic sequences suggest an obvious technological and cultural progression. As a result, North American sites are dated and classified solely from their bifacial tools; unifaces are rarely diagnostic of anything. In South America by contrast, there are few linking traits to indicate technological evolution, even where there is a stratigraphic sequence of diagnostic projectile points.[3] Where these points occur, they generally are regional types and appear with very low frequency, occupying 2 percent or less of the total stone tool collection in a site. In sum, the geographic distribution of these points in the southern hemisphere together with the presence of other bifaces such as knives and drills and of unifaces suggests complicated mosaics of technological and subsistence practices in which both bifacial and unifacial types occur independently.

What are the technological and historical linkages between unifaces and bifaces in South America? Did one grow out of the other, or do they represent separately developed traditions? Alan Bryan believes that they represent two distinct traditions; he believes, further, that the unifacial tradition was invented in South America and that the bifacial tradition was imported from North America.[4] Gustavo Politis and Hugo Nami, two Argentine archaeologists, offer a different view.[5] They see the industries as overlapping and complementary, with one predominating over the other according to context. To Politis and Nami, this complementarity indicates cultural adaptability. On the other hand, if bifaces and unifaces represent separate traditions, as Bryan believes, the question arises as to whether these traditions originated with different human migrations into South America. The distinct unifacial tradition that is unique to South America could have developed from an early mixed bifacial and unifacial industry. As humans moved into heavily vegetated environments, such as the deciduous and tropical forests of lower Central America and northwestern South America, they may have turned more to unifacial tools.

South America also contains sling stone and grooved bola stone industries, which represent a grinding and pecking tool tradition. Sling and bola stones are usually smooth, round implements that are either select water-rounded pebbles or rough stones pecked into a spherical shape. Round stones are desired because they can be thrown the farthest and the most accurately. If they are first whirled around the hunter's head in the pocket of a sling or tied to the end of a thong, their effective range is still better. Like a spear-thrower, the sling acts as an elongation of the thrower's arm. The greatest frequency and variety of these stones are found at early sites in the southern half of the continent, such as Monte Verde (12,500 B.P.) and Fell's Cave (11,000 B.P.) in Chile and several caves and rockshelters in eastern Brazil (between 11,500 and 11,000 B.P.). They thus represent one of the earliest stone tool industries in the Americas.

Although shepherds commonly used slings in controlling their flocks, we have relatively few historical examples of the use of slings among hunters. The chief exceptions were South Americans: The Araucanians of the Lake District of Chile and the Yaghans and Ona of Patagonia used them to hunt birds and other small game. The Teheulche of Patagonia, relatives of the Ona, used to throw a baseball-sized stone or bola attached to a single thong that, when released after twirling, trailed the stone like a comet's tail. This weapon could stun a guanaco or rhea, the South American equivalent of an ostrich. Some of these stones had grooves around them for attachment, a sign that they were important enough weapons to warrant careful preparation.

In addition to studying different stone tool types, archaeologists study the source material of early stone tool industries. By knowing the type and, especially, the location of raw material used to make tools, we can determine whether they were made locally, were carried for long distances, or were traded. For instance, unworked pieces of chert and quartzite of unusually high quality were often carried for hundreds of kilometers, until the supply was expended or another good source was found. And tools made of high quality material were often maintained by resharpening them, until they were dulled and could no longer be used. The kinds of raw material in a site tell us whether its inhabitants were nomads traversing a wide range of environments or colonizers staying within one region.

Most early sites in South America are not associated with sources of top quality raw material, such as chert and obsidian. Instead, quartzite, quartz, basalt, and andesite were exploited extensively in many places. Quartzite is the material from which most tools were made, although tools made of volcanic rocks and various types of silex are sometimes found. Obsidian appears rarely in the late Pleistocene record.

Regional Biface and Projectile Point Styles

A wide variety of early projectile styles are known in South America. They include bipointed forms like the El Jobo points from Venezuela and the Monte Verde points from southern Chile; the stemmed and fluted points of the Fishtail style from Ecuador, Patagonia, and other areas; the triangular and subtriangular point types from the highlands of the Andes; and an assortment of stemmed and unstemmed types from other areas (Figure 4.2).[6] The earliest forms, the bipointed Monte Verde and probably the El Jobo points, may be associated with the earliest human migrations into South America, sometime well before 11,000 B.P., or they may simply may be southern hemisphere inventions. The later Fishtail and stemmed styles correspond with human populations settling throughout the continent starting around 11,000 B.P., often adopting the generalized way of life that would characterize much of the early Archaic period.

We know that point styles began to proliferate at the outset of the eleventh millennium, particularly in the northern and central Andean mountains. The evidence of this proliferation partially reflects a sampling bias: Most archaeological work has been done in these regions. Yet it also indicates a flowering of specialized but versatile technologies adapted to fit local needs, as numerous small and localized groups adapted to a constantly changing environ-

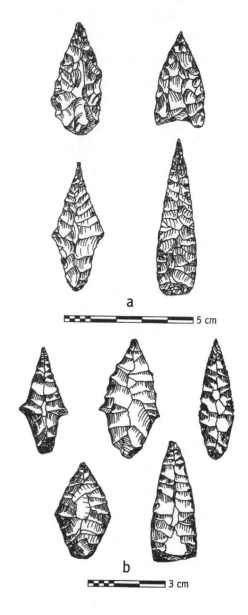

a

5 cm

b

3 cm

FIGURE 4.2   *Various Stemmed and Unstemmed Points*
(a) Stemmed and unstemmed points from the deeper levels of Guitarrero Cave,
Peru; (b) Stemmed points from cave sites of the Central Andean Hunting
Tradition.

97

ment. This localization is well documented in areas like the north coast of Peru, eastern Brazil, and southern Patagonia.

In the 1930s, Junius Bird's pioneer work at Fell's Cave and other sites in Patagonia established an important early point chronology for the continent.[7] By the 1960s, the famous Fishtail point he found at Fell's Cave had become one of the best (or at least one of the best accepted) benchmarks of early stone tool technology in South America.

Fishtails have rounded shoulders and convex-sided stems with slight corners, and they are usually fluted. It is the fluting that concerns most archaeologists, because this trait is also found on the Clovis point in North America and is thus believed to be the key link between the two continents. Unlike that in North America, however, fluting in South America shows diverse technologies and forms on both lanceolate and stemmed points.

Since the 1970s, archaeologists have found a wide variety of stemmed and lanceolate fluted points; some of them are clearly related to the Fishtail form (Figure 4.3). Scattered findings of the fluted-stem type are reported in Colombia, Venezuela, Ecuador, Chile, Argentina, Uruguay, and southern Brazil.[8] A smaller, fluted-stem form occurs at several places across Colombia and into Panama. Larger, stemmed Fishtail points, similar in form to those found by Bird at Fell's Cave, appear at the El Inga site in the central highlands of Ecuador and at a few sites on the north coast of Peru. Fishtail or fluted-like points have also been recovered from numerous sites in southeastern Brazil and in the pampa of Uruguay and Argentina. And a fluted lanceolate style closely resembling the classic Clovis forms of the Great Plains of North America has been found at several surface sites on the south coast of Chile.

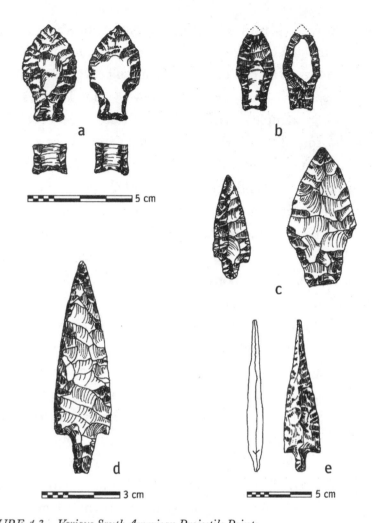

FIGURE 4.3 Various South American Projectile Points

(a) Obverse and reverse sides of a Magellan-type projectile point from Fell's Cave, Chile. Note the long, thinning flake or possible flute in the base of the points. (b) Magellan- or Fell's Cave–type Fishtail point from El Inga, Ecuador. (c) Short stemmed point from El Inga. (d) Long stemmed point without basal thinning flakes or flutes from El Inga, Ecuador. (e) Paiján point from La Cumbre, Peru. [(a)–(d) redrawn from G. Willey, An Introduction to American Archaeology, vol. 2, South America (Englewood Cliffs, N.J.: Prentice Hall, 1971), pp. 44–46; (e) redrawn from P. Ossa, "Paiján in Early Andean Prehistory: The Moche Valley, North Coast of Perú," in Early Man in America from a Circum-Pacific Perspective, ed. A. L. Bryan (Edmonton: Department of Anthropology, University of Alberta, 1978), fig. 10.]

99

How do we explain the possible bicontinental distribution of fluting? It may be the result of a shared technological knowledge having its roots in an earlier tradition among several human populations dispersing throughout the New World. Thomas Lynch believes, for example, that both the "fluted" lanceolate and stemmed forms of these artifacts, as well as their association with other bifacial tools and with various kinds of scrapers, qualifies them as variants of the fluted Clovis technology, which he thinks reached South America only 500 to 1,000 years after its initial appearance in North America.[9] But this may not be the case.

Indeed, in the 1960s and the 1970s, Irving Rouse and, later, William Mayer-Oakes both argued that Fishtails were South American inventions that diffused to North America.[10] Alan Bryan and Ruth Gruhn hold the slightly different view that the Fishtail and Clovis points were separate inventions, possibly derived from a common technology, that converged somewhere in Central America or Panama. There is growing support for this position from several archaeologists, who consider the Fishtails from Madden Lake, Panama, as more similar to the South American style than to Clovis. Luis Borrero, an Argentine archaeologist, thinks the fluted Fishtail developed independently in many centers, including Panama, Uruguay, and southern Patagonia. This would explain its distribution in several parts of the continent, if not its relationship with points in North America.

The dating and origin of the Fishtail point is controversial. Although these points have been dated by radiocarbon means between 11,000 and 10,200 B.P. in southern Patagonia, Fishtail points are no older than 10,500 B.P. in other areas of South America, where they often coexist with other stemmed, unfluted points or other stone tool industries. Furthermore, the Fishtail's technological and chronological affinity with other early point types and unifacial industries is unclear. A small handful of archaeologists presume that the fluted form is earlier than all other bifacial or unifacial industries, but there is not a single site in South America with good stratigraphic context to prove this early date. Other investigators think the Fishtail is later than other point types of South America. For instance, Gerardo Ardila, a Colombian archaeologist, believes that the stemmed Fishtails of northern South America postdate the bipointed El Jobo forms, which may be 13,000 to 11,000 B.P. years old. Furthermore, Ardila sees no connection between the fluted points of South and North America.

Some archaeologists have argued that the fluted trait does not exist at all in South America. The longitudinal groove, or fluting, on a Clovis point is designed so that it may be firmly inserted into a spearshaft. The similar groove on a Fishtail point may be nothing more than a longitudinal thinning flake removed to shape the stem or base of the point. Unlike the Clovis point, it does not always have channel flakes and "nipple" platforms to make the flute. As Gustavo Politis has observed:

> Most of the FTPPs [Fishtail Projectile Points] display only varying amounts of basal-thinning flake scars. Sometimes, a facet of an original blank [or blade] assumes the role of a channel flake. . . . Only for the Cerro La China and Cerro El Sombrero series are fluted channel flakes reported. . . . Flegenheimer [the excavator of these sites] believes that the fluting was done in the final shaping stage . . . [and thus] differs from the fluted channel of the North American points. . . .
>
> Some preliminary technological observations suggest that the manufacturing steps involved in the FTPP production process differ from those followed during the reduction of a Clovis or Folsom

preform. . . . The deep parallel flake scars, which transversely cross the fluted and unfluted early North American points, are absent on the FTPPs. Those morphological traits indicate clear-cut differences between the production of a North American fluted point and an FTPP.[11]

In a detailed comparative study of Fishtail and Clovis points, the Argentine archaeologist Hugo Nami attempted to make these points using the Ice Age methods of flint knappers. He concluded that the two types represent distinct technologies and inventions and should not be equated with either a single technology or a single human migration throughout the New World.

The Fishtail is not the only projectile point style found in multiple areas. There is also the Ayampitín point (Photo 4.1), a laurel-leaf (bipointed) shape similar to the El Jobo and Monte Verde forms. First described by Alberto Rex González, another Argentine archaeologist, from the Ayampitín site in northwest Argentina and reported from numerous sites in the central and southern Andes, this type's chronological placement has been unclear.[12] Many named laurel-leaf point types from the crest of the Andes fit the general Ayampitín pattern, but apart from their similarity to the classic form in Argentina, this relationship cannot be assessed yet. Some archaeologists have argued that the Ayampitín style dates to the late Pleistocene period; others have argued that it is later and belongs to the early Holocene.

In conclusion, the sequence of the succession of the stemmed, lanceolate, fluted, laurel-leaf, and other point styles in South America is uncertain. Fishtails, for instance, could have diffused from North America; they could have been invented in South America and diffused to the north; or they could have been devel-

5 cm

PHOTO 4.1   Ayampitín Point from
Northwest Argentina. The bases are
always slightly rounded.

oped independently in both hemispheres and converged in Central America. Part of this uncertainty comes from the way different archaeologists assign point forms to different types. Differing assignments automatically imply different origins and different ages. As I discussed in Chapter 2, these differing assignments are a manifestation of the differences between lumpers and splitters as they sort objects that are sometimes quite similar.

Uniface Technologies

Many of the early tool kits in South America are what archaeologists call simple expedient technologies, adapted not only to long-term environmental changes but to constant local fluctuations as well. We can imagine that most stone tool technologies were flexible enough to cope with adversity, so that, for example, the same activities could have been carried out at several localities with different tools if necessary. Conversely, several different activities could be performed with one all-purpose, expedient tool—a sort of Pleistocene Swiss Army knife. This technology is the uniface.

Although unifacial industries from the Andes and in much of the Amazon share some basic technological features, they also have distinctive characteristics that differentiate them by region. Thus these industries can be further subdivided into lesser regional groups and into a series of local traditions. Some of these traditions outlived the Pleistocene, continuing into the Archaic and even the proto-historic period, as in the case of pebble tool industries at many Inca period sites along the Peruvian coast. Despite these differences, however, we should view the unifacial industries as a single industry characterized primarily by edge-trimming along one face (thus the term "uniface") to produce a sharp edge for cutting, scraping, adzing, and other functions.

The flakes (smaller pieces of stone knocked from a larger stone) that are the main parts of the unifacial industries vary in shape, with round, rectangular, and pointed forms, and long parallel-sided blade flakes.[13] Many flakes show pronounced bulbs of percussion, indicating that they were probably struck off the parent core with a hammer stone. Rounded and ovoid pebbles, some 8 to 10 centimeters in diameter and battered at one or both ends, are also found at unifacial sites and suggest that this was the means used to remove flakes. Some of the more slender flakes were probably made with a wooden hammer. With the flakes are found cores of another type, made by removing one or more flakes from a suitable pebble to provide a striking platform, from which thick but sometimes approximately parallel-sided blade-flakes were then removed. A certain number of cores of both types show subsequent use as chopping tools. Chopping tools, cores, flakes, and many objects that can be described only as utilized pieces of stone are generally found in abundance at early South American sites. Bifacially shaped points are rarely found in unifacial industries, although sometimes we find pointed flakes, more or less leaf-shaped and sometimes with fairly steep retouch or regular use marks along one or both edges. These flakes could have been used as scrapers, knives, or spearheads. Crude borers or awls, worked with steep retouch on thick flakes, are also characteristic of the unifacial industries.

It has been suggested that most unifacial tools are indicative of a generalized economy in which scrapers, adzes, and tools of this sort were used to make various other tools from hard and soft woods. The general absence of stone projectile points lends itself to this suggestion. If projectile points were part of the early unifacial traditions, they may have been made from other substances, such as wood or bone. In the tropical forests today, points and knives are often made from bamboo even when metal is available. The same practice could have been present in late Pleistocene times.

CULTURAL DIVERSITY IN STONE TOOLS

There are four primary reasons for the great regional variation of late Pleistocene archaeology in South America.[14] The first reason concerns the relationship between ecology and subsistence. For example, given the range of available species between the high Andes and the lowland savannas, parklands, tropical forests, and deserts, the potential for technological variation is enormous. Thus we should expect great variation in specialized tools geared to specific local resources. Second, as the entry populations dispersed and increased and as regional variation accelerated, there was more and more likelihood of local cultural exchange from group to group. These borrowings would have brought changes in artifact form and in the inventory itself, as ideas diffused and brought about more change. Third, as people entered and dispersed throughout the continent, they settled into rich temperate environments and immediately adopted the generalized economy and technology of a proto-Archaic lifeway. The classic big-game hunting lifeway would have been restricted to specialized hunters in certain open environments. Finally, several archaeologists also would attribute some stone tool differences to the ethnic identities of the groups inhabiting different sites, although others would see the same variations simply as representing different activities taking place at different locations.

In describing this geographical and temporal variety, many archaeologists have proposed names for traditions that fit regional lifestyles and adaptations. For instance, in 1972 Gordon Willey attempted to classify the early materials into the Flake Tradition, the Chopper Tradition, and the Biface Tradition.[15] The Flake Tradition is unifacial and is scattered over the northern half of the continent and down the Pacific coastline from Colombia to the Chilean canals. The Chopper Tradition is confined to the northwest. The Biface Tradition is associated with the Andean chain, with a few lateral spreads. Later Willey expanded these three traditions into the Old South American Hunting Tradition, which is the classic Paleoindian phase in North America, followed by the Andean Hunting Collection Tradition and the East Brazilian Upland Tradition. He saw these latter traditions developing sometime after 7,000 to 6,000 B.P. The Andean Hunting Collection Tradition grew out of the Old South American Hunting Tradition and the Biface Tradition, and the East Brazilian Upland Tradition descended from the Flake Tradition. Although Willey based his scheme on scanty evidence collected more than thirty years ago and although many aspects of his ideas do not hold (for instance, the Chopper Tradition is no longer a useful category), he was one of the first archaeologists to envision the wide diversity of early stone tool economies in South America. Archaeologists after Willey have proposed numerous regional schemes of artifact classification that are far too extensive to detail here and are often based on scanty evidence. In the next two chapters, I will discuss some of the better-documented schemes in their regional context.

CHAPTER FIVE

South American Regions: The Pacific and Caribbean Sides of the Continent

T HIS CHAPTER AND THE NEXT ONE summarize the archaeological evidence available today for the late Pleistocene and early Holocene periods from roughly 12,500 to 10,000 B.P. I have divided this summary by region. In this chapter, I will focus on the regions on the Pacific and Caribbean sides of the continent, and then in Chapter 6 I will turn to the regions that face the Atlantic. Before I begin this summary, however, let me say a few words about chronology.

THE CHRONOLOGY OF SOUTH AMERICAN ARCHAEOLOGICAL SITES

Our understanding of chronology is just as tentative as our understanding of the geographical distribution of artifacts. Although the climatic effects of the late Pleistocene period faded between 14,000 and 11,000 B.P. in much of South America, to be replaced by modern Holocene conditions, archaeologists still use 10,000 B.P. to mark the end of the Pleistocene lifeway and the beginning of the Archaic period. I will use this marker as well, but, as I noted in Chapter 1, I will make a distinction between the proto-Archaic and Archaic periods.

The few late Pleistocene sites in South America that contain archaeological materials in undisturbed contexts have not been placed in a chronological framework based on radiocarbon dating and on the traditional stratigraphic succession of identifiable artifact types. The present evidence is far too limited to build a chronology that does more than distinguish early from late sites. Past schemes devised by Gordon Willey, Luis Lumbreras, and others are either too regional in focus or outdated. Instead, some specialists generally divide the late Pleistocene period into arbitrary early and late subperiods. The early subperiod ranges from at least 13,000 (but probably between 20,000 and 15,000) to 11,000 B.P., and the late subperiod from 11,000 to 10,000 B.P. The 11,000 year divide roughly marks the appearance of the "fluted" trait in South America. The early subperiod, corresponding to the first entry and dispersion of humans into the continent, is associated with the bipointed rhomboidal El Jobo (Photo 5.1) and Monte Verde points and with some unifacial or edge-trimmed industries in the Andes and the lowland eastern tropics. The late subperiod corresponds with further exploration—movement into new areas and colonization of many environments—and is associated with regional cultural variation and the adoption of a proto-Archaic way of life that set the stage for economic intensification in the following early Archaic period.

The late subperiod can be further subdivided into the periods 11,000–10,500 B.P. and 10,500–10,000 B.P. The former corre-

PHOTO 5.1   *El Jobo points from various sites in Venezuela. Note the bipointed form. (Courtesy of Alan and Ruth Gruhn.)*

sponds with the stemmed Magellan Fishtail points from southern Patagonia and various unifacial industries (for example, Amotope, Abriense, Paranaiba). The latter period is characterized by a proliferation of Fishtail point styles—fluted and unfluted forms with broad blades and constricted hafts like the Restrepo points from Colombia; fluted and unfluted lanceolate forms like the Nachaco points from southern Chile; and a wide variety of triangular, sub-triangular, willow-leaf, and laurel-leaf forms from various areas—as well as by the same unifacial industries that characterize the earlier period.

In this chapter and the next one, then, I will present a general chronological range for each site as determined by radiocarbon dates derived from archaeological material excavated in the deeper or late Pleistocene levels. I will not discuss sites dating to the early Archaic period (10,000–9,000 B.P.) unless they are relevant to the extinction of mammals or represent distinct Pleistocene cultural continuities. The Appendix gives the absolute radiocarbon dates for all sites discussed in the text, and Figures 4.1, 5.1, 5.3, and 6.1 show their locations.

I will cover most of the important areas of both past and current research and fieldwork contributing to the early and late periods and indicate some outstanding problems and areas of future research. In view of the volume of work done in the past twenty years, however, it is not possible to make this an exhaustive account, and I will cover only the most "important" sites, that is, those sites that were intact and possessed an occupation with clear stratigraphy; that contained formal or diagnostic artifacts in datable contexts; that harbored a large or well-controlled collection; or even that were reported lucidly and fully. A few sites meet all these conditions and thus are not the subject of much controversy. Other sites are highly controversial but still important in at least one of the ways described above; in the case of these sites, I will discuss how and why archaeologists either accept or reject them, though I will not present the detailed geological and archaeological data necessary to substantiate claims. This level of study is reserved for technical reports and will only be summarized here.

Because only a small handful of reliable archaeological sites date prior to 11,000 B.P., I have organized this presentation by region rather than by period. The vast majority of early sites fall into the late subperiod. When a site belongs to the early subperiod, I will point it out. In this chapter, I begin with the gateway into South America, the northern Andes and Venezuela. I then turn to the central and southern Andean coastal plains and mountains. In Chapter 6, I focus on the lowlands of Brazil and the steppes of Argentina and southern Chile.

THE NORTHWEST HIGHLANDS
AND LOWLANDS

Although there is little known evidence of human habitation in the lowland tropics of northern South America and the lower Isthmus of Panama, the presence of El Jobo points at Taima-Taima and several other sites—especially on the Paraguana Peninsula in Venezuela—and of a few Fishtail points in Panama and Colombia indicates an early human presence. The first inhabitants were probably concentrated along the Caribbean coast and piedmont and in hilly terrain. The difficulty of finding sites in the forested tropics has undoubtedly caused some sampling bias and prevented archaeologists from knowing more about the region.

Most evidence of early cultures comes from scattered remains in the savanna and tropical lowlands of Colombia and Venezuela; from the central plateau of Venezuela; and from the high mountain forests, the Sabana de Bogotá, and the Calima, Cauca, and Magdelena Valleys in Colombia. These river valleys are particularly important because they extend from the central highlands to the Caribbean lowlands in the north and probably served as major routes of early dispersion after people first entered the continent (Figure 5.1). This region may have been the site of the initial division between bifacial and unifacial stone tool industries, with the former primarily associated with open savanna and parklands and the latter with forests.

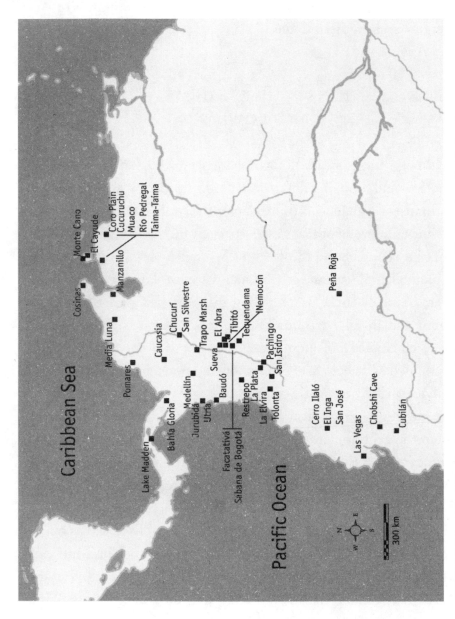

FIGURE 5.1   The Distribution of Known Archaeological Sites in Northwestern South America

Colombia

Largely neglected in the archaeological literature on the peopling of the Americas are a series of remarkable rockshelters in the highlands of Colombia that may be windows on some of the earliest hunter-gatherer cultures of the Northwest. Gonzalo Correal and Thomas van der Hammen, who investigated these shelters, have found stratified archaeological deposits ranging in age from possibly 12,000 B.P. to the present day. Tequendama and Tibitó are the two most reliable sites. Less reliable sites are El Abra, Sueva, and Nemocón, where the context and association of cultural remains are problematic and where little archaeological work has been done.

Tequendama is a rockshelter located at the edge of the present altiplano, at 2,570 meters above sea level, in a valley in the savanna that links the Magdelena River and the highlands of Bogotá.[1] The shelter is a large sandstone boulder having about 30 square meters of floor space and early deposits, and it contains an occupational deposit varying in depth from 1.5 to over 3 meters. More has been published about the sequence of human occupations at Tequendama than about any other rockshelter or cave in the northern Andes. The research at this site has allowed the reconstruction of a continuous cultural sequence of early prehistoric industries from late Pleistocene to historic times.

Beginning around 12,500 B.P., the climate in the site area began to resemble that of today's, becoming much wetter and more temperate. By 12,000 B.P. the area was forested. At 11,000 to 10,000 B.P., as the climate grew colder again, the forest became more open and thus more favorable for deer, other game, and people. During this wet period, Tequendama was located in an open woodland and mountainous terrain.

The early deposits have been divided into two major stone tool industries spanning the late Pleistocene and early Holocene periods. The earliest of the stone industries, in the deeper Zone I, was a crude flake industry called Tequendamiense, which was followed by the Abriense industry. The latter is characterized by carefully prepared, mainly pressure flaked, "edge-trimmed" unifacial tools with fine retouch along the used edges. The inhabitants of Tequendama imported stones of lidite, basalt, quartzite, and diorite found in the upper reaches of the nearby Magdelena Valley. The few unifaces are dominated by convex flake scrapers thought to have been used to work plants and wood. Also present are flaked cobbles of quartzite, limestone, and chert that could have been used for battering and chopping, as well as simple tools made of flakes that might have been used for cutting various foods.

Early sites typically contain a few bifaces, and these are found in the Tequendamiense levels. The most noteworthy pieces are a possibly reworked point fragment and two crudely shaped bifacial blades. The stone tools were associated with bone remains, primarily of deer and secondarily of mouse, rabbit, armadillo, kinkajou, and guinea pig. All of these remains were concentrated in small workshop areas and around two hearths. Charcoal from the two hearths in the deepest levels was dated between 12,500 and 10,100 B.P. Close examination of stone tools found in successive stratigraphic layers in the site demonstrates that the technology and probably other aspects of the culture changed over time. The stone tools became simpler, and more plant and animal species were added to the diet. In addition to edge-trimmed tools, the lowest levels contained battered cobble stones, sling stones, and other flake tools.

The deposits in the next younger level, Zone II containing the Abriense industry, extend from the terminal Pleistocene into his-

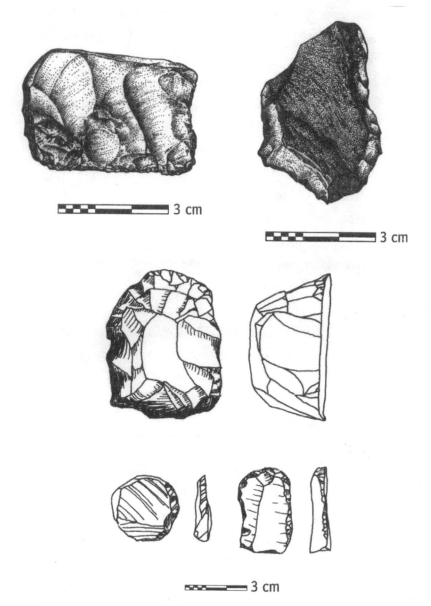

FIGURE 5.2   Edge-Trimmed Flakes Typical of the Tequendamiense and
Abriense Stone Tool Industries. (Redrawn from Julio Ariza in T. D. Dillehay et al.,
"Earliest Hunters and Gatherers of South America," Journal of World Prehistory 6
(1992):145–204.)

toric times, with the earliest dates centered between 10,000 and 8,500 B.P. This zone contains only percussion-flaked tools, no formal unifaces or bifaces. Instead, the tools consist of flakes struck from locally available pebbles or chunks of raw material, with small flakes removed from the edges to produce sharp, usable blades. The edge-trimmed tools of the Abriense tradition are also thought to reflect woodworking and processing of vegetal matter. Holding sampling bias aside, the absence of bifaces and formally worked unifaces in Zone II concerns me.

What accounts for this shift in technology from the relatively complex Tequendamiense to Abriense? Why does Zone I possess the only bifacial fragments dated to late Pleistocene times in the Sabana de Bogotá? The Tequendama bifaces are made of exotic material, probably derived from the Magdelena Valley, whereas the Abriense raw materials are local. Does this signal a technological evolution from a mixed unifacial and bifacial industry adapted to a savanna environment to exclusively edge-trimmed artifacts when climate changes create a forested environment in Abriense times?

In any case, the sample of stone tools for each industry is currently too small (just a few hundred of each type) to define two distinct technologies within such a close time span. Despite the differences between the two industries, it is probable that both belong to a single evolving technology. The pressure and percussion technologies applied to the flakes overlap chronologically and stratigraphically, and they are sometimes very similar in form. We know too little, however, to assume any stronger affinity between the makers of these two industries or to assert specific details of their way of life, other than to say they are generalized hunters and gatherers.

Unfortunately, few early sites exist in Colombia that would help us clarify the relationship between these two industries or date them more precisely. Based on the present evidence from the deeper levels of Tequendama and a similar flake tool technology at Tibitó, I would guess the date of the Tequendamiense industry sometime slightly before or around 11,000 B.P. and extending into the early Archaic period; according to another guess, the Abriense industry probably began between 10,500 and 10,000 B.P. and lasted to the historic period.

One of the oldest known and most widely accepted sites of early human occupation in Colombia is Tibitó, in a marsh north of Bogotá at an elevation of 2,500 meters above sea level.[2] The site may be as old as 11,740 years. It contains evidence of a single episode of human use associated with a unifacial industry (Photo 5.2). At this rockshelter, Gonzalo Correal excavated the bone remains of two genera of mastodon as well as fox, deer, and native horse in association with scattered chunks of charcoal and several stone, bone, and antler artifacts. He also found Tequendamiense scrapers. Associated stone tools include Abriense core scrapers, cutting flakes, and a few possible perforators. Correal found two oval activity areas containing animal remains as well as an elliptical area with artifacts and intentionally selected animal bones. Some bones show deliberate burning, cutting, and fracturing for extraction of marrow.

The bone assemblage is incomplete, implying that portions of the animals were left at nearby kill sites. Apparently the hunters at Tibitó scavenged or killed several animals nearby and brought selected parts to the boulder, where they prepared the meat. Ribs and long bones, which are meatier and easier to transport, are present, whereas the larger and heavier bones such as pelvises, shoulder blades, and skulls are missing and probably were left behind. No projectile points were found at the site. If the hunters used them, I suspect that they are located elsewhere in the marsh

PHOTO 5.2 *Excavated stone tool artifacts and bone remains of extinct animals at the Tibitó site in Colombia. (Courtesy of Gonzalo Correal and Alan Bryan.)*

near where the animals were killed. A possible butchering locality is located on the nearby banks of the marsh, where flakes have been recovered.

Tibitó has been criticized by one archaeologist, Thomas Lynch, who claims that the cultural remains may have been mixed by water deposits and that the bone and artifact remains may not be culturally related. However, all of the cultural remains were tightly clustered around a large boulder at the edge of an ancient marsh and are buried in an undisturbed geological layer overlaid by recent sediments. The geological setting is a marsh of low energy, implying slowly moving water. Thus the chances that water deposited charcoal, bone, and stone tools in the same stratum at the same place are extremely slim. Not known is whether all stone and bone materials are culturally related and whether they represent one or several human events. One criticism of the site is justified—only one radiocarbon date has been obtained from the cultural level. Although more dates are required, from both the charcoal and the burned bones, and a better understanding of the association of stone and bone artifacts is needed, I believe this site is a valid meat processing and consumption station dated to about 11,500 B.P. or slightly earlier.

El Abra—another highland rockshelter, located in the western Sabana de Bogotá—has generated much controversy.[3] The site consists of a series of small contiguous shelters associated with a narrow corridor of low parallel rock walls. Excavations by Correal and later by Wesley Hurt defined five stratigraphic units extending from the late Pleistocene to the middle Holocene period, with radiocarbon dates ranging from 12,500 to 7,250 B.P. The lower levels contained a few unifacial flakes and two small battered cobbles. The flakes are edge-trimmed and related to the Abriense tradition; the battered cobbles and one flake scraper are more characteristic of the Tequendamiense industry. But the association and context of the radiocarbon dates and the artifacts are unclear due to partially disturbed stratigraphy and the lack of detailed stratigraphic profiles. Most bones from the deeper levels are from rodents and other animals, suggesting generalized hunters and gatherers.

The site's deeper levels, associated with dates between 12,400 and 11,210 B.P., produced thirty-seven unifacial flakes. Lynch, again, has questioned these older dates and materials because nearby caves contain similar materials dating later, in the early Archaic period, that are associated with similar fauna and lithics.[4] Although the stratigraphic location of the date concerns me, too, the presence of similar fauna does not. Several early localities in South (and North) America lack bone remains of extinct mammals. To me, the presence of modern Holocene species simply indicates a temperate environment by at least 11,000 B.P., not that the site must be early Holocene. The requirement that all late Pleistocene archaeological sites must contain human artifacts in direct association with the bones of extinct animals is merely a bias of North American Paleoindian archaeology.

Some archaeologists also believe that the flakes in the deeper levels are so few that they do not represent a real site and must have filtered down from a higher, younger level. This question is difficult to answer until the site is re-excavated and the deeper flakes are subjected to analyses of dip and strike, which are designed to determine if the flakes were deposited in situ or were pulled by gravity through cracks in the stratigraphy. Flakes filtering from above are almost always small and found standing vertically in the microcracks through which they moved down. In situ flakes are larger, found lying flat, and usually located on the same habitational level. Another problem with El Abra, unlike Tequendama and Tibitó, is that the artifacts are not clustered in clear workshop areas—a point that concerns Gerardo Ardila, who has also studied the site.

I do not find either the scarcity of the alleged older deposits or their dispersion too disturbing. If the site dated prior to 11,000 or even 12,000 B.P. and was a brief hunting station, we would expect to find light, perhaps unpatterned scatters and few tools. As Lynch and others have noted, the main problem with El Abra is a lack of confidence in the stratigraphy and the associated radiocarbon dates. This is another site that needs to be restudied.

Another Colombian site also in the Sabana de Bogotá is Nemocón 4, from which Correal has obtained a sequence of unifacial industries.[5] This is a small rockshelter with a deeper level of stone tools not dated but estimated to be between 9,000 and 8,000 years old. The stone industry is edge-trimmed, of the Tequendama and Abriense technologies, and associated with hearths and with deer, rabbit, armadillo, and other modern Holocene fauna. Although this site may not date to the late Pleistocene period, I mention it here because the fauna and stone tools represent a continuity with the late Pleistocene technology and economy recorded at Tequendama, Tibitó, and El Abra.

In Sueva, on the eastern slopes of the Andes at 2,700 meters above sea level, is a small rockshelter. The deeper level containing cultural material lies immediately underneath a level radiocarbon dated at 10,090 B.P. This deeper deposit contained edge-trimmed lithics both of the Tequendama and Abriense industries, as well as hearths and the bone remains of deer, rodents, and armadillo. Based on the presence of the edge-trimmed flakes, Correal and his colleagues placed the older level between 13,000 and 11,000 B.P., but I suspect an actual age between 11,000 and 10,000 B.P., because the stone tool industry resembles the Abriense technology of that period.

Recently, a new point type, called Restrepo, has been found at several early open-air sites in central Colombia (Photo 5.3). The Restrepo is a large, stemmed point with well-defined broad shoulders and sometimes a flute or longitudinal flake removed from the base of its stem. Some scholars, primarily Warwick Bray, believe this point type has similarities with the stemmed but unfluted Paiján type found in the highlands of Ecuador and along the desert coast of Peru and dating to the late Pleistocene and early Holocene period between 10,600 and 9,000 B.P.

Restrepo points have been recovered by Carlos Llera and Crístobal Gnecco at the buried open-air sites of Tolonta and La Elvira, on terraces and hillsides in the Popayán area of Colombia.[6] These points show several flaking traits similar to the broad-stemmed and

PHOTO 5.3   Restrepo point from the highlands of Colombia. Note the flute or longitudinal thinning flake in the base. (Courtesy of Fernándo Urbina.)

5 cm

El Inga points from Ecuador, leading Llera and Gnecco to believe that a technological relationship existed between the Popayán and Ecuadorian industries. This is a reasonable hypothesis given that the sites are all in high forested areas (probably near the paramo) and were probably associated with generalized hunting and gathering societies. Radiocarbon dates from these Restrepo sites range between 9,030 and 3,430 B.P.; obsidian hydration dates on associated artifacts fall between 11,248 and 9,321 B.P. The ranges of the combined dates are too widely distributed to link the point type either to the terminal Pleistocene or early Holocene period reliably. However, based on the Restrepo point's similarity to the El Inga and Paiján forms, which date sometime between 10,500 and 9,000

B.P., I would put these sites in the same time span, but most likely between 10,000 and 9,000 B.P.

At a number of sites in the Magdelena River basin, stone artifacts have been excavated from beneath alluvial deposits near streams and rivers.[7] In some of these cases, fresh unrolled artifacts were found in situ or nearly so and lacked the water sheen of the redeposited artifacts found in many terrace gravels, which may have been transported many kilometers from the places where they were made or used. A finding of fresh unrolled tools does not in itself, however, represent an early living or working floor, especially in buried open-air sites on terraces, but it undoubtedly suggests the presence of people and indicates a locality where the potential for an undisturbed find is high. Many localities of this kind have been found in South America and elsewhere throughout the Americas, but few have stratified archaeological deposits dated by radiocarbon means.

Carlos López reports finding similar surface and buried sites yielding points and other stone tools (Photo 5.4), possibly of the late Pleistocene period.[8] Several open-air sites, including San Juan De Bedout I and La Palestina 2 and 3, contain stemmed Restrepo and Paiján-like points and, according to López, Abriense unifaces. He has also reported plano-convex scrapers and large bifacial points, which are of the Tequendamiense technology, associated with charcoal in cultural layers radiocarbon dated between 10,400 and 10,230 B.P. All of these sites require more systematic work and more dates before they can be accepted as valid late Pleistocene sites.

Other Bifacial Sites

Crístobal Gnecco has recently described an early human occupation at the open-air site of San Isidro, near Popayán in Colombia.[9] Ra-

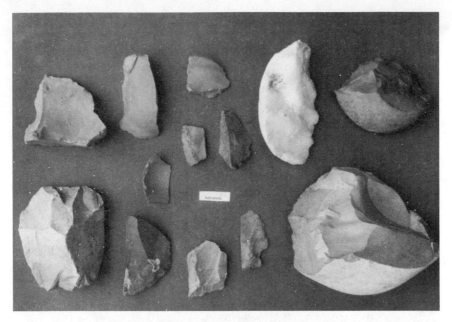

PHOTO 5.4   *Unifacial tools from various late Pleistocene and early Archaic sites in the Magdelena River Valley in Colombia. These tools are typical of the Tequendamiense and Abriense industries. (Courtesy of Carlos López.)*

diocarbon analysis of wood charcoal and charred seeds of palm fruits at this site gave dates of 10,050, 10,030, and 9,530 B.P. The site is interpreted as a lithic and plant processing station. Most of the stone tools found there are unifacial, bifacial, and grinding implements.

Peña Roja, a later site reported by Gnecco and Mora, dates to about 9,100 B.P. and reflects intensified exploitation of tropical forest resources, especially palm fruits. The abundant charcoal at this site has led Gnecco and Mora to believe either that people were deliberately clearing the forest or that a natural forest fire occurred here between 10,000 and 9,000 B.P. If they are correct, this pattern should be evident in the local pollen record, which has not been studied. Before their conclusions can be accepted, this site too needs further investigation.

Other parts of northwestern South America have yielded a wide range of stemmed projectile points with characteristics similar to Fishtail points. These include various fluted and unfluted forms from the Caribbean lowlands of Colombia,[10] Madden Lake fluted points in Panama,[11] and El Inga points in Ecuador. Confusion surrounds these points, however, because they come from disturbed contexts or surface exposures. Still, there can be little doubt that in several areas, such as the Pedregal River in northern Venezuela and the lowland tropics of both Colombia and Venezuela, there existed industries typified by broad-stemmed points akin to the Restrepo and Paiján points, but generally finer than those of the Madden Lake, El Jobo, and El Inga industries. Although rarely reported in any detail, unifacial tools are often found in similar surface collections.

A detailed understanding of all point types from the many open-air sites in Colombia, Venezuela, and Ecuador is hampered by the sparseness and uneven coverage of research, by the lack of excavated sites with intact stratigraphy, and by the complete absence of animal and plant remains. In addition, many people doubt these site's stratigraphic integrity, which forms the basis for much speculation on interregional and cross-continental linkages. A few exceptions, such as San Isidro and Peña Roja, exist along the Magdelena River and in other highland localities, where stratified deposits contain early stemmed points. Based on the radiocarbon-dated ages of these deposits and on other stemmed point types in other areas of South America, I would guess that the Colombian forms date between 10,500 and 9,000 B.P. and possibly as late as 8,500 B.P., although they may be a few centuries earlier in the northern highlands and coastal lowlands where they were perhaps used first. As for the Fishtail and El Jobo forms, only more detailed stratigraphic work at intact sites will inform us of their chronology and cultural affinity. Enough work has been done, however, to make it plausible that the El Jobo form is a precursor to the Fishtail point, as William Mayer-Oakes has suggested before.

Venezuela

An ancient water hole in northern Venezuela called Taima-Taima was the deathbed of a young mastodon—probably killed by people. The site, initially excavated by José Cruxent and later by Alan Bryan and Ruth Gruhn, appears to contain 13,000–11,000-year-old mastodon bones, with a piece of an El Jobo point lodged in the mastodon's pelvic cavity (Photo 5.5).[12] The point fragment, other stone tools, and the bones were recovered from gray sand overlain by a series of clay lenses, a context thought to be an ancient spring. They were mixed in with chipped stone tools and rounded pebbles that could only have been made by humans. Some mastodon bones reveal marks that could be cuts from stone tools used to butcher the animals.

Nineteen radiocarbon dates obtained from bone and vegetable matter in the gray sand layer range from 14,440 to 11,860 B.P., with one outlying date at 7,590 B.P. Three bone fragments have been dated at 14,200, 13,880, and 12,980 B.P. (A 1,200-year spread for bone dates of this age, even from the same animal, is not unusual.) Small twigs thought to be the remains of plants eaten by the mastodon were dated between 14,800 and 13,000 B.P. Charcoal dates from the gray sand containing the twigs, bones, and stone tools ranged between 14,000 and 12,800 B.P. Charcoal from an overlying layer of permeable black clay yielded a date between 10,200 and 9,800 B.P.

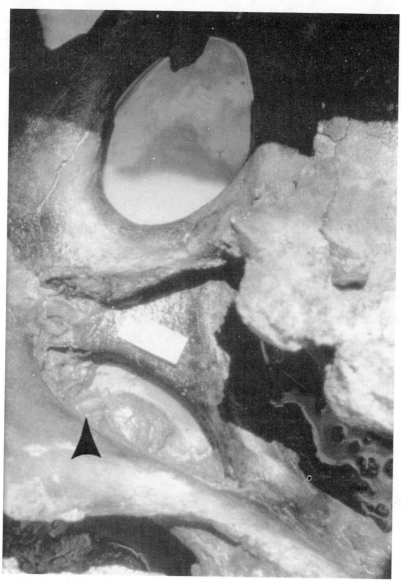

PHOTO 5.5   *The fragment of an El Jobo point (arrow) resting in the pelvic cavity of a mastodon bone at Taima-Taima, Venezuela. (Courtesy of Alan Bryan.)*

Taima-Taima has been a controversial site.[13] Some archaeologists feel the slowly upwelling spring water caused continuous remixing of the stone tools and the bones. Most seriously questioned is the broken El Jobo point in the cavity of a mastodon pelvis. Skeptics note that the supposed kill weapon is missing its tip. Only the midsection of the point is present, suggesting that it came to rest inside the cavity through water movement long after the animal's death, a possibility in this kind of geological setting. Yet, of the hundreds of bones in the site, what are the chances that natural agency would place the point fragment in just the area of the body where human hunters are most likely to have thrust it? And if not related to a kill, what are the stone tools doing there? People don't casually throw points into springs. There is no doubt that humans were doing something around the water hole in late Pleistocene times. Taima-Taima may be a case whereby some critics have employed questionable taphonomic agency to dismiss a valid archaeological context.

Another critic, Richard Morlan, asks why only mastodons were killed at the water hole.[14] The spring deposit also contains bone remains of several other species, many of which show no signs of human intervention. This does not bother me, because other species were hunted at many valid sites scattered up and down the Americas where mastodon remains are not present. Taima-Taima may simply have been an excellent place to hunt mastodons. Furthermore, any water hole will have species that died there naturally or were killed by other predators. So the questions at Taima-Taima concern whether the point and other stone tools are truly related to the death of one or more animals and, if so, the age of this relationship. The fact that the bone remains and stone artifacts were sealed in a gray sand layer overlaid by clay dating between 10,200 and 9,800 B.P. suggests a date of at least 11,000 to 10,500 B.P. Even Dena Dincauze, a noted Clovis proponent, has acknowledged that the El Jobo point and bone remains resting at the base of the old spring were sealed by an impermeable layer before 10,000 B.P., implying that mixing of older materials could have occurred only prior to this date. I believe it was most likely prior to 11,000 and 10,500 B.P.

If we applied the same standards of context and association that we apply to Clovis sites in North America, Taima-Taima would pass muster. Blackwater Draw, Naco, and other North American late Pleistocene big-game kill sites are also located in water-borne deposits. As at those sites, the association of stone artifacts (particularly the points) and bones at Taima-Taima is difficult to reject.[15] If it were located in North America and dated around or after 11,000 B.P., it would probably be accepted as a valid site. It is the pre–11,000 year dates more than the association of the bones and stone tools that has brought the site into question.

Even if the context is valid, the site's date still remains an open question. Perhaps dating the bone by accelerator mass spectrometry will help resolve its age. Whenever it happened, a mastodon was probably killed or scavenged at Taima-Taima—perhaps after it became mired in the spring. In either case, there are suggestions of butchering—the El Jobo point, which could have been either the kill-weapon or a cutting tool, and possible cut marks on several bones. Once this site has been dated and more taphonomic work has been done on the bone collection and the geological setting, it may turn out that Bryan is correct when he argues that the Taima-Taima hunter's method was to thrust lances into the animal's anuses, producing death by internal bleeding. The location of the broken point in the pelvic cavity may support this claim.

Other El Jobo localities in Venezuela have not been thoroughly investigated. Although fairly abundant remains are known to exist from surface sites, other water holes, and buried terrace deposits, there is no reliable information on their chronology. Examples of other water holes are Muaco and Cucuruchu on the Paraguana Peninsula, where El Jobo points were found in association with mastodon, glyptodon, and other extinct animals.[16] Burned bone from Muaco was dated between 14,000 and 16,000 B.P., but because modern glass is present in the same levels as the excavated bone, many archaeologists believe the site is suspect. If the bone remains show clear butchering and cutmarks, however, the radiocarbon dates cannot be denied, even though glass particles might have intruded later. This is another case in which mass spectrometry dating of bones with clear human-induced cutmarks is needed to clarify the status of a site.

Like Muaco, Taima-Taima, and Cucuruchu, other El Jobo sites have also been questioned because their "associated artifacts were too few in number to permit sound interpretation."[17] I am not convinced that this is a valid reason for dismissing these sites. Are not sites like these, with a few stone tools and worked bones, just the evidence we would expect from ephemeral occupation by highly mobile populations? Other archaeologists, such as Lynch, have other problems with these sites. They believe that the bipointed El Jobo point is too similar to the Lerma point of the desert southwest in the United States and to the Ayampitín point of the Andes, implying that all bipointed forms are of an early Holocene age. But the bipointed style is a simple form that could have been developed in many different regions and periods.[18] This is a case of misrepresenting the archaeological record by typological lumping.

Finally, it is curious that El Jobo points have not been found elsewhere in South America.[19] It may be a point type confined to the northern rim of the continent and associated with the first phase of regional specialized hunting after human entry.

ECUADOR

Moving south along the Andes from Colombia to northern Ecuador, we find the open-air site of El Inga, a high (2,600 meters elevation) terrace overlooking a river valley in the central highlands, first excavated by Robert Bell of the University of Oklahoma. In the 1960s, Bell became the first archaeologist to see "fluting" on South American projectile points. He, and later Mayer-Oakes, recognized it at El Inga, where a wide variety of points have been found, but unfortunately in undated contexts.[20] The valley below El Inga is choked with volcanic deposits dissected by rivers into steep ravines. Although the site is large and extends more than 1.5 kilometers along the terrace, survey and excavation have yielded only a few unifacial artifacts, blades, bifaces, and burins, and these were recovered from shallow deposits whose stratigraphy is not well defined.

Unfortunately, preservation at El Inga did not permit the recovery of bone and other organic remains. Although most of the attention has been on the site's bifacial tools, the unifacial artifacts could have been used to exploit a wide range of food items, including plants. The most diagnostic point type recovered here is the Fishtail or Magellan (Fell's Cave) broad-stemmed point, of the sort found at several localities in southern Patagonia dated between 11,000 and 10,500 B.P., and on the north coast of Peru in

Paiján sites dated between 10,500 and 9,000 B.P. Several points from El Inga exhibit a longitudinal flake on their bases, which Bell, Mayer-Oakes, and later Bird and Lynch compared to the fluting found on North American Clovis points. El Inga also contains laurel-leaf Ayampitín and lanceolate forms, but they are scarce and their relation to the Fishtail point is not clear.

El Inga is obviously an anomaly in late Pleistocene archaeology. It is the only early site in South America where the vast majority of the points are made of obsidian and where so many different point types are made by different technologies. Although the differing point types may represent technological change spread over several hundred years, the presence of both lanceolate and laurel-leaf forms presents a fascinating example of cultural change in one locality. This wide variety of tools suggests that El Inga may have been used more as a quarry than as a campsite.

As a result of his work at El Inga and at the nearby site of Cerro Ilaló, Mayer-Oakes has dedicated much of his career to the study of fluting in South America. He believes the technique developed from simple basal thinning into two styles: the Fishtail style and a broad-stemmed style. At El Inga, Mayer-Oakes has postulated an in situ development of projectile point forms of fluting for hafting purposes. He also believes the site contains forms that relate to all Andean projectile point styles, including both the stemmed and lanceolate forms.

Although much of his argument makes sense, there is no stratigraphic evidence at El Inga to confirm it. Thus the broader implications of the fluted and unfluted broad-stemmed, lanceolate, and leaf-shaped points are unclear. As Mayer-Oakes has suggested, the fluted stem type probably relates to the Magellan or Fell's Cave type and to other types found in Panama and at the La Esperanza site in Honduras. The lanceolate form may have been introduced by North American and Central American populations coming through the area. The leaf-shaped points may be related to the Ayampitín type scattered throughout the Andes, although this is a very general form that could have been invented several different times.

Given the variety of stone artifacts, the El Inga site appears to have been reused (or mined for stone raw material) by hunters and gatherers over a very long period of time. The radiocarbon dates on several chunks of charcoal excavated from shallow deposits range from 9,030 to 3,430 B.P., possibly suggesting redeposition by wind and water. Obsidian hydration dates obtained from several artifacts date from 11,248 to 9,321 B.P. My guess is that the Fishtail occupation at the locality dates between 10,800 and 9,800 B.P. and that the other occupations are later. With an excellent view to the river below and to the nearby rolling hills and distant mountains, the site would have been a favorite locality for people to hunt game and to gather wild plants.

San José, only a few hundred meters from El Inga, contains only flakes and unifacial tools made of obsidian. Curiously, no bifaces have been recovered from this site, although the assemblage is similar to that at El Inga. Based on the unifaces, Gruhn and Bryan believe San José belongs to the edge-trimmed tradition, but I think the points simply have not been found or have been taken by artifact collectors. Thirteen obsidian hydration dates ranged from 11,248 to 9,321 B.P., with ten older than 10,200. The dates were in stratigraphic order. Mayer-Oakes, Gruhn, and Bryan believe San José is the precursor to the El Inga site and that bifacial tools were invented sometime during the occupation of the latter. It will take a much larger sample of sites from the area, with stratigraphy containing unifacial tools beneath bifaces, to prove this hypothesis.

Other Ilaló localities near El Inga have been studied by Ernesto Salazar.[21] Although they have not been dated, these localities have stone tools similar to those at El Inga, the main Ilaló site, and at the Sueva sites. They give further evidence of the early use of obsidian tools, the importance of high-altitude grasslands and forests to early hunters in the central highlands of Ecuador, and the reuse of the same locality for several millennia.

In the southern highlands of Ecuador at an elevation of 3,100 meters is the open-air site of Cubilán, where Mathilde Temme, a German archaeologist living in Ecuador, excavated stone tools and charcoal in shallow but stratified contexts dating between 10,500 and 9,100 B.P.[22] In one area of the site, she found a lithic workshop and activity areas, and in another she found clusters of stemmed and subtriangular projectile points associated with concentrations of charcoal that she thought might represent fireplaces corresponding to a single large shelter or several small ones. She believes that the arrangement of debris and hearths suggests a close-knit social group. The Cubilán site also contains evidence of quarry activities dated in the same time range.

Another site is Chobshi Cave in the southern highlands of Ecuador where Gustavo Reinoso and later Lynch found willow-leaf, rhomboidal, and stemmed and barbed points associated with the remains of deer, rodents, and other highland species.[23] No megafauna remains or Fishtail points were recovered. Although the stratigraphy is heavily disturbed by various natural and human factors, the combined lithic and fauna assemblage suggests that the earliest occupation may date to terminal Pleistocene times but is most likely early Holocene. Lynch believes that the bone remains of local animal species indicate a continued adaptation from late Pleistocene to Holocene conditions. But the heavily mixed deposits in the cave preclude one's confidence in any interpretation of the site. Nonetheless, the single radiocarbon date Lynch obtained (10,010 B.P.) is congruent with the ages of the projectile points recovered from the site's deeper levels.

PACIFIC COASTAL LOWLANDS

In the southwestern coastal lowlands along the north shore of the present-day Guayaquil Basin of Ecuador, Karen Stothert has found a localized culture that preceded the early Valdivia culture (one of the earliest ceramic-bearing societies in the New World) and is referred to as the Las Vegas culture.[24] The early Las Vegas culture flourished from at least 9,800 to 8,000 B.P. and possibly earlier, but the scarcity of deeper material in the sites and the associated radiocarbon dates on marine shells make precise dating difficult. The artifact assemblage in the early Holocene levels of Las Vegas sites consists of large numbers of lunates, blades, decorated and slit bone tools, notched flakes and blades, pestles, mortars, basins, slabs, and a wide variety of edge-trimmed stone tools. Stothert thinks the tool assemblage was used to scale fish, butcher animals, and process plants and wood. She also found an apparent circular living structure at one site. Another feature contained an impression of a fruit of bottle gourd *(Lagenaria siceraria)*. Unlike other early sites, the early Holocene phase of the Las Vegas–type site has yielded many human skeletons, providing a relatively good picture of the morphology of the people and of the diseases that afflicted them.

In the deepest levels of one Las Vegas site, Stothert obtained dates of 10,840, 10,100, and 10,300 B.P. on charcoal. She believes that these dates may indicate an early or pre–Las Vegas occupation corresponding to the Amotope phase (11,500 and 8,000 B.P.) described by James Richardson of the University of Pittsburgh at unifacial sites on the desert coast of northern Peru.[25] Although very ephemeral and defined by simple unifacial tools and a light scatter of shell and other debris, this pre–Las Vegas phase probably dates to the late Pleistocene and represents an early coastal adaptation.

Stothert believes that both the pre–Las Vegas and Las Vegas occupations that are dated between at least 9,800 and 6,000 B.P. are associated with generalized hunter-gatherers. There is little doubt that the Las Vegas people were living in a close relationship with wild plants, sea organisms, and animals. In addition to the wide range of wild game they hunted and aquatic resources they gathered, these people expended considerable effort—as reflected in their tools—in gathering and preparing terrestrial plant foods from semi-arid parkland and savanna environments. They were clearly unspecialized hunters, fishermen, and gatherers who may have added plant cultivation between 9,700 and 8,000 B.P., as suggested by the presence of gourds, squash, and possibly corn. These people probably laid some of the cultural foundations for the later Valdivia culture around 6,000 and 5,000 B.P. in the same area of Ecuador, although there is a gap of some 1,500 years between the two cultures.

THE NORTH COAST OF PERU

The Peruvian coast to the south of Ecuador (Figure 5.3), a rich and varied environment for early prehistoric hunters and gather-

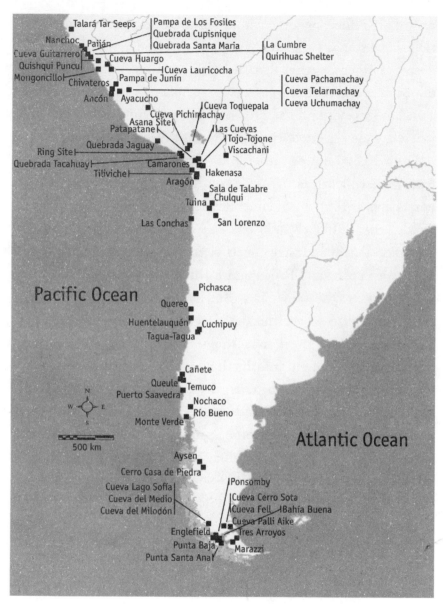

FIGURE 5.3   The Distribution of Known Archaeological Sites in Western South America

139

ers, offered four major environmental zones: the craggy lower slopes and lomas (vegetated areas) of the Andes where camelids, deer, and other game resided; the wooded valley floors, which contained deer and small game; the coastal plains where herds of wild camelids grazed; and the estuaries and wetlands along the coast where a wide variety of seafood and birds were available.

From 10,500 B.P. or earlier until Holocene times, there were at least three concurrent industries on the north coast of Peru, each employing a distinct fundamental technology and set of raw materials: the unifacial industry, the Fishtail industry, and the stemmed Paiján industry. Their sites are sometimes only a few kilometers apart, and Paiján and Fishtail points may even overlap or alternate at the same sites. But because we have few reliable temporal controls over the data, we cannot construct site networks. Confusion surrounds the sequence of these industries because so much of our information is based upon undated collections from disturbed contexts or surface exposures. Thus, it is difficult to be certain about the true distribution of any of these industries, especially when some artifacts resemble those of much later times. The Fishtail points may be related to those in Patagonia and at El Inga. Some archaeologists believe that this region will ultimately yield evidence of technological continuity from Fishtail to stemmed points.

Unifacial Industries

North of the Sechura Desert is a distinctive group of coastal midden sites associated with old beaches. These beaches were probably just being formed when the first hunters or fishermen camped among them. The lithic industries from the middens are called

Amotope and Siches and consist mainly of flakes made of quartzite; cores are represented, but they are a minor element. The majority of the finished tools are made either of flakes or of chips of raw material. There are also scrapers, a few somewhat problematic burins, and numerous utilized flakes, cores, and fragments of stone raw material. Some of these stone artifacts are reminiscent of the Tequendamiense, Abriense, and Las Vegas industries to the north. Later sites along the coast contain a small proportion of very fine projectile points, including both the stemmed and lanceolate types. Yet there is a puzzling absence of points in the Amotope and Siches industries. Why did Las Vegas, Amotope, and Siches people not use projectile points in the open environments of the coast? Was the coastal desert more vegetated than we know? Were projectile points made of wood or bone? Or is it that points made up a very small percentage of the stone tool industry and thus were not found by archaeologists? Until we find answers to these questions, we should be cautious in correlating unifaces with closed vegetated environments and bifaces with open environments.

The Sechura Desert also has campsites scattered among its ancient sand dunes. These sites provided a sheltered camping place, protected from the strong southeast winds, within reach of the sea, and near lagoons and estuaries suitable for fishing and fowling. The unifacial industries at these sites are similar to those found at Las Vegas and at later sites located father south on the Peruvian coast. The dunes were probably being formed when hunters and gatherers used them. Later, perhaps because of a slight increase in rainfall, vegetation and soil formation anchored them in place.

Some of the earliest known unifacial industries are from the Talará tar seeps near the Amotope Mountains north of Sechura. At these sites, James Richardson found more than a dozen lithic scatters located on the surface of low ridges within sight of the seeps. Bird and mammal bones taken from the tar seeps suggest a local environment of savanna woodlands or grassy plains, with gallery woodlands lining the creeks. Richardson sees the Amotope people as generalized hunter-gatherers independently developing a unifacial technology focused on the exploitation of a wide range of local resources, including plants, estuary foods, and animals feeding around the tar seeps.

The stone tool industry of Talará, which Richardson has named the Amotope Complex, primarily comprises denticulates, flakes, and cores made of small pebbles of chalcedony and quartzite that are found in local washes. He also recovered a few choppers and one mortar. With some modifications this same industry continued into the early Holocene period, with local variants known as Siches, Honda-Estero, and, farther south, Nanchoc, Casma, and Mongoncillo. The age of the Amotope Complex is based on marine shells dated between 11,200 and 8,125 B.P. Although dates on shell are notoriously unreliable, this time range generally agrees with a series of radiocarbon dates obtained from other, preceramic unifacial sites of the probably later Nanchoc and Casma industries.[26]

Around the fresh springs and fans near Nanchoc in the upper-middle Zaña Valley is a concentration of later sites (9,300 to 7,500 B.P.) with unifacial industries showing a range of variation comparable to those of Amotope and the Casma Complex farther south, which was studied by Michael Malpass. Jack Rossen's, Pat Netherly's, and my analysis of these finds suggests that these were primarily living or camp sites. Flake scrapers showing general affinities with such areas as Casma appear at several of these sites, and at one of them a small bifacial fragment was found. The Nanchoc Tradition is associated with an early Holocene adaptation to the forested slopes of the upper Zaña Valley, where there was a close juxtaposition of different environments and a wide range of resources available within a short distance.

An antecedent culture may exist in the same valley. In 1992, I found a living floor at the El Palto site in the middle Nanchoc (Zaña) Valley, buried in a hillside about 2.5 meters below the present-day surface. Ceramic and preceramic artifacts and ash lenses extended at intervals for about 60 meters along the course of the stream. Trial trenches at several points showed this layer, which contained only thin ash-and-charcoal lenses and unifacial stone tools, to be covered by the same 2.5 meter depth of alluvium along its entire length, indicating an undisturbed cultural deposit. Neither the tools nor the rubble were rolled, nor did they show signs of having moved. The tool collection included over 100 stone tools, of which finished, chiefly unifacial forms make up one third, the rest being manufacture debris and hammer stones, suggesting that the site was a factory or working area as well as a living place. So far, no organic remains have been found to give a fuller picture of the range of activities carried out there. Most of the artifacts are of basalt and andesite, which is readily available at the site, but some are of quartzite and other types of imported stone. A single radiocarbon date of 11,650 B.P. was obtained on a large chunk of charcoal taken from the deepest ash lens and associated directly with the unifacial tools. More work and more radiocarbon dates are needed to substantiate the cultural age of the site and its affinity with other north coast settlements.

No discussion of possible earlier cultures on the north coast of Peru should leave out unifacial industries recovered from old yardang land surfaces (these are remnant landforms not eroded away by glacial outwash, leaving a plateau or mesa). Although some of the yardang landforms are of the terminal Pleistocene period, many may represent older surfaces that were once inhabited by humans. The Zaña and Jequetepeque Valleys offer many good examples of yardangs with numerous unifacial lithic scatters on their surfaces. These unifaces look like crude versions of the early Amotope and Siches industries recorded by Richardson in the Talará area and may date anywhere from 15,000 to 1,000 years ago. Based on the extremely dark desert varnish on these tool's surfaces, they probably belong to the late Pleistocene period. Whatever their age may be, yardangs and other old landforms must be investigated further for environments where early archaeological records may be found.

The various unifacial industries on the north coast of Peru were undoubtedly the characteristic tools of some groups adapted to vegetated environments (but see my caution to this interpretation above). Edward Lanning, Bryan, and Richardson have suggested that these technologies indicate a woodland industry in which unifaces were used to make various tools from hard tropical trees and to process plant foods.[27] The absence of projectile points and other bifaces suggests that if these were used they were made from other substances, presumably wood or perhaps bone. The extent to which the appearance of these unifaces relates to late Pleistocene and early Holocene climatic fluctuations is a matter that requires more interdisciplinary research. The presence of sites in present-day arid regions, for example, suggests more hospitable and wooded or parkland conditions in these regions between 11,000 and 10,000 B.P. Usually these sites are situated on fossil dunes (formed during previous dry periods) and on spurs and slopes of alluvial fans or hills, particularly where these overlook permanent or seasonal water sources. Such sites vary in extent and appear to represent temporary or semipermanent seasonal camping places of families or somewhat larger groups. There are also examples of quarry sites associated with sources of raw material, such as near Cupisnique, as well as sites that contain evidence of both camping and quarry functions.

The Paiján Sites

The north coast valleys of Zaña, Jequetepeque, Cupisnique, Chicama, and Moche are especially rich in sites of various early cultures, particularly the Paiján culture, which probably coexisted with the Amotope industry to the north as well as with local unifacial industries. First described by Larco Hoyle in the 1940s from the Pampa de Los Fósiles site, and reported later from several sites in the Cupisnique Valley, Paiján is one of the best recorded early cultures in South America. Numerous Paiján sites are located on small hills or rising ground, commanding a view of the surrounding country. Others are within sight of springs inside canyons. Most of these sites yield a wide range of artifacts and waste materials, which indicates that they were the camping places or minor living sites of small groups or families. There are also a number of much larger stone tool quarry sites, which in some cases appear to have served other groups before and after the Paiján people. These sites contain local raw materials suggesting highly localized adaptations. In addition, there are two sites that appear to be more permanent, at Quirihuac Shelter and La Cumbre in the Moche Valley. These contain occupational debris in the form of small to moderate quantities of stone tools, varying amounts of bone and charcoal, and other cultural remains. Unfortunately, these cultural deposits are shallow, consisting of only a few centimeters of soil and lithics, and therefore provide little information on long-term economic and technological changes.

In the lower Cupisnique and Jequetepeque Valleys, finds of Paiján sites are so widespread that it is tempting to assume that this culture once occupied all lower valleys of the north coast of Peru, though the evidence does not support quite such a sweeping conclusion. Indications of very limited Paiján presence in the middle sections of these valleys suggest that the Paiján people were confined mainly to the coastal plains and adjacent foothills, and that their territory overlapped with some unifacial traditions. There are traces of a Paiján-like presence at the highland site of El Inga, Ecuador, but not at highland sites in northern Peru. Our surveys in the coastal foothills and plains of the Lambayeque and Zaña Valleys to the north of the Cupisnique Valley found very few Paiján sites, suggesting that they occur mainly on the north central coast. The Paiján points also diminish considerably on the central and south Peruvian coasts. This mosaic distribution suggests that Paiján may have been a specialized general foraging adaptation restricted to the grassy coastal plains and adjacent foothills in only some north coast valleys of Peru and in some highland valleys.

In the Cupisnique Valley, more than 150 Paiján sites have been found, stretching from the sea to an elevation of 2,000 meters (between 10 and 35 kilometers inland), indicating the exploitation of various environmental zones along the lower western slopes of the Andes up to about 1,500 meters in elevation. Most Paiján surface sites, however, are confined to the lower foothill zone, which contained heavier vegetation and provided habitat for an abundance of animal life. The larger sites are close to springs and to the boundaries between the coastal plains or grassland valleys and the hill zone—and not on the coastal plain itself, as Claude Chauchat once believed. Such settlements probably enabled the Paiján people to exploit the game that flourished seasonally on the coastal plains and in the hills above. Some locations were undoubtedly chosen for their access to stone raw materials.

Chauchat, a French archaeologist from Bordeaux University who has worked extensively in the Cupisnique Valley, believes that Paiján projectile points are associated with a littoral and coastal plain adaptation after the disappearance of megafauna in the region, which probably occurred during deglaciation, between 13,000 and 11,000 B.P., when the coast became extremely arid.[28] Chauchat also believes that during times of drought the Paiján culture shifted from inland to coastal resources and that as the sea level rose the Paiján makers were adapting to new landscapes after the extinction of big game such as mastodon, sloths, native horse, and paleo-llama.

Paiján campsites primarily contain the remains of lizards, snails, deer, birds, and fish. Marine mammals and bivalves were not exploited. Chauchat believes that the large Paiján points were specifically adapted to killing large fish. He bases this interpretation on the delicate needle-nosed form of the point and the acute tips (see Figure 4.3e). Yet not all Paiján forms are like this. Although a few fish bones have been found in the middens of interior sites, most Paiján points do not have a pronounced needle-nosed tip and could have been effective against deer and other game. Besides, no Paiján sites have yet been recorded along the littoral zone to substantiate his interpretation. Chauchat suggests that the interior sites simply represent secondary activities during brief forays and that many littoral sites are under water.

The Paiján industry shows a good deal of variation in lithic types, including projectile points, various unifaces, and debris. The last includes the slug or limace, which is a long, bipointed stone tool that has been resharpened until it is too small to use. These different tools reflect the varied activities carried out by the population, which evidently fished and hunted wild game. The Paiján people also relied a great deal on wild plants—judging from the presence of milling stones and a characteristic polish, known as sheen, that appears on the edges of stone tools after heavy use on vegetal matter.

Some Paiján sites suggest seasonal movement. Many of these are situated along low-altitude passes connecting the coastal grasslands with the shrubby foothills. During spring and autumn, hunters may have preyed on migrating animals that were forced to use these passes. During winter and summer, these people may have subdivided into several smaller groups, fanning out over a succession of temporary camps and special activity areas. Such a pattern is suggested by the concentration of sites and surface artifacts within the passes and near the adjacent mountain streams. It is also suggested by other findings: migratory birds, fish, and non-local chert carried in over several kilometers. There seems to have been a radial oscillating pattern of seasonal movement between adjacent environments.

In addition to the known surface sites of the Paiján culture, several excavated sites are reported. For instance, the Quirihuac Shelter, excavated by Juan Ossa and Michael Moseley, is an overhang of a large loose boulder located on a hillside in the Moche Valley about 25 kilometers from the coast.[29] The site contained a small assemblage of stone tools, including stemmed points similar to the Paiján type, biface fragments, and other debris, in association with two intrusive human skeletons of a later period. The abundance of land snails suggests that people feasted on them at the time of occupation. Radiocarbon dates on charcoal flecks from the deepest level ranged from 12,795 to 8,645 B.P. Dates on the human skeletal material were 9,930 and 9,020 B.P. In comparison, Chauchat radiocarbon dated charcoal in another grave of human remains recovered from a campsite in the Cupisnique area at approximately 10,200 B.P.

The nearby La Cumbre site gives more evidence of a Paiján occupation. In addition to recognizable Paiján points, Ossa and Moseley found a wide array of scrapers, limaces, pebble tools, and cores.[30] They also recovered a fragment of a "fluted" point from the surface collection. Radiocarbon dates from the early occupation were 12,360 and 10,535 B.P. Based on the lithic collection and on dates from other sites containing similar forms, the later date is probably a more accurate indicator of the age of La Cumbre's early cultural deposits.

The relation of the Paiján point to the Fishtail point is unclear. All radiocarbon dates from all excavated sites place the Paiján culture roughly between 10,500 and 9,000 B.P. Some archaeologists have argued that the Paiján point was contemporary with the Fishtail form; others have argued that it was slightly later. Both Lynch and Chauchat believe that Paiján points are Paleoindian points derived from the Fishtail point, but this may reflect their bias toward a fluted-point technology as the origin of all early South American cultures. Chauchat admits that there is no hard evidence for a clear technological development from the Fishtail to the Paiján form, or for that matter, from the fluted Clovis form to these forms. Each technology, however, is different in terms of the techniques that were employed to make blades and to form the point style.[31] In none of the excavations of the north coast sites so far recorded has a stratigraphic sequence of these two point types been found.

Chauchat has also suggested that people began to make Paiján points after they came from the highlands to the coast. But, as mentioned above, no Paiján or Fishtail points have been found in the highlands or on the western slopes of the Peruvian Andes above 500 meters. Because both are present at El Inga in Ecuador, however, it is likely that more will be found in the future. If the Paiján point is from the Peruvian highlands, it is different from other highland point types dated to this period.

The question of Paiján's cultural affinity is currently being reviewed at the Santa Maria sites in the Chicama Valley, just north of the Cupisnique Valley, where Jesus Briceño and his colleagues of the Instituto Nacional de Cultura in Trujillo are working.[32] Briceño has reported finding several quarry sites and small campsites containing both Paiján and Fishtail points. The campsites, about 50 meters in diameter and associated with land snails, deer bones, fish, and marine shells, contain both unifaces and bifaces of the Paiján type. Almost all of the Fishtail points are made of rock crystal and quartz; the Paiján points are made primarily of silex, quartzite, and rhyolite, though some are also made of rock crystal and quartz. Since both point types were found together and both are made of rock crystal and quartz, they may have been made at the same time, probably for different reasons. Although the mixture of the two styles in the same archaeological levels may be due to solifluction (natural mixing of sediments by rootlet and other mechanical activity), I suspect that they represent coexisting Paiján and Fishtail populations.

My guess is that Paiján already existed in Peru, having derived from another technology, when Fishtail point-bearing people passed through the area, leaving behind an archaeological record at Santa Maria showing a brief coexistence of the two point types. I do not think Paiján is earlier than approximately 10,500 to 10,200 B.P., and it probably overlaps only with late Fishtail points, after the megafauna extinction on the north coast between 11,000 and

10,500 B.P. Paiján has never been associated with bones of mastodon, paleo-llama, native horse, ground sloth, or any other species that became extinct during the late Pleistocene. It must therefore date from just after the extinction of megafauna. For the moment, it seems wise to recognize the possible affinity between Paiján and Fishtail points, regard their exact relationship as not yet settled, and retain the two as separate types overlapping in time.

In reflecting on the legacy of the Paiján culture, Michael Moseley observes that the "wider distribution [of Paiján points] coincides with the later distribution of large architectural monuments along the coastal desert. The earliest of these monuments were erected by preceramic fisherfolk who relied on nets and hooks, but not harpoons. Paiján was certainly ancestral to these later developments but rising sea levels have submerged shoreline sites which would reflect their early evolution."[33] Although there is no compelling evidence to indicate that the Paiján people were primarily coast-dwellers and that their primary sites are under water, I agree with Moseley that the Paiján people may have laid down some of the early foundations for Andean coastal civilization. Fitting into the equation also are the people associated with the Casma, Amotope, and Nanchoc unifacial traditions, who most likely exploited a wide variety of wild plants and set the stage for the later adoption of cultigens and a settled lifeway.

CENTRAL AND SOUTHERN PERU, NORTHERN CHILE

The earliest sign of people on the central coast of Peru is still a matter of debate. In the early 1960s, in the Chillón Valley just north of Lima, Lanning found remains of stone tool workshops whose surfaces were littered with debris from the manufacture of stone tools of the Luz, Ancón, Oquendo, and Chivateros styles.[34] The camps of these early coastal dwellers were situated in the valleys a little way from the hillsides where the workshops and quarries were located. The collection included steep-edged scraping and boring tools. Based on his estimate of the geological age of the hard reddish soil in which the tools were found, Lanning ascribed dates of 12,000 to 10,000 B.P. He reckoned that this soil, which he called the Red Zone, had been built up during a rainy period toward the end of the last Ice Age. Later, however, a Peruvian archaeologist, Rosa Fung Piñeda, and several geologists examined the site again, and their findings suggested that the Red Zone was laid down under climatic conditions like those of today, marked by warm summers and cool, damp winters. Lanning's date of 12,000 to 10,000 B.P. was therefore too early.

Other coastal sequences of the same order of antiquity as sites located on the north coast have been less forthcoming, although now there is some early evidence for human occupation of arid coastlines from southern Peru down to central Chile. The most detailed evidence comes from the Ring, Quebrada Jaguay, and Quebrada Tacahuay sites on the south coast of Peru and from the Tiliviche, Las Conchas Quebrada, and Huentelafquén sites on the north coast of Chile, all dated between roughly 11,000 and 9,680 B.P.

The Ring Site, excavated by Richardson, is an open shell midden associated with an old lagoon and relict shoreline radiocarbon dated between 10,000 and 7,500 B.P.[35] The site is located on a raised marine terrace about 50 meters above the present sea level. The cultural materials are contained in a large shell midden associated with worked and unworked unifacial lithics, shell remains, uncarbonized plant remains, and ash lenses. The earliest cultural levels contain few marine shells, because the shoreline was farther away, but an abundance of marine birds, mammals, and fish. Richardson thinks it likely that the site was visited on an occasional basis around 10,500 B.P. Support for this interpretation is minimal.

There is some archaeological evidence for the exchange of cultural items between the interior coastal plain and the Pleistocene coastline after 11,000 B.P. The deepest level in the Ring Site dates around 10,575 B.P. on shell. Although shell is known for producing fluctuating dates, the overlying shell and carbon dates are in some stratigraphic and chronological order. The dating of these critical levels is further complicated by a number of dating inversions in the stratigraphy. Nonetheless, it appears that this site was first occupied sometime around 10,500 B.P.

Two recent discoveries along the south coast of Peru—at the Quebrada Tacahuay site, excavated by David Keefer, and at Quebrada Jaguay, excavated by Daniel Sandweiss—have revealed bone and other material showing familiarity with sea resources.[36] At Quebrada Tacahuay, people focused on fishing for anchovies and hunting seabirds, particularly cormorants and several species of fish, suggesting a sea-oriented technology and a highly specialized maritime adaptation. The radiocarbon dates here range from 10,770 to 10,530 B.P. and are associated with hearths, unifacial tools, a few bifaces, and flakes. There also is evidence of obsidian from 130 kilometers to the east in the Andean mountains, suggesting either direct procurement or exchange with highland neighbors.

At the nearby Quebrada Jaguay site, people also gathered clams and exploited other mollusks and crustaceans. Quebrada Jaguay is dated between 11,105 and 9,850 B.P., with most dates falling between 10,700 and 10,300 B.P. The lithic remains include chipping debris, unifacial pebble tools, and a few bifaces. Again there are raw materials from the nearby highlands.

Near Antofagasta on the north coast of Chile, Agustín Llagostera has excavated the shell midden site of Huentelafquén, which, he argues, shows clear human occupation around 11,000 B.P.[37] The people here exploited a wide variety of both terrestrial and marine species. The stone tool industry is of the pebble tool type and includes small numbers of edged-trimmed unifacial tools. Llagostera has reasoned that as the sea level fell near the height of the last glacial maximum, the late Pleistocene coast expanded up to 10 kilometers to the west, and thus the frequency of visits to the coast probably increased. The late Pleistocene and early Holocene records for this site and other sites in the area demonstrate a long dependence on a broadly based marine diet. This is not surprising: The steep continental shelf and upwelling currents make the sea off Peru and Chile one of the richest marine environments in the world.

Another site in north coastal Chile is Quebrada de Las Conchas, dated between 9,680 and 9,400 B.P. and featuring a maritime economy and technology similar to that found at Huentelafquén. Tiliviche, located about 30 kilometers inland, also contains evidence of the exploitation of both land and coastal resources, suggesting seasonal movement or exchange between coastal and interior groups.

The southern Peruvian and northern Chilean coastal sites probably represent seasonal exploitation of the late Pleistocene and early Holocene coast, but with a considerably lower intensity of occupation prior to 10,000 B.P. We can infer that as the coastal plain grew increasingly arid with the end of the Ice Age, people became more dependent on marine resources and ventured less and less into the interior. With sea-level rises, most of their settlements would now be under water.

Exactly what set of archaeological traits constitute a coastal economy at this early period has yet to be clearly defined and widely accepted for South America. At several sites, the fish remains suggest net fishing, and there is evidence of gathering shellfish and hunting sea mammals and birds. We might define a coastal economy as one devoted almost exclusively to the exploitation of marine resources. Most of the late Pleistocene shell midden sites in Peru and Chile, however, show mixed exploitation of terrestrial and marine species, with an emphasis on the latter. In this case, we should perhaps look to indicators such as fish-hooks, barbs or gorgets, fish-traps, netting devices, pry-bars, and rock art showing marine animals—all of which are absent in this region's coastal sites. By 7,000 B.P., the Chinchorro maritime culture on the Chilean and Peruvian coast was producing these kinds of specialized fishing equipment. This probably represents the first true maritime economy. For earlier sites such as Quebrada Jaguay, Quebrada Tacahuay, Ring Site, and Huentelafquén, simple geographic position does not necessarily determine their full economic character, nor does an abundance of marine organisms necessarily amount to an early coastal economy or coastal adaptation. Rather, it may simply mean a mixed economy, with various marine and interior resources, that happens to be located near the coast. Clearly, the basic technology and character of a marine economy was in place by late Pleistocene times but was not fully developed until the early to middle Archaic period.

In this regard, Quebrada Tacahuay and Quebrada Jaguay do not represent the first migrants moving south along the Pacific coast.

Given the fact that older and contemporaneous sites exist in other parts of the continent, these Peruvian sites most likely represent interior groups adapting slowly to a stabilized environment shortly after 11,000 years ago.

Farther south, a late Pleistocene human presence is well established in the central coastal valley of Chile, with several sites containing the remains of early people. Among these sites is Quereo, excavated by Lautaro Núñez and located at the mouth of a small drainage near Vilos, a town on the sea.[38] In times of lowered sea level, when the coast was a large plain with meandering streams, the Vilos area would have been easily accessible and probably beautiful, rising in tiers to the east above the sea. The stone tools of the Quereo site are unifaces made by simple techniques, and most were used for various functions. Formal tool types such as projectile points are not present. Two possible human occupation layers exist at the site.

Quereo I, the deeper level, is dated between 11,600 and 11,400 B.P. and is associated with a few lithic artifacts, a few animal bones with possible cutmarks, and a collapsed horse skull. Lying above this is Quereo II, dated around 11,100 B.P. and also associated with possible cutmarks on bones, fractured bones, stone tools with used edges, flakes, blocks of stone, and marine shells. Serious doubts exist about the horse skull in the Quereo I level. The animal may have been killed by humans or by natural causes such as slumping banks carrying large boulders; or, once dead, it may have been trampled by a large animal passing through the site. I have examined the horse skull and the site setting and found the impact fracture to be too perfectly centered from directly above the cranium to easily attribute a natural agency. On the other hand, if humans had delivered the blow, why do the collapsed skull fragments remain in place? Why were they not removed to extract the brain and other soft tissue? Until this anomaly at Quereo I is explained, a human presence remains questionable. Although a few archaeologists have questioned some artifacts from Quereo II, this level of the site seems to be a valid human occupation.

CENTRAL AND SOUTHERN CHILE

Tágua-Tágua and Nochaco

One of the most informative sites in South America is at Tágua-Tágua in the central valley of Chile, some 120 kilometers south of Santiago. This open-air site was excavated by Julio Montané and later by Lautaro Núñez.[39] Two localities, known as TT–1 and TT–2, contain cultural materials and are known to have been mastodon kill and butchering sites. The first locality dates between 11,400 and 11,000 B.P., the second between 10,190 and 9,700. Both localities are represented by several major concentrations of stone tools and other artifacts occurring in buried areas that formerly bordered a small lake. The climate at the time of site use was dry and hot. Animals were mainly killed either on beaches of low promontories that jutted into the lake or on sand bars in the channels of seasonal streams draining into the lake. Although the hunters' campsites have not been found, I suspect that they are somewhere nearby, probably on a low hill or knoll from which the lagoon could have been watched for animal activity.

In 1969, when Montané first excavated the site, a cultural occupation layer buried approximately 2.5 meters below the present surface yielded about fifty stone and bone artifacts in association with the remains of horse, deer, both a juvenile and an adult mastodon, and plentiful bones of birds, frogs, fish, and other small animals. At first, the stone tool collection appeared to be unifacial because Montané recovered well-made scrapers and flake tools made of basalt, chalcedony, and obsidian. Several possible tools are made of flaked mastodon tusk and horse bones. Subsequent excavations by Núñez and his colleagues, however, recovered Fishtail projectile points, as well as an abundance of mastodon bones and stone artifacts. Núñez and his colleagues also recovered a tusk fragment etched with geometric designs. This carving represents the earliest artwork discovered in South America.

Judging from the bone evidence at both localities, portions of the butchered animals—probably ribs, tusks, and other long bones—were carried to nearby campsites. The bones remaining in the site are mainly pelvises, skulls, feet, and vertebrae. At Monte Verde, a campsite located farther south in Chile and associated with the remains of at least six mastodons, the vast majority of the bones are ribs, tusks, molars, and long bones, just the opposite of the set found at TT–2, and just what you would expect to find at a campsite instead of a kill or butcher site. At each Tágua-Tágua locality the skeletons are disarranged as if they had been tugged and hacked apart. Lying among the bones are discarded choppers and other stone tools, including points, that apparently did the butchering. Butchering also is suggested by a few possible cutmarks on bones.

We should be cautious about interpreting the skeletal collection from Tágua-Tágua. Many of the bones were recovered from an ancient shoreline of the lagoon and could have been trampled by animals watering at the hole while the bones were exposed on the surface. Trampling marks can often resemble cutmarks; and many of the marks on the bones I have seen could be attributed to trampling.

Furthermore, some of the animals at Tágua-Tágua could have died natural deaths. Núñez admits that the large number of animal bones at the site does not necessarily mean all were killed by humans.

Yet, there is good evidence for human killing and butchering at the site. Montané's earlier excavation found several concentrations of mastodon bone in direct association with four unifacial flake tools. Núñez later recovered nine concentrations of mastodon bones associated with eighteen stone tools, including three projectile points of the Fishtail type.[40] Both localities also yielded fourteen hammerstones, some with evidence of flaking, ninety-nine small flakes of rock crystal from resharpening or use, and nineteen unretouched flakes. The entire stone collection consists of a wide variety of raw material, including rock crystal, chalcedony, quartz, obsidian, basalt, silex, jasper, agnate, rhyolite, and andesite. This variety suggests the scattered origins of these tools. The Fishtail points are made of rock crystal and are remarkably similar in size and form to those made of rock crystal and found by Briceño at Santa Maria, on the north coast of Peru.

About 600 kilometers south of Tágua-Tágua, the Lake District of Chile has a few sites containing early stemmed and lanceolate point technologies. One such site is Nochaco, excavated by Zulema Seguel and Orlando Campaña in the 1960s. Nochaco is an old lagoon where bones from at least three mastodons and several lanceolate, "fluted" projectile points were found.[41] Lynch believed these to be Clovis-like points with channel flakes removed.[42] Although there is no direct association between the points and the bones, the site is a possible kill locality that requires further investigation.

Américo Gordon and I have also found Nochaco points at surface paleo-dune sites near Cañete, Puerta Saavedra, and at Queule along the south coast of Chile, approximately 250 to 550 kilometers north of Monte Verde.[43] We also excavated a Nochaco point made of chert at the Río Bueno site, which is buried in a red soil zone in a high terrace overlooking the Río Bueno River and associated with a discrete charcoal lens and chipping debris evidently related to human occupation. A single radiocarbon date of 10,450 B.P. was obtained from a single chunk of charcoal associated with the point. All of these Nochaco points are made of local chert and silex, and all were found on high riverine terraces, ancient beach terraces, or paleo-dunes along the coast. I believe that these sites are associated with human exploitation of the coastline and adjacent interior areas after they were stabilized sometime between 11,000 and 10,000 B.P.

Monte Verde

About 150 kilometers south of Río Bueno is the Monte Verde site, where the preservation of perishable early cultural remains is one of the most remarkable in the Americas.[44] It was the excavation of this site that first drew me into the study of the first Americans, in the 1970s.

Monte Verde is an open-air settlement on the banks of a small freshwater creek, surrounded by sandy knolls and infilled by a narrow bog, beneath a cool, damp forest that has been there since late Pleistocene times. The bog later developed in the creek basin, burying the abandoned settlement under a layer of peat. Because the lack of oxygen in the bog inhibited bacterial decay and because the constant saturation prevented drying for thousands of years, all kinds of perishable materials that normally disappear from the archaeological record have been preserved. An interdisciplinary research team of more than sixty scientists has studied the archaeological remains excavated from two areas at the site, called Monte Verde I and Monte Verde II.[45]

Monte Verde was discovered accidentally in the mid-1970s by local men clearing a path for their ox carts in a wooded area near a small stream, Chinchihuapi Creek. Cutting back the banks of the creek to widen their trails, the men literally stumbled upon buried wood, stone artifacts, and what later turned out to be mastodon bones (Photos 5.6–5.10). In 1977, my colleagues and I began excavation at the site. Over the years, we have uncovered a number of remarkable and unexpected finds: not only stone flakes, typical of South American unifacial sites, and animal bones but also long, bipointed projectile points and a variety of plant remains and numerous wooden objects. The organic remains indicate the importance of plants as well as animals in the inhabitants' diet. The existence of wood and wooden tools, more common at Monte Verde II than stone artifacts, provides an intriguing look at tools and equipment rarely seen in the early archaeological record.

Around 12,500 B.P., perhaps twenty to thirty people built a 20-meter-long tent-like structure out of wood and animal hides. The frame was made of logs and planks anchored by stakes, and the walls were poles covered with animal hides. Several pieces of cordage and string made of junco reed wrapped around wooden posts and stakes, recovered among the architectural remains, show that the people planned a lengthy stay. The tent's dirt floor is embedded with hundreds of microscopic flecks of hide tissue, suggesting that it was probably covered with animal skins. Inside the tent, individual living spaces were divided by planks and poles. On the floor of each living space were brazier pits lined with clay and surrounded by stone tools and the remains of edible seeds, nuts,

PHOTO 5.6   *The Monte Verde II site (dated about 12,500 B.P.), located along Chinchihuapi Creek, Chile.*

PHOTO 5.7   *The excavated wishbone-shaped foundation of a hut with chunks of mastodon hide and meat and quids of various medicinal plants at Monte Verde II. Arrows point to excavated living surface.*

PHOTO 5.8   *The foundation timbers of a long, tent-like structure at Monte Verde II. Note the pits and artifacts on the floor of the structure (arrow).*

PHOTO 5.9   *One of the human footprints excavated at Monte Verde II.*

PHOTO 5.10   *Various bifacial, unifacial, bola, and ground stone artifacts from Monte Verde II.*

and berries. Outside the tent were two large communal hearths, a store of firewood, wooden mortars with their grinding stones, and even three human footprints near a large hearth, where someone had walked across the soft, wet clay brought to the site for refurbishing the firepits. Specialists examining the prints believe they are of a small adult or large adolescent. All these remains indicate a wide range of domestic tasks, primarily food preparation and consumption, tool production and maintenance, and the construction of shelters.

In a second structure, wishbone-shaped in ground plan and made of wooden uprights set into a foundation of sand and gravel hardened with animal fat, mastodon carcasses were butchered, hides were prepared, and tools were manufactured. These activities suggest a public nonresidential area.

This was also probably a place of healing. Eighteen probable medicinal plants were found at the site—the same species the Mapuche people, who live in the region today, employ to treat skin ailments and pulmonary diseases. Although some of these plants grew locally, about half came from coastal environments approximately 70 kilometers to the west, and one was found only in arid regions about 700 kilometers to the north. Since only the medicinal parts of the plants are found in the site, we know they had only one use to the Monte Verdeans.

In addition to medicinal herbs, the remains of a wide variety of edible plants were recovered from the hearths, living floors, and small pits, along with the remains of mastodon, paleo-llama, small animals, and freshwater mollusks. Aquatic plants from the freshwater marshes, bogs, and lagoons of the flood plain and from brackish marshes of the river delta provided the greatest variety and, along with meat, the bulk of the Monte Verdeans' diet. Most of these ecological zones are located far away along the Pacific shoreline or in the Andean mountains. The presence of salt, beach-rolled pebbles used as tools, and bitumen (used to attach stone tools to wooden hafts) at the site shows that coastal habitats also provided important nonfood items to the Monte Verde economy. In short, the Monte Verdeans either traveled regularly to distant environments or were part of a web of social and exchange relationships.

The preserved remains of wild potatoes add a new dimension to the history of a food crop that has become one of the most important in the world. The presence of tuber remains at Monte Verde, left in the cracks and pits of wooden mortars and in food storage pits located in the corners of shelters, bears out the prediction of Russian botanists, who said in the 1930s that the potato originated both in Peru and in southern Chile.

The wooden artifacts excavated at Monte Verde include possible digging sticks, mortars, fragments of two lances, stakes, and the poles used for building. Bone artifacts consist of a baton for striking flakes off stones, gouges made of mastodon tusks, and digging and prying tools. Three different stone tool technologies exist at the site. Some stones were made by percussion. Others are "bola" or sling stones formed by pecking or grinding, similar to those found at other early sites. The third type of stone tools are fractured, edge-trimmed pebbles with one or more sharp edges, which the Monte Verdeans found on distant beaches and in nearby creek beds. Some of these artifacts show minimal modification by humans prior to use.

Exploiting this wide range of resources undoubtedly called for sophisticated knowledge and a division of labor. This is suggested by the separation of the residential from nonresidential areas at the site and by the association of distinct activity areas and living spaces with different tool types and food remains. The discrete living structures, features, and concentrations of specific materials indicate that occupation was continuous and that portions of the site were used more intensively than others. The many different artifacts give evidence of a wide variety of tasks to be done. There is also evidence for specific family or social unit activities, special purpose tasks, perhaps the beginnings of occupational specialization, and spatial separation between domestic and nondomestic tasks. One living space, for example, contained stone artifacts made of quartz coupled with edible fruits and tubers from plants that grow only in brackish estuaries, suggesting that the occupants may have specialized in collecting resources from the coast. Elsewhere in the living tent, stone scrapers and pieces of animal skin were found in a hide-working zone. The internal division and size of the long-tent structure suggest that a large group of people had a mixed hunting and gathering economy focused on many different ecological zones. All this evidence reveals a much more complex social and economic organization than previously expected of early New World cultures. A long sequence of radiocarbon dates on both sterile and artifact-bearing deposits, all in stratigraphic order, place this Monte Verde II occupation at some 12,500 B.P.

In the deepest levels of Monte Verde, separated from the later settlement by over 1.2 meters of sediment and buried in a different area of the site, we found a possible earlier occupation, Monte Verde I, with twenty-six unifacial and battered stone tools and three burned clay features. The burned features were possibly made by humans. Of the twenty-six fractured stones, seven of them were clearly flaked by humans, whereas four showed polish or striation on their sharp edges, possibly from the processing of meat, hides, and plant material. Radiocarbon analysis of charcoal from two of the burned features dated around 33,000 B.P. In addition, several radiocarbon dates obtained from non-cultural materials lying both above and below this layer help to bracket the age of this possible older component between 35,000 and 30,000 B.P. Although the stratigraphy is intact, the radiocarbon dates are valid, and the human artifacts are genuine, I hesitate to accept this older level without more evidence and without sites of comparable age elsewhere in the Americas.

There is no question that the younger 12,500 B.P. Monte Verde II occupation represents a human settlement practicing a generalized economy throughout most of the year. The archaeological evidence suggests that the settlement was formed by a group of exploratory or incipient colonizers who lived in the Maullín River Basin, into which the Chinchihuapi Creek flows. Although few contemporary sites have been found, it is probable that the Monte Verdeans were part of a low-density colonizing population adapted to a cool, temperate wetland-and-forest environment in times of advanced deglaciation. As for the older Monte Verde I layer dated around 33,000 B.P., the paleoecological evidence suggests a setting of beech forests and moors during a warming trend. If people were present at the site in 33,000 B.P., they were likely transient explorers of an interglacial environment.

Monte Verde has made us question the notion that all Ice Age people were nomadic big-game hunters, since the settlement was probably occupied throughout the year by at least a portion of its inhabitants, and they gathered a wide variety of plant and animal foods. The site has provided another cautionary tale as well: The stone items are rudimentary in the extreme. Many tools were no more than edge-trimmed pebbles from the creek bed or distant ocean beaches, picked up, utilized, and then discarded; others were slightly modified by splitting or by removing a few flakes. Only a few specimens, such as bifacially flaked projectile points and chopping tools, grooved sling stones, and grinding stones would be universally accepted as human tools if they had been without corroborating evidence.

CENTRAL AND SOUTH ANDES: INTERMONTANE VALLEYS, PUNA, AND GRASSLANDS

Before we move on to the intermontane valleys of Peru and the puna and altiplano grasslands of the south-central Andes, the setting needs reviewing. The north and central highlands of Peru are cut by numerous valleys whose environments range from lush meadows and grassy slopes in the north to semi-arid and puna-like conditions in the central highlands. In the north, camelids were probably sparse and deer and other game more plentiful. Farther south, camelids become more abundant, with other game restricted to lower elevations. Although the archaeological evidence is sparse, early hunters and gatherers in this region probably exploited a wide variety of plant species. Their culture is nonetheless known as the Central Andean Hunting Tradition.[46]

Unlike the wetter lowlands in the east of Peru and Bolivia and northwest Argentina, the south-central Andean altiplano and puna were probably bleak and hostile. These valleys often reach elevations of 6,500 meters. At no time can one postulate a human population as dense as that of the lusher northern Andean highlands. The land is arid, the vegetation sparse, the animal life limited, and these conditions have prevailed for at least the last ten millennia. Prior to 10,500 B.P., the region was moister; there were large lakes and, likely, many springs. There is no present archaeological evidence for people in this environment before 11,000 to 10,500 B.P. Hunter-gatherers of the South-Central Andean Tradition lived in this region.

Of the overlapping early hunter and gatherer phases, the South-Central Andean Tradition, the latest, is the least known. It is characterized by willow-leaf and triangular shaped projectile points showing considerable variety of form. The area where this tradition can be recognized encompasses southern Peru, northern Chile, western Bolivia, and parts of northwest Argentina. The fairly consistent complex of stone artifacts differs only slightly from those in the highlands to the north in Peru, and the artifacts and lifeway were tied to an ecological setting of cold and dry conditions and primarily to hunting camelids.

The Central Andean Hunting Tradition

The known early occupations in the Central Andes from southern Ecuador to south-central Peru are tightly restricted in a narrow north-south band. They are located in areas receiving adequate rainfall, with access to lakes and sometimes camelids, and at intermediate altitudes that would have offered many different possibilities for hunting and limited plant gathering. The vertical differentiation of the Andes at elevations up to 4,500 meters would have allowed food gatherers to exploit different environments and the changing seasons with a minimum of movement. Besides providing great ecological diversity, these banded environments at intermediate elevations also favored the later development of highland agriculture.

More has been published about the sequence of occupations in caves in the central highlands of Peru than about any other early highland sites in South America. Located in the mountains between 2,500 and 4,500 meters in elevation, these caves usually overlook valleys or lakes. No open sites have been found in the highlands with the exception of Quishqui Puncu in northern Peru.[47] Several tantalizing finds suggest, but do not prove, that people may have been in the central highlands as early as 20,000 to 15,000 B.P. For example, most archaeologists dismiss as aberrant the early dates of 13,460 B.P. at Lauricocha Cave, 12,560 B.P. at Guitarrero Cave, 12,040 B.P. at Telarmachay Cave, and 11,800 B.P. at Pachamachay Cave, all located in Peru. Even earlier dates come from Pikimachay Cave near Ayacucho: They range between 20,200 and 14,150 B.P. At Pachamachay Cave, Lauricocha Cave, Telarmachay Cave, and possibly Uchumachay Cave, the evidence is much more solid for the presence of humans by 10,500 B.P., al-

PHOTO 5.11   *Panaulauca Cave in the central highlands of Peru.*

though problems of stratigraphy and chronology still trouble some of these sites. Lynch, John Rick, and Danièlle Lavallée, who have carried out research at cave sites in the highlands of Peru, favor a human presence no earlier than 10,800 to 10,500 B.P.

In the north central highlands of Peru, Lynch's excavations at Quishqui Puncu, an unstratified hunting campsite located on a side river of the Callejón de Huaylas, led to the first speculation of seasonal movement between the coast and highlands. No Fishtail points were found in the deeper levels of the site; only willow-leaf-shaped Ayampitín points and modern fauna, as well as various stemmed and barbed points made of a large range of local material. Lynch notes that the site economy is represented by a wide range of resources. The oldest occupations date between 10,565 and 8,615 B.P. and, in addition to the various points, are associated with grinding stones, indicating the exploitation of plants. Caution has to be taken with this site, however, because some deposits are heavily disturbed. Modern pieces of glass and wood chips were scattered throughout the deposits, making the dates and the stone tool chronology suspect.

The excavation of Lauricocha Caves I and II in the mountains of central Peru in the 1960s by Augusto Cardich showed that people were moving into high altitude, deglaciated landscapes by at least 10,000 B.P.[48] Situated in a sheltered valley near the source of a mountain stream, these caves were found to contain several meters of cultural deposits, including hearths, both animal and human bones, and quantities of artifacts and manufacturing debris. The deeper levels contained classic triangular and willow-leaf projectile points and unifacial tools. In Layer 7, Cardich found knives, scrapers, and small flakes as well as the bone remains of paleo-llama or guanaco, vicuna, and deer radiocarbon dated to 9,575 B.P. Immediately below this layer, Layer 8 contains two bone pieces thought by Cardich to show evidence of human working. One bone is shaped like a long projectile point with one end heavily worked. The other is a rib fragment showing possible cutmarks, dated to 13,460 B.P. Knowing what we know today about bone taphonomy, especially in caves such as those at Lauricocha where predators transported body parts to their dens for consumption, it is possible that the supposed cutmarks were produced by tooth fracture and gnawing, not by humans. There also is evidence from the late Pleistocene level at Lauricocha Cave to suggest that people consumed a wide variety of local roots and tubers.

At Huargo Cave, 4,050 meters above sea level in north-central Peru, a single date of 13,460 B.P. was obtained from animal bone. The deepest levels contained bones of native horse and paleo-llama and a possible bone point and worked rib. The context of the bones is questionable and may not be associated with early human activity. This and the single radiocarbon date make the age and affinity of Huargo Cave suspect.

At Guitarrero Cave, which contains an early occupation dated possibly around 10,000 B.P., a different situation occurs.[49] In the lowest levels of the site, an early date of 12,560 B.P. is associated with four other dates ranging from 9,790 to 9,140 B.P., implying that the older measure may be inaccurate. The site is located at 2,580 meters above sea level in the Callejón de Huaylas and was excavated by Lynch and his colleagues. The scanty artifacts in the lowest levels, referred to as Complex II, include projectile points and lithics similar to other highland sites (Lauricocha and Pachamachay) located at higher elevations. Perhaps because it is located in a lower, more temperate environmental zone, Guitar-rero Cave contained a different faunal and floral assemblage. Small rodents, vizcacha, birds, deer, and occasionally camelids made up the meat diet. This cave's most remarkable feature is the excellent preservation of organic remains, including artifacts made of cordage and wood and a small assemblage of edible plants.

Possibly dating between 10,000 and 9,000 B.P. are several wild and possibly domesticated species of tubers, rhizomes, and fruits. The domesticates include common beans, lima beans, and chili pepper—nonlocal plants that were grown elsewhere and brought to the site for consumption or cultivation. Other highland caves, such as Tres Ventanas on the western slopes of the south Peruvian Andes, have yielded cultivated squash also thought to be almost 10,000 years old. Extreme caution is called for, however, because these plants' chronology is based on their stratigraphic association with diagnostic points, not on direct radiocarbon dating of the plants themselves. Small plant parts can move down through tiny cracks in the stratigraphy, often leading archaeologists to believe that they are older than they are. Although probably dating only to the early Archaic period, the plant foods and industrial cordage from Guitarrero and Tres Ventanas reveal a broadly based economy incorporating both local and exotic items.

Lynch compares elements of the Guitarrero early Archaic period with those at El Abra in Colombia, but I personally see little convincing evidence to link the technology and style of stone tool artifacts from these two sites. The only intermediate site is El Inga in Ecuador, and even Lynch admits that there is no correspondence between this site and Guitarrero, although El Inga has a strong burin component that is also found at Guitarrero. Lynch also believes that Chobshi Cave, a base camp of broad-spectrum hunters and gatherers located in the southern highlands of Ecuador and dated as early as 10,100 B.P., is culturally linked to Guitarrero.[50] Chobshi also has burins and stemmed points that link it to El Inga. Other point types link Guitarrero, Chobshi, Paiján, and El Inga, though Paiján does not have end scrapers like the sites of the Central Andean Hunting Tradition. Lynch also attempted to link Guitarrero to the Paiján sites in the Moche Valley on the north coast of Peru and to Lauricocha Cave, but with little evidence; this idea mostly reflects his effort to demonstrate contact and migration between the highlands and lowlands.

At Pikimachay Cave, there is a local series of cultural complexes that may date back to about 20,000 B.P.[51] One of the merits of Pikimachay Cave is that it is one of a few sites in South America with a long sequence of excavated cultural deposits. Richard Scotty MacNeish excavated this site in 1967, finding thirteen superimposed zones that contained forty-three separate cultural phases, extending from the historic period back to the late Pleistocene. The levels of interest here are the Paccaicasa Phase, dated around 25,000 B.P., and the Ayacucho Phase, dated at 14,000 B.P. From the contents of the later and middle levels, MacNeish sought to locate the origin of agriculture in the valleys around Ayacucho by discovering and excavating the predecessors to agricultural communities. Instead of producing information on early agriculturalists, the site yielded data on early specialized hunters and gatherers and their food resources.

The Paccaicasa Phase is defined by a small collection of bones of extinct animals (some of which possibly exhibit human cutmarks) and about 100 stone artifacts made of exotic and cave tuff distributed in several activity areas. The majority of the stone tools are made from the same stone as the cave walls. MacNeish radiocarbon dated ground sloth bones between 25,000 and 15,000 B.P. in the deeper levels. He believes these levels represent campsites of "microbands periodically residing in the region on seasonal rounds between the lowlands and the highlands." The following Ayacucho Phase is defined by 212 stone artifacts, more than 1,000 cores and chips, 517 animal bones, and nine activity areas. These were dated between 15,000 and 13,000 B.P. Fire-cracked rock and reddish burned areas suggest hearths. One other early phase is Huanta, defined by seven artifacts and six bones above the Ayacucho level, but this could be stratigraphic mixture.

I have doubts about the integrity of the oldest chronology and stratigraphy in the cave and especially about the numerous radiocarbon dates, the stone artifacts, and the possible cutmarks on bones associated with the Paccaicasa and Ayacucho phases.[52] The stones are extremely crude and made of local tuff. It is difficult to determine whether some were made by human agency, animal trampling, roof fall, or all three. Besides, tuff is a highly unusual raw material. If it was desirable for stone tools, why wasn't it used by later groups occupying the cave? Finally, none of the alleged early stone tools is diagnostic or relates to anything else I have seen. The later Ayacucho levels apparently contain exotic stones that may have been brought to the cave by humans, but from the published description, the stratigraphy is not sufficiently known to determine whether they have filtered down from higher levels. In short, it is very difficult to evaluate the earliest Pikimachay Cave data without further description and perhaps further excavation. The current importance of the deeper deposits in the site is the appearance of extinct bone remains and a sequence indicating biota possibly extending as far back as 20,000 B.P. But it is not clear whether these remains are important for archaeologists or paleontologists.

At Pikimachay, MacNeish also uncovered an early Archaic series of pebble tools, tools made out of flakes, small triangular points, and core bifaces similar to those used by the people of the central highlands. The inhabitants were primarily camelid hunters, to judge from the animal bones recovered. Also of interest are his imaginative, if sketchy, notions about the increasing human population of the valley and the accompanying changes in social life, habitation pattern, and technology. Although no one would claim that the high cultures of the Andes evolved in the Ayacucho area, MacNeish's interpretations are a valuable picture of how early highland social and technological changes might have occurred.

Like Lynch and others, MacNeish also has proposed seasonal movement between high and low elevations in the Central Andes.[53] These archaeologists have postulated wet and dry season sites at different elevations in the highlands, but the evidence is very weak in all cases. I don't doubt movement between the zones, but if there had been strong, prolonged contact we would find greater affinity between projectile point styles. Probably movement was less extreme than MacNeish and others have suggested and perhaps occurred only within highland valleys and restricted elevation zones, as John Rick's work at another highland site, Pachamachay Cave, has suggested.

Like many other cave sites, Pachamachay Cave was a base camp occupied for several millennia.[54] Its very high elevation, 4,300 meters, limited the variety of animal and plants foods. In the next-to-lowest level, Rick dated charcoal to 11,800 B.P. The date was in direct association with forty-two tools made of chert, more than 160 carbonized seeds, a small quantity of animal bones, and stone debris from making and maintaining stone tools. Most of the tools are utilized flakes, subtriangular and triangular projectile points, large non-projectile bifaces, and other stone debris. Based on the similarity of these stone tools with later ones that continue into the following early Archaic period and on the single early date with a large standard deviation, Rick believes that the lowest level is later in time, perhaps around 10,500 years or later. He also believes that the earliest occupants, his Phase I hunters, were small nomadic groups who used this and other caves.

The site, overlooking a broad basin, was ideally suited for observing the irregular movement of guanaco and other game. Between 11,000 and 7,000 B.P., the climate was more humid and colder than today's puna. Between 10,500 and 9,000 B.P., the hunters focused their efforts on vicuna and lived in the cave year round, using smaller outlying shelters as temporary hunting stations. Plants and small game were taken at the edges of lakes. Carbonized seeds recovered from levels dating to this period suggest these people collected wild grasses and other plants. To prevent overexploitation of local vicuna, Rick believes, people probably limited their group sizes.

His Phase II hunters, dating after 10,500 B.P., slowly filled in niches and moved southward, leaving the triangular points in their path. Lynch also thought that the first highland hunters could have been spreading down the north-to-south axis of the Andes but that before 10,500 "a 4,300 m elevation would have been exceedingly inhospitable or even impossible to inhabit" due to cold, harsh conditions produced by patchy ice sheets. Rick, however, does not believe the projectile point styles support Lynch's argument. He thinks people could have lived in the area in earlier times despite the ice sheets. He also thinks that the Central Andes were somewhat isolated from other areas. In this case, I agree with Lynch.

In sum, the later human occupation at Pachamachay is associated with a wide but temporally continuous suite of small triangular and subtriangular projectile points that survive until about 2,000 years ago and are characteristic of other early sites in the central highlands of Peru. Associated with these points are knives, scrapers, and various forms of utilized flakes. The site also contained abundant bone remains of camelid and guanaco and parts of several local plant species. Rick believes that good archaeological evidence exists for territorial and possibly year-round occupation as early as 10,000 to 9,000 B.P. Both wet-season camelid remains and dry-season plant species suggest that people stayed in the cave for at least several months each year. The absence of exotic plants, cherts, and other materials suggests that these peoples' economic exploitation was confined to the local environment. The many pieces of obsidian at the site, however, imported from perhaps 250 kilometers to the south, imply greater mobility than Rick admits. The presence of similar tools and food remains at nearby smaller sites suggest that Pachamachay was a large base camp where people organized their year-round exploitation of multiple resources in various habitats and that the smaller sites are associated with temporary hunting and gathering localities.

Telarmachay, another Central Andean site that yielded a long sequence of late Pleistocene and Holocene assemblages was excavated by a French team headed by Daniel Lavallée in the 1970s.[55] This is a small cave containing triangular, subtriangular, and other point styles similar to those at other puna sites. The assemblage near the bottom includes a wide variety of other lithics and the bone remains of camelids and small game and has a tiny amount of imported obsidian from 200 kilometers away. A single date of 12,040 B.P. places the occupation of the cave in the late Pleistocene, but one early outlier does not count. Most dates from Telarmachay fall after 10,000 B.P., placing the earliest reliable occupation in the terminal Pleistocene and early Archaic period.

Another site that looms large in the Peruvian literature is Uchumachay Cave, excavated by Jane Pires-Ferreira, Eduardo Pires-Ferreira, and Peter Kaulicke.[56] The lowest level contains extinct Pleistocene fauna and eight human-modified flakes. Immediately overlying this level is a cultural layer containing hundreds of stone tools and post-glacial animal species that are radiocarbon dated between 9,000 and 7,500 B.P. The eight stone tools from the lowest level could have moved down from the overlying occupational layer and mixed with the Pleistocene bone remains. The inhabitants exploited a wide range of game, including deer and small animals, and plant resources from nearby lower altitude valleys, indicating a less specialized hunting economy than Pachamachay Cave. The diversified economy reflects the lower elevation of the site, which gave its inhabitants access to more temperate highland zones where more faunal species were available.

The South-Central Andean Tradition

In the upper Moquegua drainage in the extreme southern highlands of Peru lies Toquepala Cave, dated around 9,500 B.P. and characterized by seasonal occupation and painted rock art.[57] Camelid hunting was the dominant economic activity here. Nearby, at a higher elevation, is Asana, which dates to approximately 9,580 B.P. and shows possible ritual architecture and a wet season occupation. Willow-leaf points occur at both sites, which are typical of areas to the north and south.

Farther south, in the lower puna grasslands of the south-central Andes, early highland occupation of northern Chile is suggested by Tiliviche Cave, which is associated with dates of 9,760 and 9,680 B.P.[58] Both marine and inland economies are represented there. The leaf-shaped projectile points from the site also are reminiscent of southern highland sites in Peru. Also present in this area are the Tuina–1 site at Calama, dated at 10,820 and 9,080 B.P.; the Pichasca site, dated at 9,890 B.P.; and the San Lorenzo site, dated at 10,400, 10,280, and 9,960 B.P. Across the mountains, in northwest Argentina at elevations between 3,800 and 3,400 meters, are two early sites, Inca Cueva–4 and Huachichocana, that are dated between 10,675 and 9,230 B.P. and 9,450 and 8,450 B.P., respectively.[59] All of these sites are associated with the bone remains of camelids, rodents, and other small game and with small subtriangular and triangular points. The varieties of cherts and obsidian in these sites suggest trans-Andean contact between groups living at different elevations. Núñez believes the people throughout this region moved seasonally between high and low elevation zones on the lower western slopes of the Andes. Although later in age, Huachichocana is especially important because its deeper levels contain remains of squash and chili pepper that were probably domesticated from wild forms in lower tropical elevations to the east. The presence of very young and adult camelids as well as wool fibers in these sites suggest the beginnings of animal domestication as well.

The salares (pluvial salt basins) of the high puna and altiplano of Chile and Bolivia have yielded very little late Pleistocene material. This high puna was occupied later, around 9,500 to 8,000 B.P., as evidenced at the sites of Las Cuevas, Hakenasa, and Tojo-Tojone.[60] These sites are also associated with small, subtriangular point types like those in the central and southern Peruvian highlands and at the earlier but lower sites in northern Chile. Lynch, in addition, has searched old beach ridges of pluvial lakes in the Punta Negra region but found no intact early material.

Farther south and to the east is the high puna of Bolivia, where Ice Age campsites are associated with Ayampitín points and other leaf-shaped points around ancient lake shores.[61] An important site is Viscachani, where numerous lithic industries, including Ayampitín, have been found. The Ayampitín sites in this part of Bolivia and northwest Argentina often contain an abundance of grinding stones, suggesting intensive plant exploitation. Other possible early localities are the quarry sites at Abaroa and Quetena IV, which have yielded various unifaces, lanceolate, and triangular points, but their age and cultural affinity are not known. The Bolivian high puna may have been wetter then than now, and its inhabitants may have exploited aquatic resources and been in contact with lowland populations as early as 10,800 to 10,500 B.P.

Little archaeological work has been done on late Pleistocene people in the central and southern highlands of Chile and Argentina. Archaeologists from the Universidad de Cuyo in San Juan, Argentina, report a date of 9,500 B.P. in the deeper levels of Huachún Cave. In the foothills of the central valley of Chile near Santiago, Rubén Stehberg has excavated a very deep rockshelter dating back to approximately 13,000 B.P., but human remains are associated only with dates around 9,800 B.P.

More searching in the high puna and altiplano of the central and southern Andes may bring to light more rockshelters with early occupation. Investigations to date, however, make three points clear. The first is that most caves and rockshelters we see in this region show no reliable evidence of human occupation prior to 10,800 to 10,500 B.P., although the reasons for this are not altogether apparent. Second, many rockshelters show evidence of occasional or sporadic occupation by late Pleistocene people. Again, one can only speculate why this is so. My hunch is that people began moving into these sites only after deglaciation and after soil and vegetation had formed. And third, the fact that the unifacial or core flake tradition has not yet been found in these high altitude environments, or in the cold latitudes of southern Patagonia, lends support to the idea that this tradition is adapted primarily to low, well-vegetated zones in northern and central South America.

At the same time, there remains a remote possibility that the higher-elevation cultures may be derived from the Fishtail, El Jobo, or other early cultures, even though the triangular and subtriangular points show no technological affinity with these types. To understand the total sequence of occupations in the highlands, we will need to determine whether there was cultural continuity between the coastal and highland stone technologies. Increasingly, the evidence seems to reveal that there was generally little contact between the two areas. The changing tool types portray clear differences but no major continuities. And no highland or lowland sites contain a sequence of point styles linking the two areas. The only possible exception is the El Inga site in the far northern Andes, and this may reflect coast-to-highland migration that might have occurred between 11,000 and 10,000 B.P., only a few millennia after initial human entry into South America.

If there was sporadic contact between the lowlands and highlands elsewhere in the Andes, it is not very evident in other aspects of the archaeological record.[62] With the exception of obsidian at a few sites in Peru and Chile, most highland raw material is local. And as Rick points out, the little obsidian at sites in Peru shows little north to south movement. Nor was there much east-to-west movement, judging from the scant presence of shell and other lowland materials in highland sites and of obsidian in lowland sites. Interaction between zones appears to have been minimal. Some form of contact occurred later, however, because lowland cultigens are found in different areas (such as Guitarrero and Tres Ventanas Caves), but this evidence may suggest different exchange contexts for different materials. Once again, I suspect that people did not move into the higher elevations until the glaciers had almost completely receded. The presence of megafauna and humans in the northern Andes between approximately 12,000 and 10,000 B.P. at relatively low elevations (below 2,500 meters) and in relatively lush environments, together with the absence or scarcity of megafauna in the high central and south Andes after 11,000 B.P., might indicate that human activity in higher elevations was minimal until well after deglaciation.

The return of glaciers in some highlands areas around 11,000 B.P. may have forced people to move back to lower elevations. Although camelids and people live near glaciers today in the highlands of central Peru, it is unlikely that they did in late glacial times, unless it was during the colder months. Highland temperatures were surely lower between 11,000 and 10,000 B.P. than today. It is also likely that periglacial zones in high altitudes had sporadic or continuous permafrost during this period. The lower limits of the permafrost might have been at approximately 3,500 meters, an elevation located below most known puna cave sites and consistent with the estimated lowering of snow lines throughout the region. Sometime after 12,000 to 11,000 B.P., during times of deglaciation, amelioration, and possibly megafauna extinction, there were probably outwash plains, with a drier and colder climate than now. Still, it is important to remember that the retreat of the glaciers was neither simultaneous nor uniformly paced; some lasted longer, and retreated slower, than others. Finally, many environments of the region must have become virtually uninhabitable during the final Pleistocene arid phase, between 11,000 and 10,500 B.P.

There also is the problem of cave formation and the deposition of sediments in caves. Several of the highland cave sites were probably formed in late Pleistocene times by retreating glaciers and outwash sediments. But it takes time for a cave to acquire a layer of sediment. The presence of early triangular and willow-leaf projectile points, dated no earlier than 10,800 to 10,500 B.P., and of Holocene animal species in the basal deposits of many highland and puna caves points to a relatively late arrival of humans in the highlands. The industry at these highland sites contrasts with the adjacent coastal traditions of Paiján, unifacial, and Fishtail industries. In fact, the highland sites present problems for any notion of a widespread fluted point horizon, because they date only slightly later than the Fishtail points, do not reflect a high degree of mobility, and exhibit completely different stone tool technologies. Once again, with the exception of the El Inga site, fluted points have not been found in the Andean mountains.

In summary, the current information suggests that the deeper cultural deposits in sites of some areas of the central and south Andean highlands should not be considered as accurate indications of the timing of human habitation in South America. Large-scale migration of people into these regions probably occurred after or coincident with the reinvasion of plants and animals between approximately 12,000 and 10,000 B.P. Indeed, Duccio Bonavia has suggested that camelids and humans moved into the Peruvian highlands from lower elevations at approximately the same time after deglaciation.[63] In the extreme southern Andes and Patagonia, where extensive ice sheets still remained, a similar reinvasion had to wait until several millennia later. If this scenario is correct, we should find the earliest human adaptations to central and south-central mountain environments in caves and open-air sites at elevations lower than 2,500 meters—as the current archaeological record seems to confirm. This does not mean, however, that no places in the highlands were impacted less by deglaciation and thus were habitable as early as 12,000 B.P. Rather, no evidence has been currently found to support this possibility.

CHAPTER SIX

South American Regions: The Atlantic Side of the Continent

THE EASTERN LOWLANDS AND SOUTHERN GRASSLANDS

Along the tropical Atlantic in Brazil, several sites give evidence of occupation of the arid interior during the late Pleistocene and early Holocene (Figure 6.1). At this time the coast was at least 60 to 80 kilometers east of where it is now, meaning that coastal sites older than 10,000 to 8,000 B.P. are under water. The presence of shells, however, at interior midden sites indicates some form of contact with the coast. The deeper levels of huge shell mounds, called *sambaquis,* along the Brazilian coast contain evidence of specialized gatherers in lagoons and bays once the coastline stabilized, around 6,500 to 6,000 B.P.

A number of workers since the 1960s have carried out a systematic examination of late Pleistocene sites in Brazil's Eastern Highlands. Most of these early sites are associated with a unifacial

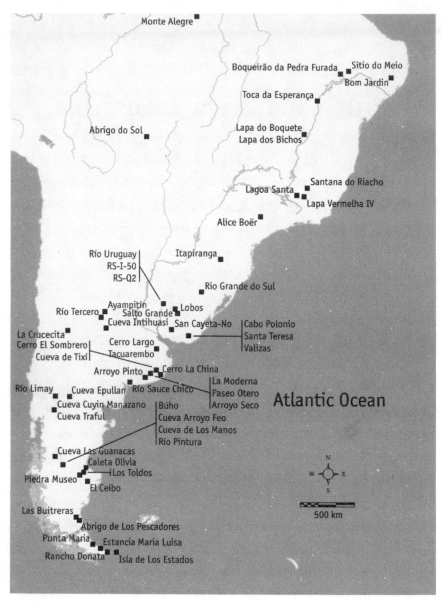

FIGURE 6.1   *The Distribution of Known Archaeological Sites in Eastern and Southern South America*

quartz and chert technology and a generalized hunting-gathering lifeway. Brazilian archaeologists considering the early record indicate that it shows a broad spectrum diet based mainly on gathered roots and fruits backed up by the hunting of game, with no clear evidence of people consistently pursuing megafauna. The vast majority of early sites are in eastern and southern Brazil. With the exception of two sites in Amazonia, the Pleistocene record of the entire western half of Brazil is unknown. Not only has very little work been done in the region, but low archaeological visibility in the tropical forest prohibits the discovery of these sites.

Despite some extravagant claims to the contrary, the Eastern Highlands lack any definite human material older than 12,000 years ago. There are two securely documented stone tool industries dated between approximately 11,500 and 9,000 B.P. and found in different regions south and east of Amazonia: the Itaparica Tradition, defined by various unifacial industries common in the eastern tropical parklands (Figure 6.2); and the Uruguai Phase, represented by stemmed projectile points and present in the open grasslands of southern Brazil. These two traditions are often well segregated; projectile points are seldom found in the forests and on the tropical savannas, whereas the unifacial industries are rare in the southern grasslands.

The wilder claims for early human occupation center on the bone remains of extinct animals associated with broken stones that the excavators interpret as human-made tools. Very early radiocarbon and other dates on these bones have led some archaeologists to speculate on a human presence in the Americas earlier than 100,000 B.P. But the only thing these sites prove is the danger of relying too much on the direct association of stones and the bones of extinct animals, particularly in the absence of detailed ge-

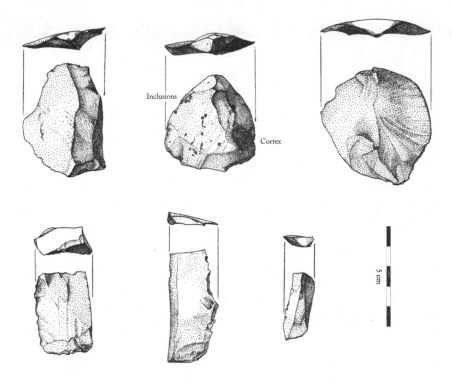

FIGURE 6.2   Unifacial Tools from Various Sites in Eastern Brazil

ological work on the sediments where they were found. Although several other sites present radiocarbon dates extending from 150,000 to 12,000 B.P., their reliability and the alleged human materials associated with them are also uncertain. No site has valid human material stratified in reliably dated deposits. Still, it's worth reviewing some of these reports.

One example, a claim of human antiquity stretching back to 300,000 B.P., comes from the famous French archaeologist Henri de Lumley and his Brazilian colleague Maria Beltrão, at Toca da Esperança Cave.[1] The deepest level is said to contain a few pebble tool flakes and a hammerstone, as well as human dental impressions, campfires, bone tools, charcoal living floors, and the bone remains from a few extinct animal species. The oldest dates, from uranium-thorium decay methods, range between 295,000 and 204,000 B.P. Although the details of this work have not yet been reported, there is no other evidence in the New World to support such an early date. The quartzite artifacts are surely naturally occurring rocks in the area. The bones were probably redeposited by flooding in the cave system and later mixed with much more recent material, including stone artifacts of the Archaic period.

More plausible but heavily disputed candidates for early human settlements are the Alice Boër and Pedra Furada sites in eastern Brazil.[2] The latter, located among dramatic sandstone cliffs in the arid outback in the São Raimundo Nonato region of northeastern Brazil (Photo 6.1), is most interesting. When Nlède Guidón of the School for the Advanced Study of Social Sciences in Paris first excavated the site in 1978, she found cave paintings and what she and her colleagues thought were ash-filled hearths and stone tools that are at least 30,000 and perhaps 50,000 years old. Unlike most other early caves and rockshelters in Brazil, Pedra Furada has not yielded any bone remains of megafauna or any conclusive evidence of human activity dated before 11,500 B.P. Other caves in the area contain bone remains of extinct animals, but these are paleontological sites. If people were here before 15,000 years ago, as Guidón and her colleagues believe, there should be some archaeological and taphonomic evidence on these bones indicating human cutmarks and fracturing, as well as stone and bone tools.

Another problem with Pedra Furada is that the alleged earliest human-made stone tools are questionable. Several archaeologists who have examined them say that they are nothing more than broken stones that were washed into the rockshelter from a gravel de-

PHOTO 6.1   *Pedra Furada, Brazil*

posit about 100 meters above. Guidón and her colleagues counter that the deeper cultural deposits in the rockshelter are protected by an overhang from falling debris and that the central portion of the shelter, where most of the disputed materials were recovered, is a meter or two higher than the adjacent terrain. Any fallen pebbles that washed in and mixed with older bones would have landed lower down. Thus, Guidón insists, the stone artifacts are real and not naturally produced rocks mimicking human chipping patterns.

However, the central area of the rockshelter is flanked by two large chimney chutes that originate at the top of the cliff where the gravel deposits are located. During heavy rainfall, loose rock falls approximately 100 meters down these chutes and shatters on the floor of the shelter. A strong flood could have easily scattered broken rocks across the entire floor, as it evidently did more than once: Stratigraphic cuts show large quantities of intact and broken gravel. Water transport tends to sort stones by size; the more violent the flow, the more of the smaller pieces it will wash away, leaving behind heavier broken rocks that often mimic human-made stone tools. Telling natural from human-made fractures is very difficult in this kind of geological setting.

Critics also have doubts about discrete concentrations of charcoal, which Guidón believes represent ancient fireplaces associated with the stone tools. It is impossible to tell whether the charcoal was in fact swept into the rockshelter by winds during natural fires. Guidón has claimed that if the charcoal had been left by forest fires, carbon deposits would have been found scattered across a wide area rather than in discrete concentrations. Yet the now-buried stratigraphic floors of the rockshelter may once have had a wide distribution of charcoal, most of which was subsequently washed away or redeposited by rainwater, leaving flecks protected within clusters of stones. The fact that in many areas of the rockshelter the charcoal is ringed by stones, Guidón counters, is strong supporting evidence for human-made hearths, not natural formations filled by wind-blown flecks of charcoal from natural fires. She argues that at 30,000 B.P. the area was a humid tropical rain forest, in which natural fires would have had a hard time getting started. But palynological studies from nearby peat bogs suggest that the area was much drier, with gallery forests located along streams—an environment susceptible to natural fires. (Even if the region was a rain forest, an El Niño-like climatic event could have caused sufficient drought to permit a widespread fire, as it did in many parts of the world in 1998.) Lastly, if the hearths are valid, burned sediment should have been found below them, but none was.

At first, the excavators of Pedra Furada also claimed the early rock art at the site dated back 35,000 years or more. This claim was based on a fragment of painted rock found in the deeper levels, but this fragment may not have fallen from the wall 35,000 years ago; it could have filtered down through the deposits. Guidón and her colleagues have now recanted this claim and believe that people were painting walls at the shelter by 12,000 B.P.

Despite the heavy criticism levied against Pedra Furada, it is possible that the shelter may indeed have been used by people around 12,000 B.P. or earlier. If so, it may not have been a campsite as postulated by Guidón and her colleagues, but a quarry site where broken and unbroken stones were readily available. If the floor of the shelter was moist, people may have avoided it and camped elsewhere. Such a scenario would offset some of the geological and archaeological criticisms of the site and account for the presence of any convincing human-used or human-made artifacts there. The status of the site thus hinges on the validity of the stone tool artifacts. Having seen a representative sample of the collection from the site, I admit that a few very early stones appear to have been made by humans. They resemble human-made flakes and hammerstones that are similar in form, raw material, and edge damage to some stones recovered from the deeper, possible cultural level at Monte Verde, which is dated around 33,000 B.P.

On the other hand, I also saw, in the pile at the base of the two chutes at Pedra Furada, thousands of broken rocks that look like they might have been worked by humans but clearly were not. The context is important here. In the deeper Pedra Furada stratigraphy, natural and possible human deposits overlap very closely, and there are few reliable external checks on the site—such as human-induced cutmarks on animal bone, exotic chert imported to the site, or carbonized and imported seeds—to substantiate the claims for a very early culture. The later Pedra Furada cultures are associated with valid human artifacts made of chert and other exotic materials and dating after 12,000 B.P.

To me, the solution to Pedra Furada depends on detailed publication of all geological and archaeological evidence before we can pass final judgment. Yet I suspect that the real answer lies in the excavation of other nearby rockshelters. If people were at Pedra Furada before 12,000 B.P., they were also at other sites in the vicinity. Several candidate localities excavated by Guidón and her coworkers have yet to yield evidence of pre-11,500 B.P. occupation. This does not mean, however, that people were not in eastern Brazil before that. People moved around a great deal, and many localities undoubtedly were never occupied or were not reused for hundreds or thousands of years. The answer to Pedra Furada is buried in other shelters, perhaps ones less contaminated by criticism and less subject to natural forces that can mimic human activity.

In the same region, Guidón and her colleagues also report early dates from the deeper levels of the Toca do Sitio do Meio Cave.[3] This site has yielded radiocarbon dates on four hearths ranging from about 14,300 to 12,200 B.P. Charcoal dates on three of these, of 13,900, 12,440, and 12,200 B.P., are associated with a small group of cultural flakes in a lower level, and a date of 14,300 B.P. occurs on an even deeper level. Bryan, who re-excavated Toca do Sitio do Meio Cave, believes that there is good evidence for the presence of late Pleistocene people. He found a bone with two possible cutmarks in association with unifacial flake tools. Unfortunately, the bone was too badly deteriorated to be dated by radiocarbon means. No additional hearths that would yield charcoal for dating purposes were found in the cave. Bryan believes that the simple pebble tools and flake tools of quartz, chert, and quartzite he took from the site show minimum human modification without intentional shaping of the pieces. Other sites excavated by Guidón and her associates, such as Toca do Caldeirão Dos Rodrigues I, date to approximately 18,000 B.P. and also contain fractured stones. None of these sites, however, is securely dated or associated with human related lithics or bone remains.[4]

Farther north, Anna Roosevelt's excavations in the Caverna da Pedra Pintada or the Monte Alegre site, in the lower Amazon River, have uncovered evidence that humans inhabited the humid tropical forest about 10,400 B.P. and that they practiced a mixed plant gathering and hunting lifeway.[5] Situated in a sheltered valley near the source of a mountain stream, this cave was found to contain 3 meters or more of occupation deposit, including a great deal of cultural and organic material such as hearths, bones, plant remains, and quantities of artifacts. The people here gathered fruit, caught fish, and hunted a wide variety of land animals. Finds at the cave include thousands of carbonized fruits and wood fragments from tropical trees as well as the remains of fish, birds, reptiles, large forest game, and freshwater shellfish. Excavations also uncovered lumps and drops of red pigment, apparently used in wall paintings. Roosevelt and her crew also recovered twenty-four stone implements, including a possible biface fragment, in the deeper levels, along with a wide variety of debris produced during tool making.

Farther south, in the southwestern state of Goiás, Pedro Schmitz has divided the early unifacial period into the Itaparica Tradition and the Paranaiba Phase, dated 11,000–8,500 B.P. and 10,700–9,000 B.P., respectively.[6] Larger tools, such as scrapers and utilized flakes, cores of all kinds, and fragments of quartz are abundant throughout this region, and both awls and burins are also found. What is remarkable about the unifaces is the wide variety of flake tools. These tools grade into one another and also into smaller groups of edge-trimmed flakes. Discoidal cores prepared for the removal of flakes, similar cores already struck, and the flakes produced from them are all present in some number. The most diagnostic tool for the Itaparica Tradition is the limace or slug. Bifacially-worked artifacts are very rare, and they are usually Tanged or contracting stem points. This tradition represents a generalized hunter-gatherer culture during the terminal Pleistocene and early Holocene period.

The Itaparica Tradition sites are adapted to a wide variety of environments, including savannas and forests. Most sites are temporary campsites, though more permanent localities are associated with caves and rockshelters. The Itaparica people exploited large and small game, various fruits and other plants, but no extinct megafaunal remains or kill sites are reported. In age and form, the unifacial industries of the Itaparica Tradition are roughly similar to those of the Andean region. Isolated projectile points are rare in these assemblages, appearing only in the later Paranaiba Phase, between 9,000 and 8,500 B.P., but their presence shows that the technique for making them was at least known. Rock art, predominantly geometric designs and animal scenes, is thought to be widespread at these sites.

The Paranaiba Phase saw a more intensified hunting and gathering lifeway that left behind limaces, a few bifacial tools, and occasionally bone projectile points, which were probably used to hunt rodents, tapir, and rheas and other birds. Wherever the limaces have been found, they have been considered primarily as a technological anomaly, marking a consistent change in the way people made stone tools. This change probably reflects changes in associated crafts such as working wood, bone, and leather. We do not know if limaces are also related to changes in hunting or gathering methods.

At a number of other Itaparica sites in central Brazil, unifacial assemblages have been excavated from mixed and intact Pleistocene deposits in caves near streams. In fact, the record from central Brazil among several sites dating between 11,500 and 10,000 B.P. in the areas of Rondonopolis, Mato Grosso, Cerra de Capivara, Paiui, and Vale do Peruacu in Minas Gerais shows clear cultural evidence that people here were primarily gatherers and secondarily hunters.

Several other rockshelters and caves from central and southeastern Brazil have yielded radiocarbon dates in excess of 11,000 years. None of the localities, however, has been studied extensively enough to relate the stratigraphy and artifacts to a secure late Pleistocene human presence.

Grande Abrigo da Santana do Riacho, Lapa dos Bichos, and Lapa do Boquete in the state of Minas Gerais are rockshelters with good preservation and well-stratified cultural deposits. These sites are primarily unifacial, although a few rare projectile points are found at Grande Abrigo da Santana do Riacho.[7]

Lapa do Boquete has produced abundant stone artifacts in its lower levels typical of the Paranaiba Phase of the Goiás state, dated between 12,070 and 9,000 B.P. Use-wear studies of the edges of the tools suggest they were used to work plants and wood. Most of these artifacts were flaked unifaces and cores made of chert, quartzite, and limestone. Also found were small bifacial thinning flakes; the tip of a projectile point; thick, elongated, plano-convex tools or limaces; many retouched or utilized flakes; charred palm nuts; and several nutcrackers for breaking open palm nuts or seeds. André Prous and his team also excavated a 10-

centimeter-thick layer of silt containing well-preserved materials, including hearths with ash and charcoal. This site presents a broad spectrum foraging economy associated with deer and small game such as armadillo, rodent, fish, and lizards.

The Grande Abrigo da Santana do Riacho north of Lagoa Santa, also excavated by Prous, is dated between 9,460 and 7,900 B.P. and associated with human skeletons. A deeper level, dated at 11,960 B.P., contained a hearth and exotic flakes of rock crystal, all in stratigraphic and chronological order. Although the skeletons are in bad condition, they may be some of the oldest yet found in South America. Several flakes, hearths, and pigment fragments were also recovered in the deeper levels of the rockshelter, as well as animal bones possibly worked by humans. The context of the deeper level has not been sufficiently studied to confirm the presence of humans around 12,000 B.P.

At Lapa Vermelha IV, Annette Laming-Emperaire, a French archaeologist, found a simple flake and core tool industry associated with ground sloth bone dated between 10,200 and 9,580 B.P.[8] Her Franco-Brazilian team also reported, in the deepest levels, a possible human occupation dated between 25,000 and 15,300 B.P. and associated with quartz cores and flakes and unifacial scrapers. Prous later excavated, from levels above this, some exotic quartz flakes that he dated between 15,300 and 11,680 B.P. A human skeleton was found in a stratum dating between 11,960 and 10,200 B.P. The stratigraphic context and dating of all these finds requires more work before the late Pleistocene occupation can be fully accepted.[9]

Buried in a deep alluvial deposit radiocarbon dated between 14,200 and 6,085 B.P. is the Alice Boër site, first excavated by Maria Beltrão and later by Wesley Hurt. Levels 8 and 9 in Layer 3 contained a large stemmed point, two broken stems, leaf-shaped projectile points, a unifacial flake, and a discoidal core-scraper.[10] Below this level were found unifaces, broken bifaces, a core, and a scraper made from a flake, which dated around 14,000 B.P.

Questions arise, however, about the context and age of this site. Maria Beltrão has dated more than forty culturally burned chert artifacts from the Alice Boër site. She believes that the older dates, which range from 12,190 to 11,000 B.P., are in agreement with the estimated geological and paleoclimatic age for the deepest layer and with the human artifacts, which are estimated to date between 14,000 and 11,000 B.P. Many archaeologists believe that the stone tool artifacts and radiocarbon dates have been disturbed by fluvial action and thus represent a mixed and invalid context, which is a reasonable possibility given the location of the site in a buried terrace where the stratigraphy can be mixed by flooding.

The single point recovered from Level III has been identified as the Tanged point type. This type is known to date after 11,000 B.P. Moreover, the single radiocarbon date of 14,200 may not be in accurate stratigraphic association with the older stone tools. Two thermoluminescence dates of 10,970 and 10,950 B.P. were determined from fire-treated chert artifacts, but a radiocarbon date from the same level was just 6,085 B.P. Based on the diagnostic tools from this site, the deeper level appears to date in terminal Pleistocene to early Holocene times, probably between 11,000 and 9,000 B.P. Only extensive excavation in the deeper levels and more geological work on the site stratigraphy will shed more light on the Alice Boër site. Furthermore, microscopic examination for water polish would indicate whether the stone assemblage was deposited or disturbed by water.

The poorly defined industry of the Ibicui Phase is evident primarily from two open-air sites excavated by Eurico Miller in terraces along the Río Uruguay and its tributaries in extreme southern Brazil.[11] This phase is known for its poorly made unifacial tools of basalt and sandstone and is dated by only two radiocarbon ages: 12,770 and 12,690 B.P. at the RS-Q2 and RS-I-50 sites, respectively. The dates are derived from charcoal buried in presumed human habitational layers covered by alluvial deposits. One site has yielded bone remains of extinct fauna, possibly associated with human activity. The chronology and stratigraphy of these sites need to be better understood, however, before human activity can be securely related to exploitation of megafauna.

The Uruguai Phase sites date between 11,555 and 8,585 B.P., with most dates falling between 10,180 and 9,000 B.P. The phase is represented by more than twenty open-air sites found along rivers. The type site is RS-I-69 on the Río Uruguai in southeast Brazil, which contains stone tool clusters and hearths containing the carbonized pits of wild fruits. Other sites are RS-I-68, RS-I-66, and RS-I-98, which contain bones of deer and small game, some showing human modification. The most defining tools are small, stemmed projectile points and triangular points made from chalcedony; other bifacial tools; scrapers; and a wide variety of small flake tools. People of this phase were generalized hunters and gatherers.

Bifacially flaked points of the contracting or Tanged Point Tradition appear in certain areas by 10,000 B.P.[12] This tradition gradually spread throughout the eastern lowlands of Brazil and Uruguay, as Bryan has suggested, and was probably an independent development in southern Brazil, where it was associated with hunters of deer, armadillo, large rodents, rheas, and tapir. The same people also gathered wild plant food.

Possible late Pleistocene finds are reported from several other localities in eastern and southern Brazil. For instance, in southwestern

Brazil, Miguel Bombín and Bryan have found a human skull fragment in association with unifacial tools dated from 12,770 to 11,010 B.P.[13] At Furna do Estrago in Pernambuco, Enrique Lima reports a date of 11,060 B.P. associated with stemmed points typical of southern Brazil. These two localities also require much more work before they can be accepted as valid late Pleistocene contexts.

Preliminary archaeological investigations by Agüeda Vilhena Vialou and Denis Vialou at the Santa Elina site in the tropical Rondonopolis region of Mato Grosso in southwest Brazil have revealed early cultural deposits associated with pigments of rock paintings, a unifacial stone tool assemblage, and bone remains of extinct megafauna and modern animal species.[14] One radiocarbon date places the oldest level at 10,120 years ago. Overlying this level are cultural layers dating from 7,940 to 275 years ago, suggesting a long succession of human occupation at the site.

Work by Wesley Hurt in the floodplain terrace of the Uruguay River near Salto Grande, Uruguay, has revealed pressure flaked artifacts, including Tanged points, in deep levels dated to about 10,000 B.P.[15] Also in the Uruguay Basin, Bombín and Bryan found thick bifaces dated around 12,770 B.P. associated with unifacial tools and a glossotherium (sloth) skull. Two thin bifaces were excavated at the Arroyo Dos Fóseles site associated with bone remains of extinct animals and dated at 11,010 B.P. Tanged and fluted Fishtail points have been recovered from the surface of several localities in the vicinity of Lobos, Cabo Polonio, Santa Teresa, and Valizas, Uruguay. The contexts of cultural remains at these sites are uncertain, either because they were excavated in terrace deposits and have not been well dated or because they are surface finds.

In summary, the late Pleistocene occupation of Brazil becomes much clearer after 12,000 B.P. Our knowledge of any place before this date is limited to Pedra Furada and a few other sites; but the later phases dated between approximately 11,500 and 10,000 B.P. have been well recorded at several rockshelter sites, especially Lapa do Boquete and Grande Abrigo da Santana do Riacho. In general, these sites are characterized by quartz lithics together with tools, such as edge-trimmed flakes, pounders, choppers, and hammers, made of various kinds of stones. Where conditions permitted, there are also preserved bones of small and medium-sized animals. There is no question that the Brazilian record is predominated by a generalized hunter and gatherer lifeway, characterized by both a unifacial and a bifacial tradition, dating to at least 11,500 B.P. The absence of evidence linking extinct fauna with humans in the early Brazilian archaeological record once again reminds us not to require the bone remains of these animals to validate a late Pleistocene cultural site. The Brazilian record also features numerous sites with pre–12,000 B.P. dates on bones or flecks of charcoal that are allegedly associated with human artifacts. However, as discussed above, there are many doubts as to how securely these dates can be applied.

The rarity of bone remains of extinct animals in Brazilian sites suggests that people probably came to some areas of eastern, central, and south Brazil shortly after extinction. Pedro Schmitz thinks the late Pleistocene people in these regions hunted tapir, peccaries, deer, anteaters, armadillos, turtles, birds, rhea, and other game, supplemented by fruits and nuts, especially from palm trees. Various wild fruits are found in such sites as Grande Abrigo da Santana do Riacho, Lapa do Boquete, and Monte Alegre.

Many Brazilian archaeologists believe the modern tribes who once inhabited the remoter eastern hills where many of these sites are found are direct descendants of the late Pleistocene inhabitants of the excavated caves. Some doubt can be cast on this belief, on account of the intermixture of later peoples, but there can be no doubt that the Pleistocene cultures represent a continuous tradition of hunting, gathering, and living for part of each year in caves, which in many areas eventually gave way to the pressures of horticulture and industry at the beginning of this century. Ever since the beginning of the ceramic period more than 5,000 years ago, the hunting and gathering tribes must have been steadily drawn into economic relations with more advanced communities. Like many such groups in the lowland tropical forest, however, they may have managed to retain their own cultural identity.

THE PAMPA AND PATAGONIAN GRASSLANDS

To the south of Brazil stretches the Pampa and Patagonian plains, a vast area that covers not only northeast Argentina but most of Uruguay. The archaeology of this area is fairly well known. There are numerous sites characterized by surface finds of Fishtail points, other stemmed points (Tanged), and other stone debris. Here people hunted horse, guanaco, armadillo, rhea, and other game and gathered a wide variety of wild plants.

Between 10,000 and possibly 11,600 B.P., a series of hunting and gathering societies flourished on the grasslands and varied terrain of Argentina and southern Chile. If any place in South America is similar to the hunting phases of North America, this is the place. Missing from the archaeological record of the southern grasslands, however, are the big-game jump sites and massive kill sites associated with bison hunting on the North American Great Plains. Many open-air sites, however, particularly in the Pampa region, are places that were used repeatedly for single kills. These are strategic points where animals routinely passed or where communal game drives occurred. Smaller communal hunts were probably commonplace. Many local groups apparently shared this large region; some adapted to the northerly temperate grasslands of the Pampa and others to the frigid, open plains of southern Patagonia. Still others resided in caves and wooded areas along the eastern slopes of the Andes in the far south. Many of their campsites contain guanaco bones and, when preserved, wild plants. Most hunters exploited a wide range of late Pleistocene animals, from rabbits to giant ground sloth.

A wide array of archaeological information comes from southern Patagonia and Tierra del Fuego. These vast steppes were a much less hospitable environment for hunter-gatherers than the well-watered valleys of the Andes or the rich Pampa grasslands. There were caves and rockshelters in a few convenient places, but for warmth and shelter many inhabitants of these areas probably built artificial dwellings. Early human activity appears to have been focused on a generalized foraging economy with primary emphasis given to hunting guanaco, rodents, rhea, waterfowl, and probably carnivores. Some plant foods were eaten as well, but they were not always preserved and, when present, can often be found only by floatation studies. Many sites are located along secondary waterways. They may have been campsites or kill sites, but unfortunately few have been excavated.

Seemingly absent from the southern grasslands of South America are the unifacial industries characteristic of the northern and central Andes and of many parts of Brazil. There are, however, a wide variety of projectile point types and associated stone tools for processing hides and meat, which show clear technological advances through time. These advances may have played a decisive role in people's adaptations to low latitudes. They allowed not only more efficient hunting weaponry but also the development of such important weapons as the bola and sling stones, highly effective for killing or capturing small mammals and birds.

The Pampa

Gustavo Politis's excavations on the Pampa at Arroyo Seco and La Moderna document communal kill sites.[16] About 9,000 to 7,000 B.P., a group of foragers repeatedly visited small gullies at Arroyo Seco where animals congregated or passed and where hunters trapped and killed them. The site, which shows several episodes of use separated by decades or centuries of abandonment, contains in its deeper levels edge-trimmed unifacial flakes associated with the bone remains of extinct horse, giant ground sloth, and armadillo. Although projectile points have not been found at the site, they may have been used and carried away or have been made of bone or wood. The bones have been dated between 8,890, 8,390, and 7,320 B.P. Stratigraphically below this level is a layer containing twenty human skeletons, all representing different burials. The skeletons range in radiocarbon age from 8,980 to 6,880 B.P. It is not known whether the later dates are correct and whether megafaunal species survived into the early Holocene period.

The La Moderna site, also excavated by Politis and Fernándo Palanca, is a complex open-air site that also has yielded simple flake tools made of rock crystal and associated with two genera of extinct giant armadillo, dated at 12,330 and 6,550 B.P.[17] Politis believes that the earlier date is too early and that the later is contaminated. Given that they are both Pleistocene species, it is likely that both armadillos were killed between 11,000 and 10,000 B.P. Once again, the explanation for the absence of points may be the same as that at the Arroyo Seco site.

Gustavo Martínez recently has reported on the Paso Otero 5 site, where he found biface fragments and another lithic tool associated with ground sloth, native horse, guanaco, and armadillo.[18] One date on bone was processed at 10,190 B.P.

Arroyo Seco, La Moderna, and Paso Otero 5 all require more precise radiocarbon dating before their cultural materials can be placed securely in the late Pleistocene. It is also unclear whether the stone tools from Arroyo Seco and La Moderna represent true unifacial industries or whether bifacial tools were present but not recovered.

Recent work by Nora Flegenheimer at two sites in the Tandilia Hills, Cerro La China and Cerro El Sombrero, has shed new light on the southern Fishtail point. Cerro La China is actually a complex of small sites located on a little hill isolated on the Pampa plains.[19] One of the deepest levels, Layer 2 at Site 1, contained broken Fishtail points, other stone tools, and one bone fragment of a guanaco. This layer dated between 10,790 and 10,720 B.P. Two other sites yielded similar materials or radiocarbon dates around 10,610 B.P. Flegenheimer believes this area was used repeatedly by the same peoples as a temporary shelter from which to make hunting forays on the surrounding plains. At Cerro El Sombrero, Flegenheimer has recovered more than thirty Fishtail point fragments. The dates here range from 10,725 to 8,060 B.P. El Sombrero appears to be similar in age and function to Cerro La China.

Another site reported from the Tandilia Range is Cueva Tixí, excavated by Diana L. Mazzanti and dated to 10,045 and 10,375 B.P.[20] The dates are derived from burned areas and associated with the bone remains of guanaco, deer, armadillo, and other game animals and with stone tool manufacturing debris, including scraping tools, cores, hammerstones, flakes, and red ochre. Like the other Tandilia sites, Cueva Tixí reflects a series of short-term hunting episodes.

Patagonia

Northern Patagonia is represented by three caves located along the Limay River Basin on the eastern flanks of the Argentine Andes. Trafúl Cave contains unifacial and bifacial artifacts associated with the bone remains of guanaco and small game animals, dated between 9,400 and 9,200 B.P.[21] Cuyín Manzano Cave is dated to 9,300 B.P. and contains guanaco bones and end scrapers in the deeper levels.[22] Farther east, in the steppe grasslands, is Epullán Cave also associated with guanaco remains, unifaces, and hearths dated between 9,900 and 7,500 B.P.[23]

In southern Patagonia, the end of the Pleistocene period is well defined geologically and archaeologically. Ernesto Piasano believes that once deglaciation began, around 13,000 B.P., the movement of plants and animals into the region was slow and highly selective. The first serious archaeological research in Patagonia was done in the 1920s by Junius Bird, who spent several seasons excavating in various caves.[24] Bird worked for short periods of time at Fell's Cave, where he unearthed the first proof of a human presence in Pleistocene South America. Since those investigations, abundant information has been gathered on the earliest occupations in the region, especially by Chilean and Argentinean archaeologists working in the extreme south. As a result, there is now sufficient information to construct a picture of the early human presence in Patagonia.

The most important sites in the region are Los Toldos, Piedra Museo, Mylodon Cave, Las Buitreras, Tres Arroyo, Fell's Cave, Palli Aike Cave, Cueva de las Manos, Cueva Grande del Arroyo Feo, and Cueva del Medio (see Figures 5.3 and 6.1). At those rare places, such as Fell's Cave, where Fishtail points are overlaid by later materials, we can observe a long sequence of occupation. The date of the first Fishtail points in the southern cone is uncertain, but it is now clear that these points were not the earliest in South America and probably have slightly more antiquity in the south than the north. One site shedding new light on the age and affinity of the Fishtail point in Piedra Museo, on the eastern side of the Andes in Argentina. The earliest occupation apparently has unifacial flakes overlaid by Fishtail points and is probably associated with the retreat of the ice sheets. It is dated, by radiocarbon means, to more than 12,000 years ago. Other sites are almost as informative.

At Los Toldos or Cave 3 in southern Patagonia, for example, Augusto Cardich has excavated early materials possibly dating to 12,600 B.P.[25] This date is associated with unifacial tools and camelid bones in the lowest level of the site. The tools are broad flakes and a few blade-like specimens, with one possibly reworked as a projectile point, in Level 11. The level immediately overlying Level 11 contained large blades and Fishtail points, which Cardich called the Toldense industry. This industry compares in form to the earliest materials from Fell's Cave, and Level 11 in Los Toldos Cave 3 may be earlier than the first occupation at Fell's Cave.

The large unifacial flakes recovered from Level 11 of Los Toldos are just the sort of technology one would expect to precede the appearance of Fishtail points and blades. This deeper level is not, however, without its critics. Lynch has rejected it, arguing that the Toldense and Level 11 industries are stratigraphically inseparable, with the latter simply a part of the former. But this inseparability characterizes any rockshelter with tight microstratigraphic levels. Besides, the broad flakes in the deeper levels are not found in the layers overlying Level 11. Another problem with the site is that the radiocarbon dates from the overlying levels were obtained from scattered flecks of charcoal not always well associated with flake artifacts and bone remains. In any case, Level 11 is an anomaly that requires more work. This is another site where more extensive excavation and dating of the deeper deposits needs to be done before its role in late Pleistocene prehistory can be understood.

At Cueva 7 de El Ceibo, another site excavated by Cardich, it is hard to determine whether the stratigraphy is intact. In the deeper levels of this site, large, thick flake tools and bifacial points were found in association with guanaco and extinct horse and camelid. These levels are overlaid stratigraphically by bifacial core tools, pressure-flaked Fishtail points, and bone awls like those found at Los Toldos. Before this sequence can be accepted, we need to know whether the flakes were lying flat or dipping and whether they are of the same material as the fluted points of the overlying Toldense culture. These are very large flakes that would not filter down easily. Also, this site has not been radiocarbon dated.

Laura Miotti is carrying out important excavations at two caves at the Piedra Museo locality near Los Toldos in southern Patagonia.[26] She has found several Fishtail points overlying a unifacial industry in the deeper levels of one cave and has obtained a date of 12,890 B.P. from charcoal in the deepest unifacial level, Stratum 6, below the Fishtail points. Stratum 6 also contains a large bifacial thinning flake, five knives, eleven secondary flakes, nine other pieces of lithic debris, one possible bone tool, and the bone remains of extinct native horse, ground sloth, rhea, and camelids.

The overlying Strata 4 and 5 are dated at approximately 10,400 B.P. and contain broken Fell's fluted points, unifacial tools, end scrapers, and knives. These levels are also associated with the bone remains of native horse, guanaco, paleo-camelid, and rhea. Subsequent levels, dated at 10,400, 9,700, and 7,670 B.P., are all in stratigraphic order. Miotti believes that before the Fishtail occupation the site was occupied by generalized foragers with a broad technological knowledge. Although more details are needed, the stratigraphic placement of bifacial levels over unifacial levels probably dated around 12,900 years ago requires us to look more closely at Level 11 in Los Toldos. Of further interest is a date of 8,750 B.P. on a layer overlying a level containing the last remains of American horse at the site. This may suggest that by 9,000 B.P. this animal was becoming or had become extinct.

Farther south, Bird's work at Fell's Cave, overlooking the Strait of Magellan, contains early deposits sealed from later materials by a fallen roof. Underlying the roof-fall were Magellan or Fishtail points associated with the bones of horse, giant ground sloth, and camel. Radiocarbon dates on charcoal from the deepest levels were about 11,000 and 10,720 B.P. The Fell's Cave industry has many small flakes as well as small scrapers, gravers, and notched pieces. The local quartzite was unsuitable for making such delicate tools, and finer grain materials were carefully sought and collected. Not surprisingly, the Fells' Cave people hunted guanaco more than other game. Plant food was probably collected but was either not preserved or not found by Bird.

Mauricio Massone has argued that the human sequence at Tres Arroyos Cave extends back to 10,280 and possibly to 11,880 B.P.[27] This cave's deepest level yielded dates on charcoal from four human hearths, of which the oldest was 12,400 B.P. Given the presence of four hearths close together but vertically separated by several centimeters, he believes they are not contemporaneous. Also, given the restricted space, it is unlikely that a small group needed four hearths. Even though the 12,400 date is from the deeper level of the cave, Massone rejects it in favor of 10,600–10,280 B.P. for a human presence. However, a date of 11,880 B.P. was recently obtained from the deeper level, suggesting that people may indeed have first utilized the cave around 12,000 years ago. In a deeper, non-human level on the talus slope of the cave is a precultural deposit of native American horse and camelids dated around 12,280 B.P., indicating the presence of vegetation and animals in the region soon after deglaciation.

The archaeologist Hugo Nami recently excavated the Cueva del Medio site in the same area.[28] The deepest levels yielded two complete Fishtail points, numerous other stone tools, and abundant bone remains of the American horse as well as evidence of ground sloth, deer, feline, canid, and guanaco. Associated with these remains was a hearth. Two dates on charcoal from the hearth were processed at 12,390 and 10,550 B.P. Other dates were 10,850 and 10,450 B.P. It is most likely that the younger date of 10,550 B.P. is most accurate, since two other dates from the same level as the hearth came out at 10,310 and 9,595 B.P.

Another well-known locality in the vicinity is Mylodon Cave, an enormous cavern excavated by numerous archaeologists since the last century and famous for the large quantities of sloth dung removed from the late Pleistocene and early Holocene levels.[29] Radiocarbon dates on dung, bone, and charcoal range widely from approximately 13,500–10,200 B.P. in the deeper levels—which are absent human evidence—to approximately 5,300 B.P. in the middle levels. Although the stratigraphy in many parts of this cave is heavily disturbed by human and animal activity, there is some evidence that the ground sloth may have survived in this area until about 6,000 B.P. It is unclear whether humans hunted the sloth, although Guillermo Mengoni and others report cutmarks on a few sloth, guanaco, and horse bones. The date humans first occupied the cave is also not well understood. The wide variety of stone tools found there are not very helpful in establishing cultural affiliation and chronology. One pattern, however, seems clear: By at least 13,000 B.P., a variety of game animals were living in southwestern Patagonia. A human presence at the site probably began around 10,385 B.P. when valid stone tools and worked animal bones of ground sloth appear in the deeper levels.

In commenting on the giant ground sloth at Mylodon Cave, Las Buitreras, and Palli Aike, Mengoni suggested that humans probably stalked the giant sloth until it entered its cave den and then killed it there.[30] Mengoni points out that people hunted other animals too, including rodents, rhea, waterfowl, and other birds, and gathered plants, although the latter have not been studied extensively.

At other cave sites in southern Patagonia, the earliest human occupations range from approximately 8,639 B.P. at Palli Aike to at least 9,300 B.P. at Las Buitreras, Cueva de Los Manos, and Cueva Grande del Arroyo Feo. A variety of later stemmed and triangular points, occasional bola stones, and the bones of extinct and modern animals are found in the deeper levels of these sites. Older dates have recently been reported by Alfredo Prieto from Cueva 1 del Lago Sofía, dated to 11,570 B.P., and Cueva 4, dated to 11,590 B.P.[31] The stone and bone tool assemblages and food remains from these sites show adaptations similar to those at other early sites in the region, except that the inhabitants exploited a wider variety of animal species. All of these sites also require more excavation and more radiocarbon dates before they can be put into chronological sequence with the better-known sites. Nonetheless, the preponderance of pre–11,000 B.P. evidence in good stratigraphic context is building up to make a strong case for the human exploitation of a wide variety of environments in Patagonia before the appearance of the Fishtail point.

People living in arid, open terrain such as the Patagonian steppes probably had to cover large expanses to find their food. It has been estimated that a range of up to 16 square kilometers was needed to support one person; a group of thirty, therefore, might have needed a range of 500 square kilometers just to supply itself with meat and plant foods. We should keep in mind that even if late Ice Age groups were as successful as hunting groups are today, through most of the year meat probably provided no more than half the food a group needed. The rest had to be supplied by vegetable food, implying that people probably observed and recorded all aspects of their environment in order to survive.

CHAPTER SEVEN

Patterns and Prospects

IN THE LAST TWO CHAPTERS, I presented a large mass of archaeological information of varying quality, ranging from the results of modern scientific excavations to inferences pieced together from undated artifacts picked up off the ground. The information is overwhelmingly dominated by site type and location and by stone tool technologies. It is time to stand back from these details and attempt to view the picture as a whole.

One of the greatest problems facing late Pleistocene archaeology in South America is the limitation of our data. We simply do not have enough detailed archaeological and geological information to build a more precise chronology from the early subperiod (before 11,000 B.P.) to the late subperiod (11,000 to 10,000 B.P.). People probably first entered the continent between 20,000 and 15,000 B.P., but the earliest secure traces of a human presence are at Monte Verde around 12,500 B.P. and at a small number of other sites a few hundred years later: Lapa do Boquete, Lapa dos Bichos, Grande Abrigo de Santana do Riacho, and possibly other rockshelters in eastern Brazil; possibly Tibitó in Colombia and Taima-

Taima in Venezuela; and maybe the Piedra Museo, Cueva Sofía I, and other sites in Patagonia. Our evidence of pre-Clovis people in South America is limited to at most eight and perhaps as few as three well-established sites. Other sites scattered across the continent have deeper levels radiocarbon dated slightly before 11,000 B.P. but either have not been reported in sufficient detail, have questions regarding their stratigraphic context, or are poorly dated. Many sites fall into the subperiod between 11,000 and 10,500 B.P.

Still, we have enough evidence to be sure that virtually all parts of the continent were at least traversed, if not occupied, by the end of the Pleistocene, around 10,500 B.P.[1] At this point, people began to exploit a wider range of environments and settle into more productive habitats such as bays, temperate forests, and mangroves. The obvious results of this widespread diversification were the steady proliferation of local technological industries and the accompanying faster rate of cultural change that we recognize in the archaeological record between 11,000 and 10,000 B.P. Demographically, this process probably led to increases both in the size of individual groups and in overall population levels in some areas—and thus in the number of archaeological sites recorded between 10,500 and 10,000 years ago. By the end of the Pleistocene, many of the foundations for the diverse richness of later South American cultures had been laid.

Early sites dating before 11,000 B.P. are mostly small, reflecting brief episodes of short-term occupation. Signs of more complex and long-term occupation (postholes representing living huts, storage pits, hearths) are generally lacking with the exception of the Monte Verde site, where preservation is excellent and perishables are preserved. Although earlier sites were simpler, and thus are harder to find, than later ones, they were not necessarily different in artifact content and function.

Many more early sites may have been found but not recognized. For example, a number of cave and rockshelter sites in the Andes contain evidence of possible human activity in their basal levels, which date between 13,000 and 11,000 B.P.: Tequendama in Colombia; Pachamachay Cave and Uchumachay Cave in Peru; several rockshelters in eastern Brazil; Los Toldos, El Ceibo, and Museo Piedra in Argentina; and Tres Arroyo and Cueva del Medio in southern Patagonia. Most archaeologists have dismissed this deeper evidence because it is ephemeral, usually consisting of just one or two pre–11,000-year radiocarbon dates, a few flakes, and perhaps some animal bones that may (or may not) have been modified by humans. Archaeological reasoning has it that these are younger materials that have been mixed with older, deeper strata by animal burrowing or other some natural agency. Light or sporadic human activity is not seriously considered. Yet is not this light scatter of material exactly what we would expect from an initial exploratory phase of human entry? This would be particularly true in the higher elevations and higher latitudes of the Andes, especially if people were following plants and animals on a seasonal basis as the ice sheets gradually retreated. This is not to deny that older geological deposits may have gotten mixed with younger cultural materials in these caves. But too many archaeologists have used taphonomy as a handy excuse to reject ephemeral records rather than test them more thoroughly by carrying out more extensive horizontal excavation to determine their geological integrity and archaeological validity. Here again, in the absence of modern site formation studies, we can only ponder the status of these records.

BACK TO TECHNOLOGY

Given that the first people to cross the Being Strait were probably from northeastern Asia and had unifacial and bifacial technologies, we would expect that they brought both with them. Yet no good unifacial industry existed in North America, unless it is revealed in pre-Clovis sites whose validity is still questioned in some archaeological circles. Despite obvious local variations, some technological developments followed parallel courses throughout the Americas. Others did not. Some parallel developments are the proliferation of lanceolate, stemmed, unstemmed, and fluted points on both continents between 11,000 and 10,000 years ago. Some independent developments in South America are the unifacial industries and the bola and sling stones.

Archaeologists are still far from being able to explain why *any* parallel developments occurred; at the outset of human movement into the continent, technologies were most likely to diffuse from a common source. In several areas where unifaces developed independently, there may have been an accompanying shift to hunting smaller, more solitary creatures and gathering plants in closed habitats, and away from hunting the gregarious herbivores that dominated open areas. These developments are often seen in the late Pleistocene and early Holocene periods, when wooded environments reached their maximum extent. Without proposing a simplistic cause-and-effect correlation, we can partially associate the adoption of more expedient unifacial technologies with this change in lifeways. The very ubiquity of this technology in South America shows that it suited a wide variety of environments.

The coexistence of unifacial and bifacial industries in South America is more reminiscent of late Pleistocene technologies in

Australia and parts of Asia than of North America. Does South America have a greater cultural affinity with these regions, or is it simply that sampling and typology biases have led us to overemphasize bifaces in the north and unifaces in the south? We do not know.

The first South Americans most likely had a bifacial industry. Yet, with the possible exception of fluted points, not all bifacial technologies are clearly derived from North America. And the fluted tradition appears to be later than El Jobo and Monte Verde points; it coexists with a wide variety of stemmed and unstemmed points. The unifacial traditions, on the other hand, have no known antecedent in North America, and it is not known whether they derived from the bifacial tradition or developed independently from an earlier pebble tool tradition. Curiously, these same unifacial traditions occasionally exhibit rare bifaces and can often be traced to bifacial traditions, suggesting that unifaces, which at first glance appear more primitive, are actually a later development. Yet bifaces and projectile points do not dominate the early stone tool collections in South America as they do in North America. So questions regarding the origin and affinity of these two traditions persist.

Unfortunately, no current site has a stratigraphic sequence showing clear technological continuities from unifacial to bifacial industries or vice versa. Nor are there sites containing stratigraphy to document a sequence from El Jobo to Monte Verde or vice versa, or from these point types to others such as El Inga, Fishtails, subtriangular, triangular, and Tanged points. All we can conclude is that diverse technologies developed both in parallel and independently throughout South America.

I do not wish to leave the impression, however, that the two dominant technologies were somehow opposed. There probably were not, for instance, two different sets of people who each employed one of those technologies exclusively. As I discussed in Chapter 4, I follow the thinking of my Argentine colleagues Gustavo Politis and Hugo Nami, who believe that unifaces and bifaces are complementary technologies whose use depended on the situation. People could make either one—and did—to varying degrees, depending on what resources the local environment offered and on how they chose to exploit them.

Seldom in South America can we document a broad uniformity of stone tool technologies over a wide range of geographical and environmental regions. The only exceptions are the unifacial industries of Colombia and eastern Brazil, the Fishtail points, and the Ayampitín-like points. Recent radiocarbon dating suggests that the Fishtail form, for example, became widespread within a surprisingly short time, probably between 11,000 and 10,400 B.P. This distribution implies interregional contacts among existing populations over a period of a few hundred years. The Fishtail is later replaced by a few variants with crude fluting but generally disappears by 10,000 B.P. in most parts of the continent. Thus the fluted trait probably represents a short-lived trend associated with a late coastal migration that may have left North America (assuming its origin there for the moment) sometime between 11,500 and 11,000 B.P. and blended with existing local groups such as the Paiján people along the coast of Peru.

It's important not to overestimate the value of stone tools in Pleistocene and early Holocene economies. The early stone tools are mostly made from local raw materials, primarily quartz, quartzite, basalt, and occasionally chert and obsidian. I believe the high frequencies of unifaces in many site's assemblages reflect the more regular use and discard of expedient tools made from local material and the conserving of tools made from better, nonlocal material. Thus a high proportion of unifaces is just what we should expect.

For some archaeologists, however, this argument may make little sense. They would argue that a society's settlement and subsistence pattern would reflect their heavy dependence on high quality materials to procure plant and animal resources. In other words, stone is just as important as food. But this may not always be the case. Other technologies, such as basketry, cordage, bamboo, bone, or wooden points, may be equally crucial. And whereas high quality stone, capable of holding a sharp point, can be procured directly or indirectly from distant sources, high quality foods are often less transportable. Meat rots in tropical heat; stone does not. Although it remains unclear just how these decisions were made, I doubt that the availability of high quality stone material dictated where people settled. When it came to good food or good stone, I suspect food took precedence.

A wide variety of stone, wood, and bone tools could have been used to process plants. At Monte Verde, for instance, there is solid evidence of a generalized diet focused on wetland resources, including large and small game, a wide variety of terrestrial plants, and a few marine plants, including seaweeds. Several other late Pleistocene sites, including Huentelafquén in northern Chile, the Quebrada de Taguay and Quebrada Jaguay sites on the Peruvian coast, and numerous rockshelter sites in eastern Brazil, represent a generalized hunting and gathering lifeway.

Direct evidence of other technologies is very sparse but not completely absent. At Monte Verde and Guitarrero Cave, wooden artifacts and cordage are preserved. Pieces of animal hide, tied reed, and wooden timbers and poles at Monte Verde remain from the long tent structure that housed at least twenty people. Hearths and pits reflect the extensive use of fire and perhaps the need to store food and other items. The important point, however, is that whenever organic remains are preserved, a broad spectrum economy is always documented.

PROTO-ARCHAIC ECONOMIES

Almost all current evidence indicates that the first people to enter South America employed a generalized, or proto-Archaic, economic strategy encompassing a wide range of plant and animal resources and employing a variety of technologies and inventions utilizing many raw materials. They were not just big-game hunters. As these people spread, their subsistence probably varied from season to season, as they focused first on one species or one environment and then on others. Eventually, groups spread throughout the continent and, in areas such as the puna grasslands and Patagonian steppes, developed specialized economies based on one or more mammal species supplemented by local plants. When groups specialized for different environments, they intensified their exploitation of resources. This intensification led to new techniques of food preparation and to the use of an even broader range of raw materials.

One basic innovation of the late Pleistocene period is the use of some form of a milling slab for crushing or grinding hard-shelled nuts or plants. The slab made available new vegetable foods, such as roots and nuts, and must have necessitated new cooking techniques such as boiling. The slab and grinding stone also indicate plant manipulation and the eventual development of domesticated crops, a process that probably had its beginning in the late Pleistocene and early Holocene period in both the east and west sides of South America.

With the exception of parts of Patagonia, there is good evidence from all over the continent to show that people had developed the proto-Archaic way of life by 11,000 to 10,500 B.P. In some areas they intensively exploited one primary food source, such as palm nuts in the eastern lowland tropics and marine resources along the Pacific coast. This intensive exploitation can be seen most clearly at sites where organic remains are well preserved: Peña Roja, Monte Verde, Monte Alegre, Lapa do Boquete, Quebrada Jaguay, and Huentelafquén. People seemed to have crossed a kind of dietary threshold about 10,500 B.P., when more sites appear containing a wider variety of plant and animal remains. The occasional big-game hunters favored specific game in specific environments, just as other groups favored particular plants or small animals. The fauna assemblages recovered from many sites suggest a heavy bias in favor of one particular species, such as guanaco, mastodon, and sloth. This bias is difficult to explain if we assume, as many archaeologists have, that the earliest Americans were hunters who selected their game at random.

Diversification from the proto-Archaic lifeway probably began earlier in the warmer latitudes and at lower elevations. The primary factors in this diversification were probably the disappearance of megafauna, the increase in temperature and rainfall between 11,000 and 10,000 B.P., and social changes resulting from increased economic intensity and occasional specialization.

The latter two features must have heightened the competition for primary resources and perhaps social territory. By 10,500 B.P., a number of localized stone tool industries had developed, such as the

Paiján points in northern Peru, the Tanged points in southern Brazil and Uruguay, and the Fishtails in southern Patagonia. These differing points hint at territorial ranges of groups living in those areas. Territoriality may have developed even earlier in the temperate bays along the Pacific coast, where predictable year-round resources would have permitted a stable lifeway by 11,000 B.P.

Exploitation of marine resources in general is commonly associated with demographic, technological, and social patterns that are different from those usually found among foragers subsisting exclusively on the land. The sea is easily accessible, and success is more reliable. Mastodons could be taken at only a few scattered spots, but, particularly off the west coast of South America, fish could be caught almost anywhere. And the land has no analogue of a stationary protein source such as a clam bed. Although it may not have been the case everywhere, the Pacific coast would certainly have supported many habitats for shellfish and sea mammals and provided many points of access to the sea, particularly once the shoreline was stabilized after 6,000 B.P. In some areas, the coastline may have served as a highway between adjacent interior environments such as those on the coast of Ecuador and Peru, later the scene of the first impulses of Andean civilization.

Over and over, I have suggested the cultural diversity in late Pleistocene South America. Cultural change may take place because of invention, cultural drift, the adaptation of people to an environment, or diffusion of new ideas into an area. During the early times of entry and dispersion, when groups were constantly on the move, change due to contact between groups was probably minimal. Adaptation to new environments was probably the main force causing traditions to change. When people carrying a particular tradition reached the edge of a new environmental zone, they would have slowly adapted to that zone by discarding, changing, and inventing habits as necessary. They would either have rapidly moved through the new zone or, if it was rich in resources, settled in. We can account for the widespread diversity seen between 11,500 and 10,500 B.P. only by supposing that splinter groups of small, dispersed founding populations must have been isolated geographically and maintained only sporadic contact with others. Yet although we generally know what these groups looked like archaeologically, we know next to nothing about their genetics and biology.

CHAPTER EIGHT

Skeletons, Genes, and Languages

WE ARE EXTRAORDINARILY IGNORANT about certain aspects of the first immigrants to the Americas: their anatomical features, their religious beliefs, where and how they buried their dead, and the kinds of languages they spoke. Direct evidence on the physical and genetic makeup of the first Pleistocene Americans, especially South Americans, is scant or entirely missing.[1] In fact, perhaps only one reliable human skeleton of late Pleistocene age has been excavated in South America, and only two have been recovered in North America, making these the only continents on the planet where our knowledge of an early human presence comes almost exclusively from traces of artifacts and not from human skeletal remains. Why are human skeletons from this era so elusive in the Americas, particularly when those from the early Archaic period (10,000 to 7,000 B.P.) are relatively abundant? Perhaps the answer to this question will give us the key to understanding other elusive aspects of the peopling of the Americas.

Most likely, the founding population entered the New World in very small groups. Since there was no competition for food from other human groups, these first people could have expanded their population and geographic range rapidly. According to Paul Martin and his followers, a group as small as twenty-five people probably could have occupied the entire New World within 1,000 to 1,500 years. Although calculations are interesting, however, they are not evidence.

There is some archaeological, skeletal, and modern-day genetic evidence to suggest that there were multiple migrations into the Americas. Each migration may have been small, and, as David Meltzer has pointed out, some could have failed and thus not made a genetic contribution. Still, they might have left behind an archaeological record, if it can be found. Every time a group successfully entered the New World they would have brought with them new gene combinations. Early arrivals may have been proto-Mongoloids, later ones perhaps more like modern Mongoloids or Asians.[2]

Two types of human skeletons, a robust form and a gracile form, apparently coexisted in early Holocene South America. This early diversity of human types raises questions about the date and direction of entry and about the kinds of people moving into the New World. Recent cranial morphological studies of early human remains from various places in the Western Hemisphere suggest that the earliest South Americans may not be morphologically linked with northeastern Asians or Siberians. They may more closely resemble South Pacific and South Asian populations. At the same time, some genetic studies also suggest affinities between South American and South Asian populations as well as Asian populations in general. These results only add to the unanswered questions.

WHERE ARE THE ICE AGE SKELETONS?

Of all the possible archaeological indicators of late Pleistocene people in the Americas, their burial of the dead is the worst documented. We know of possibly only one deliberately meaningful burial before the beginning of the early Archaic period between 10,000 and 9,000 B.P. Although archaeologists and physical anthropologists allude to human skeletal remains dating to late Ice Age times, perhaps only one has actually been found. A few human bones have been recovered from possible Ice Age sites, but these remains are fragmentary, derived from questionable contexts, and few have been securely radiocarbon dated. For instance, Erwin Taylor and associates have radiocarbon dated human bone from various early North American localities.[3] Although these remains had previously been assigned ages ranging from 15,000 to 70,000 B.P., only one of the dated skeletons turned out to be older than 10,600 B.P. Two sites dated to the mid-tenth millennium: the Wilson Butte Site in Montana and the Mostin Site in California. In South America, the earliest known human skeletal evidence comes from Las Vegas in Ecuador, Lauricocha and Paiján in Peru, Lapa Vermelha IV Lucia skeleton in Brazil, and La Moderna in Argentina. With the exception of Lapa Vermelha IV possibly dated around 11,500 B.P., the others face between 10,200 and 7,000 B.P. Admittedly, these and other early Archaic skeletons are direct descendants of the first Americans, but they are not the founding population. As I will discuss later, this point is important because each skeletal population has its own genetic and migratory history that require understanding.

The diversity of burial treatment at these early Archaic sites (and later ones) suggests that burial of the dead was a formal custom. People were placed in shallow pits within a few meters of a dwelling, probably the structures where they had last lived. In general, people of the early Archaic period treated the dead carefully and thoughtfully, which suggests that similar practices, albeit less sophisticated, may also have existed in late Pleistocene times. Yet the skeletons are missing.[4]

The missing skeletal evidence is particularly intriguing because the archaeological record of the Old World contains prehuman and human remains extending as far back as 3 million years ago. Well-defined burial patterns and rituals are commonplace after about 50,000 B.P. In fact, it was the Neanderthal people in Europe and Asia (ca. 60,000 B.P.) who first performed ritual burials—a uniquely human activity. Archaeologists have found dedicatory offerings of flowers, exotic flints, red ochre, and other curiosities within the carefully prepared graves of Neanderthal people.

Compared with those of the first modern humans *(Homo sapiens)*, Neanderthal burials were simple and crude. Nevertheless, the presence of any ritual at all in Neanderthal times testifies to people's awareness of life and death—and of something transcendental in life itself. This, surely, is a criterion by which we identify human activity—perhaps more so than the presence of lithics or other artifacts. The earlier prehistoric record of the Old World contains nothing like it. The Neanderthals seem to have invented an important human feature.

Similar burial patterns appear in Australia. The archaeological evidence suggests people arrived there about 40,000 or possibly 50,000 to 60,000 B.P.,[5] and several sites have produced human remains dating between 30,000 and 10,000 B.P. These remains consist of individual and group burials, often associated with rituals and grave offerings, regularly found at sites buried in alluvial stream terraces, caves and rockshelters, and swamps.

Given that burials of modern humans have been found all through Europe, Asia, and Australia since at least 40,000 B.P. and that some of these people are the ancestors of the first Americans, why don't we find more Ice Age human remains in the New World? Their absence suggests several possibilities:

1. Paradigm bias: we simply are not looking in the right places for human remains because we mistakenly believe we know where early people lived and interred their dead
2. Archaeological invisibility: geological activity has concealed or destroyed many early burial sites
3. Destructive or inconspicuous burial practices: the first Americans destroyed the remains of their dead, did not practice burial, or possessed a different ideology and mortuary practice
4. Contaminated radiocarbon dated human bones: we possibly already have found some of the first Americans but the radiocarbon measures derived from them are contaminated and giving younger dates (this is unlikely given our sophisticated means to detect contaminates)
5. Any combination of the above or other factors

The first Americans need not have always buried their dead and performed patterned ritual burials as their Old World predecessors and Archaic period descendants did. Some of them may have killed and eaten one another, not out of hunger but as part of cannibalistic ritual. But if this were the case, we would have found at least some collections of human bone remains near living areas, which we have not. They also may have cremated bodies and disposed of the remains in special places, such as bogs, swamps, or rocky crevices, located away from habitation sites. If so, then few intact skeletal remains would be found by archaeologists, who tend to look for living sites, quarry sites, and other conspicuous places of human activity.

Some Clovis proponents have attributed the lack of early skeletal material to the first Americans' land use pattern. The Clovis people apparently avoided living in caves and rockshelters —a popular locality of human occupation throughout the rest of the world in all time periods.[6] Robert Kelly and Larry Todd have proposed that the first immigrants (i.e., the Clovis people) avoided caves primarily because they moved through the land so rapidly that they never found any. According to Kelly and Todd, people simply would not have had time to familiarize themselves with local landscapes, and so would not have occupied hospitable caves and rockshelters. But this does not really explain the absence of human skeletons in the most archaeologically conspicuous and excavated type of early site.

On the other hand, we could argue that in the face of high mobility in changing environments, the lack of burial patterns and rituals became adaptive traits. Deliberate burial and ritual may have involved too much social energy and a commitment to a homeland. If this is correct, we should not find human burials in caverns or other sites. Still, human remains should be located somewhere—perhaps along migratory trails or in places where bodies could be disposed of quickly. These burial patterns do not call for a sophisticated ideology or commitment. This argument, however, makes little sense to me. The Neanderthals, their predecessors, and the ancestors of the first Americans were surely just as mobile as the Clovis (and pre-Clovis) people, and we find their skeletal remains not only in cavernous sites but in open-air sites as well. In fact, it was a highly mobile human population coming out of northeast Asia that most likely first inhabited the New World. The avoidance of cavernous sites by Clovis peoples is in direct contrast to early Asian ancestral populations, who lived and buried their dead in these places.

Moreover, how could unfamiliarity with the local landscape prevent the early immigrants from finding caves, when these same people had a sufficiently intimate knowledge of local stone raw material to make tools and of local food resources to find enough to eat? If they knew the local terrain well enough to find these crucial resources, they surely could have occasionally found caverns, which often were in the same rock formations where they found stone for their tools. In short, although the rapid movement of groups undoubtedly explains why some early people did not live or bury their dead in caves, it probably played only a minor role in our inability to find early human remains in the Americas. The more likely reasons are archaeologists' poor identification and sampling of early sites and burials of the first immigrants, and perhaps the immigrants' practice of a belief and burial system different from that of some Old World populations.

Given the rather simple technology of some early Americans, we might expect to find bodies placed in areas where it was easy to dig a pit or where the body could have been placed conveniently without much work. The intent may simply have been to inter the dead in an expedient place protected from elements and predators. Such localities may have been sand dunes or other sandy or soft sediment deposits, under rock ledges or in rocky crevices, in swamps and bogs, or perhaps in sinkholes, arroyos, or canyons. Whatever the case may be, one pattern seems constant: The first Americans rarely used the most conspicuous places—the habitation sites, quarries, and kill sites—to bury the dead. This implies that the paucity of early human skeletal evidence may simply be a function of archaeological sampling.

The paucity also may be explained by the first Americans' different experience. They achieved something never before done by modern humans (except for the early Australians)—they conquered a previously uninhabited landscape. Surely, the demands of this unique adventure accelerated invention and socialization, as well as caused the abandonment or suspension of some cultural practices. Was the deliberate burial of the dead in habitation sites one of these practices? We already know that some early Americans, the Clovis people, possessed a distinctive stone tool technology, the fluted point industry. Perhaps they also possessed a distinctive way of treating their dead, at least at the outset of spreading into new environments. It is possible, then, that not all early Americans buried their dead, that some buried them only from time to time and from place to place, depending on local circumstances, or that archaeologically conspicuous burial may not have been performed. But is it possible that they did not bury their dead at all?

The notion of a society not interring its dead in late Ice Age times challenges some of our accepted Western notions of what makes us human. It also seems to imply some form of cultural "devolution" in Pleistocene America, given that early Europeans, Asians, and Australians were burying their dead in graves and often performing internment rituals. Without arguing for such devolutions, however, I would suggest that the migration into and through the Americas called forth a different set of traits—traits possibly related to different forms of social organization, technology, and land use patterns, and presently not well understood. When we have a better understanding of these aspects of the peopling record and how they relate to changing biological adaptations (such as body size and acclimatization to high altitude), we may then find more skeletons. In the meantime, we must begin to look in a wider variety of new places, and we must keep our minds open and our field strategies flexible and highly interdisciplinary. Until we find more Ice Age skeletons, archaeologists and bioanthropologists must depend on early Archaic skeletons to reconstruct the biological makeup of the first Americans.

SKELETONS OF THE EARLY ARCHAIC PERIOD

Until recently, the best accepted scenario for the settlement of the Americas was synthesized by Christy Turner's "Three Migration Model",[7] which rested on the assumptions that the Western Hemisphere was occupied in recent times (ca. 11,000 B.P.), that three separate migrations led to the high biological and cultural diversity of the native American populations, and that all founding populations are of Mongoloid (northeast Asian and Siberian) descent. According to Turner, South America was reached first by groups of the first migration, called "Paleoindian," sometime around 10,000 B.P. Two later migrations to the south are associated with Holocene populations, called the Amerindians.

In recent years, the Three Migration Model has been seriously questioned by both physical anthropologists and archaeologists. Several physical anthropologists studying the cranial morphology of human remains from early Archaic sites in both South and North America are now suggesting that non-Mongoloids entered the New World prior to Mongoloids. This suggests an earlier fourth migration, which coincides well with firm archaeological evidence of pre-Clovis populations. Osteological and molecular studies have also recently challenged both the timing and number of migrations in the Three Migration Model.[8] People have argued for as many as four and as few as one migration.

Brazilians Walter Neves, Marta Lahr, and others have made extensive statistical comparisons of cranial measurements taken from early human skeletons and from modern native South Americans.[9] Neves has found that cranial measurements taken from a single skeleton from Lapa Vermelha IV (probably dated around 11,500 B.P.) in eastern Brazil do not closely resemble similar measurements taken from living Native Americans. The Lapa Vermelha IV cranium, Neves believes, shows stronger affinity with modern skulls from Africa, the South Pacific, Australia, and early modern humans from Zhoukoudien Cave in China. Neves also thinks a non-Mongoloid population, possibly related to South Pacific or more generalized Mongoloid groups, first inhabited east Asia before the classic Mongoloids and that this population moved into the Americas ahead of the Mongoloids. These populations later mixed in the Americas to form a complex American type. (I find it odd that they did not mix in Asia before arriving in the Americas.) This admixture is evident in South America, Lahr suggests, in the Fuegian population, which she sees as being closer to late Pleistocene skeletal material in Brazil because these people were isolated from the rest of the continent.

Ties between various Asian populations and contemporary North American tribal groups are also suggested by Loring Brace and other physical anthropologists' studies of skull and facial features.[10] Brace has suggested that Athapaskan-speaking peoples of parts of North America and Tibeto-Chinese speakers from east Asia share similarities that include long faces, narrow heads, and other skeletal features. The classic Mongol populations of northeast Asia, by contrast, have short faces and round heads. Most Native American groups are of the short face and round headed type, but not all.

In 1998, Neves reported that the Lapa Vermelha IV skeleton, known as "Lucia" in the press, shared the long face and narrow head appearance with southern Asians and Australians. And most recently, the puzzling find of the Kennewick Man (dated to the early Archaic period) in an eroded bank of the Colombia River in the northwestern United States shows possible affinities with ancient, long- and narrow-headed non-Mongoloids. These patterns suggest that late Pleistocene populations did not closely resemble modern-day Native Americans. Other physical anthropologists, such as Gentry Steele and Joseph Powell, also believe that the first Americans differed greatly from recent Native Americans.[11] They too have found strong cranial affinities between ancient Native Americans and southeast Asians rather than northeast Asians.

How do we explain various affinities? Many researchers point to different migrations at different times by different people, which would have brought different physical types. These differences should appear in the genetic record of both past and present Native Americans. Another reason for the differences is offered by Claude Chauchat, the French archaeologist working on the early Paiján culture of Peru. Chauchat has observed morphological differences between early Archaic skeletons from the Pacific and Atlantic sides of South America. He attributes these differences to regional subsistence and adaptive patterns rather than to genetic and migration patterns:

> At the beginning of the Pleistocene almost all remains are dolicho-cephalic [robust], while during the later period [early Archaic] skeletons are short and brachycephalic [gracile] because of the massive contribution of Mongoloid-type skulls. In spite of this sharp difference, without a trace of evolution, racial difference exists already at the beginning of the peopling of the continent, the Paiján type being different from other known remains (Lauricocha, Lagoa Santa, La Moderna). But distribution and habitat as well as dietary habits are certain factors to account for this diversity.[12]

We obviously need much more skeletal evidence from systematically studied sites before we can fully understand the meaning of morphological differences between skeletal populations. It is simply too speculative to derive hemisphere-long patterns from a single skeleton, as some researchers have done. We also need new methods to evaluate these measurements and some sense of how much weight can be assigned to them. Although some physical anthropologists place great confidence in such measurements for defining the differences between early populations, others view them more ambivalently, relying more on genetic and other physical patterns. And some physical anthropologists are uncomfortable with the robust, gracile, and other classifications, believing that true types do not exist. These anthropologists also believe the amount of variation that is known to exist among and within modern and fossil human groups suggests that the few skeletal remains from early America available for study might have biased our conclusions. Whatever the true entry date(s), number of migrations, and geographical vectors of movement into the Americas, the morphological differences observed in the existing early Archaic skeletal record surely contain clues to the patterns of gene flow and the gross biological type of *Homo sapiens* that first settled South America.

THE GENETIC RECORD

Both genetic and physical anthropological studies indicate that the early colonization of the Americas was much more complex than the Clovis model of a single population of hunters passing between continental glaciers to populate the New World. In an effort to resolve the number of early migrations into the Americas, geneticists today are examining variability among modern Native Americans, primarily using single locus markers like mitochondrial DNA (mtDNA) and markers on the Y chromosome. These markers carry a molecular clock; if a single population splits into isolated groups, the buildup of random mutations allows geneticists to estimate how long ago the split occurred.

Besides timing the arrival of the first Americans, geneticists are asking other questions. How many ancestral populations colonized the Americas? What are their sources? Do these populations correspond to current physical, linguistic, and archaeological groups? What factors brought about genetic change? Every human population is subject to the effects of mutation, adaptation, genetic drift, gene flow, and natural selection. But we don't know what determines the sequencing of mutations in populations or how disease, migration, and demography affect these differences. Nor do geneticists know how mutation rates were affected by population size and geographic isolation.

Human populations and their genetic makeup were undoubtedly affected by disease. According to Alexander Cockburn, a leading epidemiologist, one class of disease would have been caused by those organisms that had adapted to earlier human populations and persisted with them as they traveled throughout the New World.[13] This class would include head and body lice, pinworms, yaws, and possibly malaria, as well as such bacteria as salmonella, typhi, and staphylococci. Although many anthropological epidemiologists dismiss the potential of malaria in early hunters and gatherers because of their small population sizes and because they had adapted to nontropical areas, founding groups passing through tropical areas of Central and South America would have been exposed to mosquitoes that carry the malaria parasite. Zoonoses are another class of disease that might have affected the early settlers of the Americas. Zoonotic diseases have nonhuman animals as their primary host and only occasionally infect humans. Zoonoses can strike humans through insect bites, consumption of contaminated flesh, and from wounds inflicted by animals. Tetanus, sleeping sickness, scrub typhus, trichinosis, tuberculosis, and schistosomiasis are among the zoonotic diseases that could have affected early hunter-gatherers. The problem for geneticists and physical anthropologists is that these diseases leave few signatures on skeletons and thus are extremely difficult to detect.

Diseases not only could have reduced the size of a migrating population but also altered certain genetic patterns, thus making some groups appear more similar or dissimilar than others. This genetic alteration and other changes make it even more difficult to understand rates of genetic change, estimate times of gene divergence, and link geographically isolated populations.

Like archaeologists and physical anthropologists, geneticists also have differing viewpoints on the tenure of humans in the Americas, the number of source populations, and their points of origin. Most models suggest great biological diversity both prior to and after initial migration, which requires a time depth of 20,000 years or more. Other models propose a number of long-distance migrations, all arriving relatively recently. Much like the lumper and splitter typologies in archaeology, geneticists read the gene patterns differently. Some see one to two founding lineages; others see four or more. For instance, there is the three-wave model of Joseph Greenberg, Christy Turner, and Stephen Segura and its broad implications;[14] the single-wave model of Andrew Merriweather,[15] Anne Stone,[16] and others; the two- to four-lineage model of Antonio Torroni,[17] Douglas Wallace,[18] Theodore Schurr,[19] and Ryk Ward;[20] and others.[21] The proposed source areas range from Siberia, Mongolia, and Southeast Asia to the South Pacific. These models suggest the retention of very old lineages (as Asians moved into and dispersed throughout the Americas), common genetic sources somewhere in Asia, and/or direct oceanic contact between Asian and American populations. Some models speculate that a single founding population from Asia splintered, with one group becoming isolated in North America while the other kept moving farther south. Although most geneticists point to long-distance migration from Asia as the likely source of genetic diversity, Emöke Szathmary warns that some change is also due to highly local population movements by small groups.[22]

There are problems with using genetic diversity to estimate the date of entry of early populations. The molecular clock must be calibrated on absolute archaeological dating by radiocarbon or other means. The precise date of entry is especially significant. If it was before 40,000 B.P., as some archaeologists, geneticists, and linguists believe, one would have to conclude that a premodern physical type (most likely Neanderthal) was the pioneering human species in the New World. Up to now, however, no human skeletal remains or archaeological sites have been found to support this possibility.

Looking specifically to South America, Rebecca Stone suggests that there was one wave of Asian immigrants coming directly from the Old World and passing through North America to reach the south. Considering where the first South American immigrants settled, Francisco Rothhammer and his colleagues have studied allelic, craniometric, and blood variation among living people and early archaeological skeletons in South America.[23] They have reconstructed gene frequency maps that suggest two possible areas of initial settlement: One area is located in Colombia and Ecuador, along the eastern slopes of the Andes and in the adjacent tropical lowlands; the other is central Amazonia, where Rothhammer thinks the west Andean populations originated. The studies of Rothhammer and his colleagues also suggest stronger affinities between southern Andean and northeastern South American groups and between northern Andean and northeastern South American groups, hinting at initial movement along the Pacific and Caribbean coastlines, respectively.

Other genetic studies hint at oceanic contacts between Asia and South America. For instance, after studying newly discovered alleles and virus strains among the living Cayapa (or Chachi) of Ecuador, Elizabeth Trachtenberg and her colleagues have determined that they have some molecular similarities to those in southeast Asians and Japanese, but these similarities are absent in northeast Asian populations.[24] The alleles and strains from Japan also are related in their molecular structure to those found in Native South Americans in Chile, Colombia, and Brazil. Other strains present in native South Americans and in some Japanese groups also appear in the far eastern part of Siberia. Further similarities are observed in Japanese, Polynesian, and other South American groups but are absent in eastern Siberia. For some researchers, these southern affinities add strength to the proposal that ancient voyagers could have followed Pacific sea currents from Japan and the South Pacific to South America. Many other genetic and virus studies also suggest different degrees of distant contacts.[25]

I cannot leave out recent discussion of a possible ancient migration of western Europeans to the Atlantic side of the Americas.[26] Stylistic similarities between stone tools of the Clovis culture and the Solutrean culture of Spain and France (dating between 20,000 and 16,000 B.P.), plus a few genetic linkages between living native populations in these regions, have led several scholars to revive an old hypothesis that Europeans landed on the eastern shoreline of North America in late Ice Age times. Strangely, about 3 percent of present-day Native Americans have a genetic trait that occurs elsewhere only in a few places in Europe. Does this mean that Ice Age Europeans may have trickled into the New World many thousands of years ago, perhaps by skirting the Arctic ice pack over the North Atlantic?

A problem I have with these genetic models is that the genetic patterning may not be the result of ancient common ancestry but a consequence of population contact in the Archaic period or even in recent historic times. Some similarities, anomalies, and admixtures might be due to European colonization since the 1500s. To solve this problem, we need to know the mtDNA signatures of the first or founding immigrants, their homelands in the Old World, and their routes of migration throughout the New World. This information will help us sort out whether the observed genetic patterns are associated with the first migration or with later mixing of different populations. There also is the problem of admixture resulting from New World populations possibly migrating back into Siberia and northeast Asia.[27] If this happened, current native residents of Alaska and Siberia may be descendants of more recent migrations across the Bering Strait or from migrations back into the area from within the interior of the New World. And if this occurred, it may make the date of genetic divergence seem later than it really was.

A back-migration assumes that groups below the ice sheets in North America are older than populations living in now deglaciated areas of the northern hemisphere. This scenario also requires people being south of the ice sheets prior to deglaciation between 13,000 and 11,000 B.P. and having led to the formation of Eskimos and Athapaskans by 8,000 B.P. Geographic and genetic isolation may also account for different gracile and robust skeletons and for the presence of non–Mongoloid and later Mongoloid forms, if indeed such distinctions existed.

In sum, the genetic data are puzzling and, along with the physical and linguistic evidence, highly thought-provoking, but we must await further solid evidence and refinement of methods before the patterns the data suggest become facts. As the evidence mounts, however, certain truths about Native American populations are becoming apparent. First, with the exception of much later Eskimo and Aleut populations, most Native Americans share a number of distinctive physical and genetic traits that must have been passed down from a small founding population. Second, the mtDNA in the blood cells of many present-day Native Americans differs so much from group to group that a single, relatively recent entry into the Americas seems unlikely.

THE LINGUISTIC RECORD

The linguistic data also provide compelling support for two or more prehistoric migrations in the Americas. Greenberg's model has been the most dominant linguistic interpretation of the peopling of the Americas. When Europeans first reached the New World, there were probably more than 1,000 languages spoken by Native Americans. Greenberg classified these numerous and diverse languages into three waves or families: Amerind, Na-Dene, and Eskimo-Aleut. Each of these families appears to be more closely related to an Old World family than to the other two, thus suggesting three separate migrations from the Old World to the New. Several lines of evidence indicate that the Amerind speakers were the first to arrive. The second migration brought the Na-Dene language to the New World, and the final migration gave rise to the Eskimo-Aleut family. Following popular archaeological opinion, Greenberg and his colleagues supposed that the first American migration corresponded to the Clovis people and that it took place around 11,000 B.P. The second wave followed shortly.

Contrary to Greenberg's model, several linguists have recently argued that modern American indigenous languages probably evolved from a single ancestral tongue, and because they differ so greatly it is hard to imagine how this could have happened in the short time frame proposed by Greenberg. Led by Johanna

Nichols at Berkeley, several linguists now claim that a human presence of much more than 12,000 years is needed to explain this diversity.[28] Nichols counts 143 Native American language stocks from Alaska to the tip of South America that are completely unintelligible to one another, as different as French is from Japanese. Nichols believes that it takes about 6,000 years for two languages to diverge that far from a common ancestral tongue and lose all resemblance to each other. Allowing for how fast people tend to subdivide and migrate, she calculates that 60,000 years are needed for 143 languages to emerge from a single founding group. Even assuming multiple migrations of people using different languages, she figures that people first showed up in the Americas at least 30,000 years ago. Nichols suggests a coastal route of migration into the New World, rather than an interior route, because the centers of greatest language diversity are located along the Pacific coast of North America and the northwest corner of South America.[29]

Diversity may have been greater than we presently know. In areas where preindustrial states later developed, such as the Maya and Aztec regions of Mexico and the Inca region of Peru, regional language diversity was obscured by the state-imposed language. For instance, we know from historical records that in Peru the Quechua language of the Inca replaced numerous regional dialects that were not recorded by early European chroniclers and have not survived today. These kinds of historical transformations greatly affected the diversity and density of Native American languages now studied by linguists. Much more work needs to be done on the historical variables accounting for language diversity before we can fully understand the kinds of models proposed by Greenberg, Nichols, and others.

EPILOGUE

Solid archaeological evidence indicates that humans made it to the New World long before 12,000 B.P. and that the Clovis people were not the first to migrate from Alaska to Tierra del Fuego. Our inability to locate the dead of the first Americans, including the later Clovis people, suggests a uniqueness inherent either to the first people or to the methods by which we study their past record. It will be very important to discover where and how the early Americans buried their dead: what landforms they used, how these related to their living areas and other activity sites, and what if any rituals they used. Once these localities are found, we can further reconstruct the early biological, genetic, and religious patterns of these people and perhaps also gain a better understanding of their social, linguistic, and cultural achievements.

In the meantime, bioanthropologists and archaeologists must be cautious in the employment of a few anomalous skeletons, such as Kennewick and Lucia, to draw new conclusions about the ethnic affinity of the first Americans. Once a larger sample of earlier skeletal remains are found, we may discover that the genetic and anatomical differences between the true first Americans are as pronounced as those between the early Archaic and present-day Native American populations.

CHAPTER NINE

Migration, Adaptation, and Diversity

A T VARIOUS POINTS DURING THE LATE ICE AGE, some areas of South America were periodically or permanently occupied by people, but others never were. Ice sheets, severe cold, high elevation, drought, impenetrable wetlands, and forest kept humans out for long periods of time, even up to the present. Certain high Andean valleys, for instance, and some fjords or canals of southern Chile have never been occupied. Other areas were inhabited sporadically, or occupied once or twice and then permanently abandoned.

Our understanding of the movements of the first immigrants to South America is incomplete. From their artifacts we have learned something of their behavior, of the places they lived and the foods they ate. Their tools, when made of imperishable materials, have told us something about their technology. Yet the list of what we do not know about them is far longer. What was the social basis of the groups that made base camps in the large rockshelters in highland Peru or at Monte Verde in Chile? Was there any social or economic unit larger than such groups? If so, were these associations permanent? How did these social organizations affect people's decisions about when to move, how long to stay, and when and where to settle? And how did the environment, and climate and climatic change, influence these same decisions?

As I discussed earlier, different opinions exist about the role of the environment in determining movements and lifeways. Many archaeologists are reductionists, believing that late Pleistocene people were strictly controlled by climatic change. Others, such as Luis Borrero, suggest that these early populations were not greatly affected by environmental changes—that early immigrants were used to adjusting quickly to new environments and could adapt to almost any change in almost any setting.[1] We know that in some regions, for instance the steppes of northern Patagonia, there was no great change of the climate in the late Pleistocene, so it could have had at most a limited effect on people's movements and adaptations. Still, local environment plays an important role in determining the kinds of foods and other resources people may exploit, and these local adaptations are in turn a key to people's movements, both seasonal and not.

Three variables determine differences in local adaptations; environment, food type, and technology. Environmental differences are differences in space and resources. These include what ecologists call coarse-scaled or macrohabitat differences (for example, broad vegetation zones such as savannas and forests) and relatively fine-scaled or microhabitat differences (for example, seasonal variations in resource availability, volume and quality of usable stone raw material in a quarry, local availability of water, or the kinds of shellfish living along a particular stretch of coast). Food differences involve food size, food availability, food type, the homogeneity of the environment, and the make up of microenvironments. Finally, technological differences include not only such obvious matters as uni-faces versus bifaces but also less well-represented technologies and their patterns of use—for instance, the way hunting parties were organized.

Depending on local circumstances, any one or two of these factors may dominate the others. The Clovis people in North America, whose technology and big-game hunting probably took precedence over environment type, can be considered a "technology-oriented" group.[2] These people hunted big game and gathered foods in many different environments, which explains much of the ubiquity of Clovis points. David Anderson's early eastern United States groups, who settled into highly productive areas and set up staging areas for the exploration of adjacent zones, are an example of an environment or "place-oriented" group.[3] The staging area, Anderson says, was a frontier for expansion into new territories. Other people may have preferred what I call a "food-oriented" adaptation, focused on a specific type of food and habitat, such as palm nuts in the tropical forests of eastern Brazil, camelids in grasslands, or marine resources in bays. For these peoples, environment and especially technology may have been less important.

A comparable way of making the same distinction is via John Beaton's notions of "transient explorers" and "estate settlers." Partly in response to the long-held assumption that the first Americans spread rapidly without restraints throughout the New World, Beaton has proposed that the initial dispersion in both the Americas and Australia was a slow, complex process characterized by preference for certain kinds of habitats and certain kinds of resources within those habitats.[4] He views the first people as risk managers out to minimize loss and maximize gain. Different types of populations could have managed their risks in different ways. One type was the "transient explorer" who traversed one familiar habitat after another in search of similar resources, moving long distances and producing ephemeral archaeological sites. The other type, "estate settlers," attached themselves to a familiar territory. Radiating colonizers who filled local habitats and left conspicuous archaeological records provide a typical example of this type.

Although the first explorers and settlers undoubtedly emphasized varying technologies and subsistence strategies, I would guess that each type can generally be identified with a specific economy. Transient explorers were probably "technology-oriented" big-game hunters passing through open environments such as savannas and grasslands in search of a relatively homogeneous set of resources. Estate settlers were probably "environment-oriented" generalists, searching for specific kinds of plant and animal resources. They may also have moved up and down river valleys where resources are generally heterogeneous and richest. Explorers may have practiced a more random and opportunistic movement in open grasslands and savanna environments where resources are relatively more homogeneous. Although broad in scope, both my model and Beaton's model of population types provide us with different ways to consider the early archaeological record.

In addition to the variables of environment, food type, and technology that influenced local adaptations, small founding populations also had demographic requirements. Other people were a crucial resource that probably placed limits on how far away a group could venture from its nearest neighbor. Any small founding group needed to maintain networks of potential mates, social interaction, and exchange of information on foods and other resources.[5] Such social ties would help to explain the general uniformity of a technology across vast areas of the continent, such as the similarities in the unifacial industries stretching from the Pacific to the Atlantic coast. I believe the most important factor determining the long-term and long-distance movement of founding populations across different landscapes was their ability to adapt their technologies and social organization to the exploitation of new food sources and yet maintain social ties with neighboring or splinter groups. Any constraints on this movement were likely to be greatest where resources were limited. In homogeneous, relatively static environments such as the grasslands and coastal deserts of Peru and Chile or the arid savannas and grasslands of Brazil and Argentina, where resources were patchy in time and space, groups probably had little choice but to move more often. The lowland deciduous forests of the Andes, Brazil, and Venezuela, which were more heterogeneous and richer in foods, may have supported many different economies, and groups may have stayed longer in some areas. Furthermore, because people would have spent more time exploring these areas and getting to know the variety of resources available, these longer stays would have led to the beginnings of permanent settlement. Wetlands and temperate and tropical forests, in particular, probably gave people many subsistence options and the opportunity to reside longer, but less incentive to specialize or concentrate on particular resources.

MODELING EARLY MOVEMENT

The movement of early hunter-gatherers is often portrayed as something that underwent a uniform stage of development from rapid entry to colonization. Many archaeologists apply a single model to all early people, a model that generally involves small mobile groups carefully adapting their own numbers to the capacity of locally changing food sources, with rather fluid though important social relations beyond the immediate group. This model does not make sense to me. Although much of the variations in the archaeological record can be explained by time depth, local adaptations, and cultural change, much of the variation is also a product of differences in human movements. Instead of just one pattern, I would argue that there are at least four patterns of human movement within an environment: initial entry, opportunistic dispersion, migration, and eventually settling in or colonization. Each of these patterns had characteristic effects on the ways people organized their technology, economy, and social organization.

Entry, the first human presence in an area, is probably followed by random but opportunistic dispersion and exploration in virgin territories, with no particular goal in mind. After people have gained some knowledge of regional environments, they may begin to migrate. This is a relatively permanent moving away from a geographical location to a known destination. The last stage is colonization, when a budding population, previously on the move, explores and eventually settles into a home territory for good.

These movements probably were not the same for dispersing and colonizing populations of the twelfth or fifteenth millennium as they were for those of the eleventh millennium or the tenth. Nor were they the same across North and South America. Furthermore, these movements were not necessarily sequenced or uniform across a continent but probably occurred in a mosaic of simultaneous and occasionally overlapping stages. While some hunter-gatherer groups were dispersing, migrating, or colonizing in certain environments, others were making the first movement into virgin territories. And still other parts of the continent remained unexplored.

We don't know how much overlap existed between these movements or whether the archaeological record truly reflects adaptive differences among distinct dispersing, migrating, or colonizing populations. It's reasonable to suppose that different types of population movements must have been associated with different rates and different purposes and therefore must have produced different archaeological signatures. For instance, entry and dispersion probably produced more ephemeral records than did migration and colonization. Technology would have been more generalized and the sites would have been small, with smaller amounts of cultural debris and less internal patterning of material into specialized activity areas. This stage may be represented by the deeper levels in caves such as those at Pachamachay in the highlands of Peru or Tres Arroyos in southern Patagonia, which contain only a few flakes and a firepit.

Migration and colonization should be associated with more conspicuous records characterized by both generalized and specialized technologies and large sites with a high degree of internal artifact patterning, such as some Paiján sites, the Monte Verde site, and perhaps the pre–Las Vegas site. The archaeological record should ideally reflect a chronological sequence from entry to colonizing populations, with the population at each stage employing different types of adaptive mobility. Unfortunately, we presently do not have the hard evidence to identify and sequence these movements. Nonetheless, what the different records suggest about early people's movements in different periods is an important, even if hypothetical, record of the settling of South America.

Enough settlement and economic data exist in South America to let us speculate that different patterns between sites may represent different stages of human dispersion, migration, and colonization, each of which probably manipulated technology, environment, and food type differently. We can begin to make some correlations between these stages and the economic orientations proposed by Anderson, Beaton, and others. At least three different types of populations may have existed, either sequentially or simultaneously, depending on whether an area was being explored initially or being colonized.

First, some populations were equipped with a bifacial stone tool technology adapted primarily to hunting game in multiple habitats. These would be Beaton's transient explorers, and they were probably the first people to disperse into some newly explored areas. They were highly mobile interlopers operating primarily in open savannas, steppes, deserts, and parklands inhabited by both large and small animals. For these people, a specific set of food resources (mastodons, sloths, native horses, camelids) and the technology they used to hunt them (projectile points) were more central to their lives than specific locales or even a type of environment. Their primary archaeological traces are the El Jobo, Fishtail, and Paiján types of projectile points, at sites usually located in open to semiopen habitats. Other evidence for this type of adaptation includes ephemeral butchering or camping sites used for brief but sometimes repeated episodes, such as the sites of Taima-Taima in Venezuela, many Paiján sites in coastal Peru, Tágua-Tágua in Chile, and the Cerro La China and El Sombrero sites in the Argentine Pampa. These sites generally have little intra-site patterning of artifacts and different activity areas. Floral and faunal diversity are generally low, comprising mainly large, nomadic prey animals, and a low to moderate proportion of the stone tools are made from exotic raw material. With the exception of Taima-Taima (possibly dated between 13,000 and 11,000 B.P.), these sites generally range in age between 11,000 and 10,000 B.P. and probably represent different periods of initial movement into various areas of the continent.

A second population possessed both unifacial and bifacial technologies and was adapted to multiple resources in specific habitats, such as arid grasslands and the high Andean puna. These people moved seasonally within a home territory or migrated from their home to another territory and back on a yearly basis. Here, technology and habitat probably took precedence over food type. Since Beaton has no category for this population type, I will call them immigrants. They moved from a known territory to a known destination and may have practiced a loose form of territoriality. They used a wide variety of plant and animal resources from both open and closed environments and were probably adept at exploiting environmental boundaries such as the edge of a forest or desert. Compared to the transient explorers, immigrants were probably fine-grained in their response to environments, meaning that instead of looking for the same few things everywhere, they paid close attention to the different resources that the different settings offered.

Seasonal scheduling of movement was undoubtedly very important to these people. In the temperate forests of eastern Brazil, for example, they learned to exploit a widening spectrum of resources with ever-increasing skill. As people seasonally harvested wild palm nuts, fruits, and other vegetable foods, they continuously hunted. By 11,000 B.P., at the beginning of the archaeological record, they employed a local diversity of unifacial stone tools, but the tool kit eventually included a few bifaces. The variety of plant and animal species taken increased continuously as the centuries passed, and there was a multiplication of specialized tools of every sort, eventually including bifacial projectile points; technological skill also increased. The rise of cultural diversity in this region by 10,500 B.P. points to increased innovation by local peoples rather than to culture diffusion from elsewhere.

Another example of an immigrant culture is the Central Andean Hunting Tradition of the puna grasslands of Peru and northern Chile, which dates between 11,000 and 10,000 B.P. This type of culture appears to be habitat specific and is best documented at Pachamachay and other caves in central Peru. During the late Pleistocene and early Holocene, camelids were the inhabitants' major food source, accounting for 90 percent of the bones found in sites. (These people also ate small game and plants.) Campsites were chosen so that the animals would be close enough to be hunted for as much of the year as possible. Early hunters and gatherers of the puna probably adjusted their seasonal movements according to the waxing and waning of resource availability through an annual cycle. Camelids lived in highly localized areas, and this may have enabled people to experiment with managing wild or semiwild herds. The people who first domesticated the herds were probably descended from these early hunters and gatherers.

The last group is represented primarily by unifacial and secondarily by curated bifacial technologies adapted to multiple resources in multiple zones. Here habitat and food type take precedence over technology. In Beaton's terms, this group is called colonizing estate settlers. These settlers manipulated specific environments and various food types and maintained a curated technology for specialized tasks. They generally occupied large territories with limited movement. For settlers, seasonal scheduling probably involved integrating the exploitation of a wide array of resources, so that each resource was managed as a separate entity having a different pattern in time and space.

This adaptation produced an archaeological record of intensively occupied sites—some large, others quite small—containing a moderately high diversity of faunal and floral resources and predominately local stone raw material. Some examples are the Monte Verde site of south-central Chile (12,500 B.P.), several sites of the Itaparica Phase of Brazil, the late Pleistocene midden sites on the south coast of Peru and the north coast of Chile, and the pre–Las Vegas site of southwest Ecuador. The estate settlers exploited a wide variety of marine and terrestrial foods in closely juxtaposed environments. At Monte Verde, for instance, the people gathered a wide variety of plant and animal food from various estuary, mountain, and riverine environments both nearby and at some distance. Another good example is the early maritime people associated with the shell midden cultures of coastal Peru and Chile, which date as early as 11,000 to 10,500 B.P. Each of these sites shows a generalized subsistence pattern seasonally focused on plant, animal, and, in the case of Las Vegas, marine foods.

HUMAN MIGRATION AND CULTURAL DIVERSITY

These scenarios of different population movements are highly speculative. I cannot give a chronological sequence of types because each region of South America had its own history. There is not a single site or set of sites to suggest a clear chronological trend between these hypothetical scenarios, except perhaps in the semiforested and forested regions of eastern Brazil. In these areas, there may have been a trend from transient explorers and immigrants equipped with expedient unifacial technologies to exploit a wide range of resources in a few habitats, to colonizing settlers equipped with bifacial and unifacial technologies to exploit an even wider range of resources in many habitats.

Yet perhaps we should not expect to find a clear sequence. While some areas were being colonized, others surely were being explored for the first time. I suspect that many highland areas of the Andes were explored long after temperate northern lowlands had already been colonized. Thus, some of the "first entrant" remains in some areas may date later than those of some colonizing estate settlers in other areas. There currently is no record at all of the actual first entrants into the continent, and even if we found it, we may not recognize it as such. In short, whatever the chronology and sequence of different groups may have been, two things are clear: People were engaged in different kinds of exploratory and colonizing movements, and they had a proto-Archaic lifestyle at the outset of human occupation in much of South America.

The archaeological evidence for a proto-Archaic economy is weak in some areas. Only in the past twenty years we have come to realize how widespread this type of economy was in Pleistocene South America. This new realization is probably a result of better recovery techniques (i.e., flotation studies). These techniques have led to the discovery of new foods and have opened archaeologists' minds to the idea that not all early people were big-game hunters. Examples of "new" foods are the thousands of snails recovered from Paiján sites; the variety of seeds, nuts, soft leafy plants, tubers, and seaweeds recovered from residential floors at Monte Verde; and the abundant remains of palm nuts and other plant types found at caves in Brazil dating between 11,500 and 10,000 B.P. Despite these new foods, other groups developed economic practices that relied on a specific species, for instance hunting high quantities of camelids (guanaco) or a few other species. These different practices may have come from partly conscious cultural decisions.

Although the early appearance of a proto-Archaic lifeway and a broader subsistence base is important, what caused it by 12,500 B.P. in South America is difficult to say. The disappearance of big game between 13,000 and 11,000 B.P. may have been a major cause in some cases. Climatic change may also have been instrumental, but the relationship between culture and climate is not clear. Deglaciation had begun by 13,000 B.P. in several areas, after which the climate became warmer and wetter until it approximated today's conditions by about 8,000 B.P.

The proliferation of a greater number of archaeological sites and the exploitation of a wider variety of food resources after 11,000 to 10,500 B.P. reflects a broadening of the subsistence base to include progressively greater amounts of plants, as well as smaller animals, birds, aquatic creatures, and invertebrates. People who used these consistently available resources probably stayed in one place longer than those who relied heavily on hunting mobile game. Thus, people began to settle and to develop local traditions of technology. Being in one location also enabled them to develop nonportable equipment, such as heavy ground stone tools, and possibly means of storing food.

Many of the cultural advances made by the proto-Archaic hunters and gatherers at the end of the Pleistocene became more important and widespread with the succeeding cultures in both the Andean region and the tropical lowlands to the east.[6] The cultigens discovered in the highlands and on the coast of Peru and

Ecuador and dated between 9,000 and 7,000 B.P. have generally implied an origin elsewhere, because most of the plants are lowland or tropical species. Their adaptation to drier and seasonally cooler higher altitude climates must therefore reflect an earlier domestication in their original environments. Large, seemingly semipermanent base camps, limited storage facilities, and food processing equipment were no longer rare by 10,000 to 9,000 B.P. but were integral to the cultural inventory of many South American groups. Although people still lived in caves, the proportion of open sites increased after 10,000 B.P., and caves declined as major places of community activity. It is in the remains of intensive food collectors and camelid pastoralism that archaeologists find the evidence for the birth of South American village life between 8,000 and 6,000 B.P., with all of its technological and organizational implications. This change was neither universal nor irreversible; but those who successfully settled in villages took a step that changed the course of history, especially in the Andes.

CHAPTER TEN

The Social and Cognitive Settlers

So far, I have spoken about the first Americans largely in environmental, demographic, economic, and technological terms. Now it is time to say something about their social and cognitive skills. How did they communicate and transmit cultural information? How did they cooperate economically and maintain social cohesion, particularly during prolonged treks across long distances through previously uninhabited lands?

COGNITIVE MAPS

Exploration is a complex skill. As psychologists have shown, it is entirely mental and perceptual, requiring no instruments of any kind. It is based on inference within the framework of a cognitive map—a mental picture of the environment that may be studied at leisure by the mind's eye. In many areas of the world, for instance among desert nomads such as the Australian aborigines, there are navigation traditions that rely on cognitive maps and cues (particularly of direction) derived from natural phenomena. Celestial movement in particular must have been important for retreating back to a known world in Ice Age times. Once they stabilized, rivers and coastlines in South America must have become important landmarks as well.

During the late Pleistocene period, such exploration must have involved the following scenarios. First, the traveling group would have begun in territory it currently knew and of which it already had a cognitive map. There was, in other words, an idea of a local place or home and its relation to other places, including distant unknown lands. But this idea of home, this cognitive map, was not merely for navigation. An elder's knowledge of the best places to hunt would have included other knowledge as well: of what animals came there, and when, and what they did; of the best techniques for killing them; of how to make the tools those techniques required; and of the materials from which those tools should be made. The map of the best places to gather plants included the knowledge of which plants grew there, and when, and in what abundance; of how to tell edible species from inedible, and ripe from unripe; of how to prepare them, how long they lasted before going bad, and how long one could live off them in times of starvation. The map of ritual places included a knowledge of the rituals conducted there and of the history and mythology supporting them.

An exploratory group must also have added to its cognitive map a destination, or at the very least a direction of travel, whether along a visible mountain range like the Andes, a river like the Amazon, or a coastal shoreline. Perhaps these travelers knew that at any point along their journey they could have turned back and returned home—or perhaps they could not. On a journey taking many generations, the cognitive map of "home" would have changed with each generation, possibly beyond recognition. To reduce risk, people probably traveled when they could in environments that most closely resembled those they knew, and when they moved into poor resource areas, they may have turned back—or, depending on the lure of their destination, they may have soldiered on. Most movement was probably imbricated; the strange and the familiar probably overlapped when people gradually and perhaps deliberately adapted from known to unknown, as climate change caused local environments to shift beneath their feet.

The initial dispersion into the continent was probably made possible by a small number of innovations that made it easier for separate groups to reproduce and move into unoccupied lands. Within a generation or two, I suspect that people adopted numerous innovations (possibly including no found burial of the dead) in response to changing local conditions. New plant types had to be learned and new ways to hunt new animals had to be evaluated in light of more familiar ones. The stage was then set for further expansion and adaptation as groups of settlers leapfrogged to more distant lands that approximated familiar environments.

Archaeologists usually ignore the importance of this kind of cognitive mapping, human observation, and culture memory of environments, treating them as unknown factors that had a vague role in adjusting humans to their landscape. Social organization and culture are assumed to have simply responded mechanically to environmental stimuli such as climatic change. The role of human observation and decisionmaking is often unappreciated. It is important to remember that information about environments is culturally transmitted in both time and space and, more importantly, that cultural transmission allows people to pool their knowledge and compare information drawn from the experiences of multiple groups in different places over several generations. Social events such as feasts and rituals may have served as clearing houses for crucial information, especially when groups were exploring new territories. The expansion into new environments was perhaps high adventure that gave people a strong sense of mission (imagine our space program continuing for some millennia).

SOCIAL NETWORKS

Clearly, early cultural development required adaptations to new situations, including new social environments created by exploration. People probably took an active role in setting up social networks to ensure prolonged contact between splintered groups residing in known and unknown territories. The creation of such networks probably was one of the most significant contributions people made to the early cultural development in South America—or in any continent.

As people dispersed into new territories and as relatives maintained contact with one another, the social networks that linked individual groups probably strengthened. In this social web that joined members of a mobile group, both the reciprocal sharing of the spoils of hunting and gathering and marriages may have been the strongest filament. To this basic structure, hunting and gathering added a material dependence between males and females and between distant groups, thus tying family knots even tighter. Most probably this pattern laid the foundation for the long-term material dependence that we see through the accumulation of prestige possessions (such as jewelry, precious stones, and elaborate textiles) that characterized later agricultural societies. Eventually, once environments were being colonized more permanently, social groups probably came to depend increasingly upon their neighbors. This broadening of social interdependence must have strengthened and improved people's adaptations in many different ways. And this kind of group interdependence was perhaps the most important of the new kinds of social bonds among early people migrating long distances. However ancient its beginnings, this interdependence eventually became a basic unit of early South American society.

I would guess that the first populations moving into the New World were very small kin groups of perhaps no more than twenty to thirty people. Their social organization, based on constant movement, depended on kinship branching and extended cooperation between splintering groups, rather than on formal alliances. Small, localized kin groups may have constantly budded, branched, and reformulated with new membership and structural arrangements. Later, once people settled into homelands and began to manage resources, they probably formed territorial systems or a more hierarchical social order. These territorial groups most likely created more formal and larger alliances to facilitate the exchange of mates and resources. This shift—from a kinship branching system based on the availability of resources across a vast territory, to a territorial system based on management of those resources across common borders—was a major divide in South American prehistory. Some groups could perhaps shift between these two kinds of social organization, depending on the seasonal availability of resources or on the kind of environment they were exploring. These are the types of territorial and social structures that probably led to new social ideas and innovations, such as the use of rock art and iconography to communicate ideas. Based on the regional artifact styles that we observe between 10,500 and 10,000 B.P., I would guess that territorial kinship systems began developing between 11,000 and 10,000 years ago, depending on local circumstances.

We know from the work of ethnographers that we cannot draw a direct correlation between a particular tool type and a specific cultural type, migratory population, social structure, or subsistence pattern. Nevertheless, as we begin to piece together a mosaic of different point or artifact style zones in North and South America, we begin to see ways to relate various stone tool industries to certain aspects of territorial and social organization. For instance, some regional economies in Colombia, Venezuela, and eastern Brazil, where local populations were adapted to a variety of forest, savanna, or parkland environments, possessed unique unifacial or bifacial technologies. On the other hand, societies in the Central Andes and in the arid lowlands of Peru, Argentina, and Chile may have been more habitat specific, hunting camelids in open areas. Many of these groups, in addition to being highly mobile, may have also had constantly shifting memberships. Because of the constant interaction and perhaps mixing of groups, we should not expect clear artifact style differences between groups.

The archaeological record permits few conclusions about the specific character of social cohesion, or even its existence, across vast distances in different kinds of environments. Some generalizations can be proposed from the Old World, where much more archaeology has been done on early human migration. For example, John Speth has suggested that the social organization of anatomically modern *Homo sapiens* might have emerged as a solution to the problem of exploring low productivity environments of the far north, such as tundra and polar desert.[1] The archaeological records of these environments suggest that small groups of early human foragers tended to fuse into larger corporate groups at scheduled intervals. Speth speculated that it was the ability of these anatomically modern populations to extend cooperation for a long time across considerable distances that reduced their risks and permitted greater resiliency in the face of adverse environmental conditions. If these supercooperative modern humans of the Old World were socially, biologically, and, I would presume, cognitively successful in the cold, harsh environments of the north, they would have brought this trait to the lush temperate environments of South America.

Clive Gamble of Southampton University also believes that large networks of complex social interactions were necessary in the glaciated northern latitudes of the Old World.[2] He suggests that these networks assured continued access to mates and to information on resources. Surely there is a limit, however, to the distance over which such contacts may be effectively maintained. Further, when groups moved, did they coordinate their moves into approximate zones? Such coordination takes time, so much so that quick movement may have been impossible for some groups.

Robert Whallon has anticipated the difficulty of alliance-building and how it may have slowed long-distance movement:

> At a certain threshold of population density and local group size it must become impossible to obtain adequate information for continuous survival through direct perception and immediate, face-to-face communication. Such inability would constitute an effective block to colonization and sustained occupation of such environments by any human groups not capable of indirect communication and circulation of information. . . . There must be a threshold below which the risks of failure become too great in the absence of

assured access to permit sustained human presence in an environment. Lack of a means to guarantee access to known mates and resources thus becomes a block to the colonization and long-term occupation of such environments.

Both the Arctic tundra and the Australian desert appear in general to be such environments. The climatic, vegetational, and faunal differences between them make it highly unlikely that their colonization and the subsequent maintenance and expansion of human populations in both areas in the earlier Upper Paleolithic was due simply to the invention in this period of the requisite technical means for their exploitation.[3]

With limited technology and little information about new environments, the first groups moving into the Americas probably spent the first few years overcoming problems associated with new environments. They probably relied on reducing risk and being highly flexible, staying in touch with each other on an extended basis and eventually forming alliances in some areas, most likely in open arid lands where resources would have been patchier than in parkland and wooded environments. The size of cooperative networks probably varied inversely with the richness of the environment and the extent of the area affected when resources grew scarce. In environmentally diverse areas, a cooperative network might have extended only to a neighboring group or to the neighbors' neighbors. In very marginal areas, however—on the dry steppes of Patagonia or the cold forests of southern Chile—networks may have extended for hundreds of kilometers. Because networks must have been essential for survival, it is hard to imagine any Pleistocene hunters and gatherers existing without them. These networks were a vitally important social and technological means of obtaining information, food, and other resources during critical periods of initial dispersion. Yet such networks (especially formal alliances) also may have created problems of another kind—potential conflict between groups—and, as Whallon notes, they slowed movement considerably.

More formal, less periodic alliances may have arisen after groups had settled into permanent territories but probably not at the outset, when people were moving long distances, population densities were low, and one could resolve conflicts simply by moving to a more productive environment. In later times, such alliances may have alleviated periodic severe food shortages by establishing sharing on a regional scale. When resources dwindled so far that group members were incapable of supporting themselves in their own home range, they may have left temporarily to visit allies in an area where resources were not so critically affected. Even in earlier periods, when the group could move into an unoccupied environment, they would have needed some advance knowledge in order not to expend excessive energy searching for food.

Large-scale exchange networks are probably the most important difference between the late Pleistocene records of North and South America. The presence of exotic cherts and other materials at Clovis sites in North America, some more than 1,000 kilometers from their source, suggest far ranging networks of exchange or mobility. In South America, most materials are local; only in later times do we see the exchange or direct procurement of exotics, such as obsidian in the Peruvian highlands, and even then from no more than 200 kilometers away. Still, the great similarity in the form of Clovis points in North America, the Fishtail, Ayampitín, highland triangular points, and unifacial limaces in South America, and the styles of rock art in both continents suggest that even if goods did not travel, ideas and cultural styles traversed vast distances.

ART AND BELIEF SYSTEMS

Every society has a system of shared beliefs, a cosmology or world-view that expresses its answers to profound questions. Most world-views offer a view of the nature of the present world, its origins, and the role and destiny of humans. Most also show how people can live in harmony with the world and how, through ritual practice, they can influence the world in a manner favorable to their needs and desires. These beliefs naturally have a strong influence on people's behavior, social actions, and economic strategies.

In many living hunter and gatherer societies, activities related to land and territory involved in hunting are a part of a religious way of life. In our own culture, people conceive of their relationship to their physical environment, and even sometimes their human environment, as mechanistic and manipulative. What is for us land tenure or the rights of use and disposal of natural resources is for hunter and gatherer societies an intimate sense of belonging. Some groups see themselves as belonging to the land in the same way that the plants and animals belong to it.

We can presuppose that people's religious experiences and beliefs in late Pleistocene times resembled those of aboriginal peoples today. This is difficult to demonstrate archaeologically, although such an experience is certainly plausible as a motivating force for some of the symbolic art found in the French caves of the Upper Paleolithic period. Steven Mithen believes that art and symbols in this period were part of an exchange of information that served to educate the young and help hunters cope with scarcity and unpredictable food supplies.[4] It may be that rock artists were preoccupied with animals because of the greater risk and unpredictability of pursuing them. Less immediate rituals were needed in gathering or fishing because the element of chance lay not in momentary events of the hunt but in the general cycle of the weather. If this cycle varies annually, one may hold anticipatory rites, relieving anxiety over the availability of the food source. The early appearance of rock art in South America, if it can be dated to the late Pleistocene period, would coincide with evidence of food shortages brought about by a combination of environmental and demographic factors related to deglaciation.

On the other hand, one of the clichés of archaeology is that improved stability and a more dependable and easily obtained food supply bring leisure time, and with it an enrichment of life in such areas as religion and art. If this link between leisure and art occurred in some late Pleistocene societies of South America it is not overly apparent, unless we can infer it from the development of rock art or skill in sculpting and polishing stone. Perhaps the cordage design in the deeper levels of Guitarrero Cave or the geometric designs on the tusk fragment at Tágua-Tágua, both dated around 10,500 B.P., are signs of increased wealth and leisure.

South America is rich with rock art. However, rock art is difficult to date. Several archaeologists—including Niède Guidón and Anna Roosevelt, working at Pedra Furada and Monte Alegre in Brazil, respectively—believe that they can assign it a late Pleistocene age based on the presence of pigment spalls in the deeper levels of caves, but these could have migrated down from upper levels and are dated only as they appear stratigraphically. In the early Archaic period, however, caves and rockshelters begin to show a distinctive form of rock art. Many of the rockshelters that were inhabited during early Archaic times and that have protected rock surfaces have been decorated with single scenes or figures. Animals—camelids, felines, deer, birds, snakes, and capybara—are the most frequent subjects, either alone on a small flat area of rock or in larger groups such as herds or in hunting scenes. The stylized figures are full of life and action. People are sometimes shown with bows and arrows and spears. Other subjects include anthropomorphic figures, heavily stylized human figures, and geometric designs—but all this art probably dates to the early Archaic Period.

In summary, there is little evidence from which to study belief systems and how they may have influenced human behavior in late Pleistocene South America. Most archaeologists working with this period avoid considering worldviews and social institutions as important aspects of the peopling of the Americas, preferring instead to see human responses to changing environments. They thus commit the fallacy, common throughout the sciences, of assuming that the most easily studied factors are therefore the most important. But it seems to me that when we are speaking of the fear, exploration, social cohesion, and core institutions necessary to human survival in unknown worlds, we must see this survival as a social and ideological phenomenon, not just as a matter of technological and economic adjustments. Recently, archaeologists have begun to show more interest in the human mind, in what people learned from different kinds of experiences and how these experiences led to different cultural patterns in different environments. In general, the wider role of people's knowledge systems, how they are expressed in rock art and other symbolic media, and the changes they underwent as migratory groups adapted to new areas may have been much more important to human adaptation than archaeologists have previously thought.

CULTURE DIVERSITY AND CULTURAL CHANGE

Until recently, there had been little global interest in the peopling of the Americas because the New World represented the caboose, so to speak, of the human train of migration. What took place in the Americas was seen as a continuation of the much earlier migration and adaptation in the Old World. Besides, who cared? We already knew what had happened. The first Americans were simply nomadic Mongols, culturally unelaborate people who migrated from the plains of northeast Asia into the unknown landscape of the New World. But the situation is much more complex than this.

What makes the New World so fascinating is that some of the first pulses of human civilization—permanently occupied sites, the appearance of architecture and art, and the use of plant and animal domesticates—developed only five to ten millennia after people first arrived. In contrast, in the Old World, people were present for hundreds of thousands of years before the beginnings of preindustrial civilization. In Australia, first inhabited 40,000 to 50,000 years ago, preindustrial civilizations never developed at all. As one of the last continents occupied by humans but one of the first sites of preindustrial civilization, America offers an important study of rapid cultural change. Although we do not know when people first arrived in the New World, we know that these changes accelerated quickly between 11,500 and 10,000 B.P., once humans moved into lush temperate environments. What brought about this rapid cultural change?

The earliest period, between at least 13,000 and 11,000 years ago, South America was inhabited by a small number of groups probably connected by tenuous contacts. This geographic isolation would have meant there were few inhibitions on the range of cultural variation. As populations increased in size and groups moved into more predictable and abundant habitats, they probably maintained more contacts and borrowed more from each other as social relationships increased. After 10,500 B.P. we see both more sites and more shared artifact styles. Similarities in unifacial industries across the continent and the subcontinental distribution of Fishtail, Ayampitín, triangular Andean forms, and Tanged points all date from this period.

Local adaptation, utility, cultural tradition, social contact, and stone raw material also played their parts in generating the heterogeneous mixture of early stone tool industries. Beginning around 10,500 B.P., as the mixture of technologies became much richer, there were cultural transitions similar to those elsewhere in the world. We can only assume that by the time people reached the New World, the pace of cultural change had already sped up. Thus cultural change and its pace, as we find it expressed in stone, bone, wood, and other tool technologies, was in part imported from the Old World.

Most archaeologists invest the transition from the Pleistocene to the early Holocene periods, dated at 10,000 B.P., with an almost mystical significance. To archaeologists, this turn of eras connotes great social and environmental change. Yet this transition actually means nothing: It represents neither a major environmental shift nor a change in patterns of life. The really major environmental changes occurred between 14,000 and 11,000 B.P. The major human changes took place between 11,500 and 10,500 B.P., especially around the latter dates, when new ecosystems had stabilized after deglaciation and when colonization and social contact had begun their rapid increase. Thus, for me, the crucial transition took place between 11,500 and 10,500 B.P. The greater abundance of sites after 10,500 years ago probably has less to do with the presence or absence of humans than with the exploitation of more environments, greater archaeological visibility due to more stable landforms, and a larger human population.

As I discussed in Chapter 3, explanations for the changes that appear in the record of late Pleistocene sites have generally appealed to climatic change, population pressure, and technological innovation. As for climatic change, we cannot deny the importance of the environment in human prehistory. At the same time, it is clear that if the environmental changes during the late Pleistocene preceded these cultural transitions by some 500 to 4,000 years, then they cannot have always been the major causative factor in shaping people's lives.

Models of population pressure are also popular among archaeologists for explaining rapid shifts in culture, especially the adoption of a sedentary agricultural lifestyle. Yet we have no single instance in the archaeological record of population pressure having produced any important cultural shift in late Pleistocene times. Such pressure probably helped stimulate change in some cases, but it is most likely that increases in human numbers occurred after a shift in technology or a move into more productive environments, rather than before.

No doubt, technological innovation and new economic patterns developed as groups colonized new areas and acquired new knowledge of animals and plants. The detailed monitoring of environmental changes and fine-tuned cultural adjustments in response are among the most impressive accomplishments of early hunters and gatherers. These groups evidently used a wide array of highly specific observations of animal behavior and plant life to anticipate animal movements and other subtle local changes. New knowledge of this sort and the accompanying technological innovations helped to create different local and regional cultures. Of course the question remains whether technological innovation occurred first and thus allowed groups to take advantage of new territories, or whether advances into new territories resulted in technological innovation. In any case, it is certainly likely that the sheer diversity of South American environments stimulated cultural change as much as climate or population pressure did.

For instance, the cultural changes that coincided with the adoption of plants as part of the diet occurred in the continent's imbricated or overlapping environments, characterized as they were by abundant and predictable resources in temperate and tropical areas. These overlapping environments, which could support a wide variety of different economic strategies, provided the pattern for overlapping cultures, which were probably stimulated by economic diversification, experimentation, specialization, and intensification. These diverging economic strategies arose before the close of the late Pleistocene, beginning between 12,500 and 11,000 B.P. Ties of extended cooperation, and later exchange alliances, probably helped diffuse knowledge of technologies and ideas and favored still more change and innovation as groups partitioned and settled into new areas. Plant manipulation, experimentation, and domestication were part of the rapid changes taking place locally in many different environments.

On a global scale, the peopling of new environments by anatomically and socially modern *Homo sapiens* presents a complex spatial and temporal mosaic of many different cultures. The rapid peopling of the Americas and the accompanying rapid cultural change must be related to some radical and far-reaching shift in human behavior that occurred broadly within the time range between 100,000 and 30,000 years ago. It is impossible to account for all changes in the late Pleistocene period entirely in terms of economic shifts requiring different tools. The colonization of new areas with little diversity or predictability of resources became possible only after new cognitive capacities had evolved. These capacities were undoubtedly social, permitting the development of extended cooperation and exchange alliances. Rather than new technologies alone, was it these new social, cognitive, and cultural strategies that permitted humans to move into new and challenging environments?

It is my belief that the first immigrants adapted to South America very quickly, creating a mosaic of different types of hunters and gatherers (such as big-game hunters, general foragers, littoral foragers) immediately after they entered new territory. The key issue, then, is not the rapidity of a blitzkrieg migration but rapid social change—the adaptation of technological, socioeconomic, and cognitive processes over several generations. As the early archaeological record of South America suggests, this rapid social change was not a unitary process but varied from region to region. While hunter and gatherer groups were colonizing one new territory, others were just penetrating neighboring areas for the first time. All of these processes must have begun sometime before 15,000 B.P.

CHAPTER ELEVEN

Lingering Questions

THIS BOOK HAS BEEN ABOUT early human diversity in the New World; more specifically, it has been about the cultural, social, and biological variations of the first people to settle in the various regions of South America. Our problems in understanding human and cultural diversity are complex, widespread, and ongoing. One purpose of this book has been to present a new view of the earliest cultural diversity in South America and, by extension, North America. To conclude, then, let us return to some lingering questions about the who, when, and where of the first Americans.

Who were the first Americans? The most reliable archaeological, genetic, skeletal, and linguistic evidence all suggests that the first people entering the New World were Asians. Yet the skeletal and genetic evidence in particular suggests a great deal of variability. Some physical anthropologists think the earliest Americans physically resembled southeast Asians, early Asians, or early Archaic North American populations more than north Asians or modern-day Native Americans. The simple fact may be that the early human skeletons in the Americas do not closely resemble any living groups and show little similarity among themselves. The first Americans were probably Asians, but not the kinds of Asians we know today. They were most likely mixtures of different populations of anatomically modern *Homo sapiens* who had been roaming and mating across various regions of the Old World before crossing into the New World.

How did the first Americans get here? Again, our most confident answers are the vaguest: They likely came from somewhere in Asia. There are a few hints in the genetic and archaeological records of a late Ice Age migration from ancient Europe as well. We don't know whether people came by way of the Bering land bridge or followed the Pacific coastline into the New World. Yet whether by land or by sea, archaeologists often suppose that people followed a straight path from Alaska to Tierra del Fuego, as if they had been issued a road map or the force of gravity pulled them toward Antarctica. In reality, there was undoubtedly much backtracking and lateral movement as people spread out into new environments. In fact, recent genetic evidence suggests that North American populations may have been migrating back into Siberia around 10,000 B.P. or earlier. And as David Meltzer has pointed out, some migrations may have failed, leaving behind no genetic or linguistic traces.[1] And any archaeological remains they left behind would be hard to detect or understand.

Geography is a barrier to understanding the peopling of the Americas. During the last Ice Age, the northern reaches of the New World were pretty much closed to foot traffic. In late Pleistocene times the "ice-free" northwest corridor in Canada would have been filled with glaciers, and much of Beringia would also have been covered with ice. Though late Pleistocene people might have mastered the corridor, big game animals almost certainly did not, and finding food and shelter under those conditions would have been difficult at best. This difficulty makes the idea that the first Americans traveled by boat appealing to many archaeologists, who now think that people using skin covered boats made their way along the Pacific rim (which was then one continuous coastline) from Asia to Tierra del Fuego. A few other archaeologists believe that late Ice Age Europeans may have skirted along the edges of ice sheets across the north Atlantic, and so found the eastern shores of North America. A migration of this sort would mean that the initial peopling of the Americas was tied to a littoral or maritime lifeway, most likely characterized by simple unifacial tools rather than large, elaborate projectile points like Clovis.

When did people first arrive in the Americas? The question lingers. An earlier generation of archaeologists postulated Pleistocene antiquity for human settlement, perhaps as far back as 50,000 years ago. Until very recently, most archaeologists of the current generation thought that the New World was inhabited no earlier than 11,500 years ago and that early cultural achievements in South America had been carried from North America by Clovis people. Our thinking about the peopling of the New World once required a belief not only in rapid migration of humans from Beringia to Tierra del Fuego but also in extremely rapid cultural change. We now know that this belief was misplaced.

People were in Monte Verde, Chile, by 12,500 B.P., which means that they had to have reached North America by at least 20,000 to 15,000 years ago—if, once again, we assume that people migrated from north to south by way of land. People could have been in the Americas even earlier, as hinted by the possible presence of human signatures at several sites in both North and South America (including the deeper level of Monte Verde I) dating as far back as 50,000 to 20,000 B.P. But these sites, however intriguing, remain controversial and must be shelved until more archaeological work is done.

If sites exist earlier than 15,000 years ago, why have we not found them? One reason may lie with archaeological visibility. Between 14,000 and 10,000 B.P., the melting of ice sheets created many new rivers and deltas. These were favorite places of occupation. Changing weather patterns, changing origins of meltwater as glaciers receded, and occasional tectonic activity may have altered many river courses and deltas. Many sites from before this period may have been washed away or covered by sediment. In fact, it is interesting that the 10,500 B.P. time line is so visible in the South American archaeological record. In addition to the stabilizing landscape, there may also have been an increase in the human population and people may have started to aggregate in lush temperate environments. All three factors would make the archaeological record more visible and explain why more sites are found around this time.

A second reason for the lack of sites earlier than 15,000 B.P. may be our archaeological research design. Until recently, most excavations in the New World stopped when the Clovis or other late Pleistocene deposits were reached; archaeologists simply assumed that nothing lay deeper. I suspect that as more archaeological attention is given to older and different kinds of geological landscapes and people become attuned to the possibility of deeper and older cultural deposits, more ancient sites will be found.

The reason many archaeologists have not turned their attention to these older and different landscapes until recently is that their work has been influenced by a paradigm bias in favor of the Clovis model. In the past, most archaeologists were eager and able to fit their data to Clovis theory and to readily dismiss data that did not fit it. Even today some die-hard Clovis advocates refuse to see the South American record as being distinct from North America.[2] They insist on the primacy of Clovis and cultural linkages between the fluted trait, despite what expert South American specialists think.

Paradigm bias has been abetted by cultural bias. The opinions of Latin American investigators, who have worked extensively with early collections in their respective countries and are often skeptical of Clovis, generally have been ignored by North American archaeologists. This bias is another barrier to understanding the diversity and versatility of the first South Americans.

With few exceptions, when archaeologists have discussed the peopling of South America they have not talked about models of human migration and diffusion but about models of the distribution of Clovis points and of the mobile big-game hunters who made them. This allegiance to a particular type of model makes the gathering and interpretation of data into a self-fulfilling prophecy. In effect, we have treated the first American cultures like a hunting machine with unbounded movement and distribution in time and space, although that thinking is beginning to change.[3] Worse, we have taken a simple aspect of a surmised culture—the fluted projectile point—as the sole basis for broad scenarios of early lifeways. We have made an explicit assertion, not always critically questioned, that the spatial distribution of a particular artifact trait—the flute—is the spatial distribution of an actual culture and society. But as archaeologists, we know that we cannot always make a direct correlation between a particular trait and a particular society, any more than we can say that the distribution of cowboy hats equals the distribution of Texans. If a particular trait does not represent a society, how can it represent a distinct culture? And if it does not necessarily represent a culture, what does it really say about early human migration in the New World? Many different projectile point styles, other artifact styles, and settlement and subsistence practices must be combined into coherent pictures of the past before we can reconstruct the hemisphere-long history of the first Americans.

The peopling of the New World was clearly much more complex than we had realized. Moving people through the Americas is a different issue from moving the fluted trait from North America to South America. My hunch is that people were coming into the Americas by different routes at different times, and that once better geological evidence is available, we will see that both coastal and interior routes were used, and more than once. I also suspect that the Clovis fluted trait is unrelated to the initial peopling of the New World but is important to the late Ice Age migration of one segment of the North American population into South America. In fact, I am becoming more convinced that the fluted trait, in both its lanceolate and stemmed forms, was associated with a southerly coastal movement of fluted trait–bearing people sometime between 11,000 and 10,500 B.P.

I also believe that the people who brought the fluted point south were rapidly moving interlopers who coexisted with several existing native regional populations in South America, including those in Brazil who made unifaces and those along the west coast of South America who made Paiján points. Future studies of the peopling of the New World should give close attention to the archaeological and human skeletal diversity that is showing up increasingly in eastern Brazil. Physical anomalies in the skeletons at Lapa Vermelha IV and other Brazilian sites may suggest early contacts with Africa, Australia, and Oceania. Although we should be critical of new evidence, we also should keep our minds open to new possibilities and ideas.

However and wherever they came to the New World, perhaps the most important key to the first Americans' survival was that they had to sustain a minimum population size in order to reproduce biologically. There probably were no more than a handful of first immigrants moving into the northern hemisphere, and they may have been thinly dispersed across the landscape. It must have been difficult for them to maintain the size and reproductive viability of their groups. Families or groups that moved ahead would have faced long periods of isolation, low social connectivity, and, if things went wrong, extinction.

The severity of these risks would have depended on several factors, not the least of which was how rapidly they were moving from their homeland and fissioning into smaller groups. If they reduced the risks by keeping in regular contact with distant groups, then they would have markedly slowed their overall migration. Given these constraints, I would guess that it took several millennia for people to reach Tierra del Fuego and fill the major regions of North America. By 10,500 B.P., the New World was full of cultural variability, especially in South America. No doubt, the onset of more Holocene-like temperate environments by 12,500 B.P. in South America brought cultural and social advances to many regions. By then, these people had reached a threshold of social, cognitive, technological, and organizational skills that led to the cultural diversity of the late Pleistocene period and laid the foundation for the development of more complex societies after 10,000 B.P.

THE LEGACY OF EARLY AMERICAN CULTURE

As I noted at the beginning of this book, what makes the New World so fascinating is that the first pulses of human civilization developed within just a few millennia after human arrival. In contrast, in the Old World, people were present for hundreds of thousands of years before they began to build civilization—essentially at the same time that civilization originated in the New World. It's a curious and provocative fact of world prehistory that agriculture and early civilization appeared independently in China, Mesopotamia, south and Southeast Asia, and parts of the Americas at almost the same time.

What explains this worldwide cultural explosion at the end of the Pleistocene period? Why then? What set the stage for these changes? Over the years, archaeologists have put forth many answers, including environmental change, population pressure, and the slow accumulation of social complexity. The example of South America throws these questions into a particularly intriguing light because the stress of environmental change was partly self-induced, the population pressure was not that great, and the social complexity was itself partly a survival tactic adopted for a largely voluntary exploration of new territory. America thus offers an important study of rapid cultural adaptation and change in the context of what can only be called a worldwide cognitive explosion.

The beginning of food production—of agriculture and animal domestication—was one of the catalytic events of human prehistory. As an economic strategy that greatly increased both the quantity and reliability of food supplies, food production ultimately resulted in much higher population densities in many locations, a settled way of life, more long-distance exchange of raw materials, specialization of labor, and other forms of increased human social complexity, eventually culminating in the rise of preindustrial states and then urban societies.

Research in several regions of Mexico has shown that portions of the Northern Hemisphere were developing food production between 9,000 and 7,000 B.P. Advanced bands of hunters and gatherers were settling into farming villages by 7,000 and 3,500 B.P. The earliest evidence of maize, beans, and squash probably occurs at Tamaulipas, Oaxaca, and Tehuacan, respectively.[4] These major domesticates and animals probably formed the nutritional basis for the New World's first complex societies, including the Olmec of Mexico, the Hopewell of the eastern United States, and the Anasazi and Hohokam of the American Southwest.

It is not really surprising that the most highly developed cultures were restricted to the same regions where agriculture had flourished for hundreds of years. High civilizations such as the Zapotec, Toltec, Maya, and Aztec had their origins in these regions. Earthen mounds, built by different cultures at different times, also emerged around 5,000 B.P. in parts of the Mississippi River Valley. They grew increasingly elaborate over the succeeding centuries, becoming easily recognizable monuments of early civilizations.

South American civilizations were far older and more sophisticated than we once imagined.[5] As early as 12,500 to 11,000 B.P., ancient South Americans were exploiting a wide range of resources and living in lands ranging from high mountains to green river valleys and from the largest tropical rain forest on Earth to one of the driest deserts. By at least 11,000 B.P., hunters and gatherers were surviving in the harsh southern regions of Chile and Argentina. New excavations in Peru and Ecuador have turned up large pyramids and other monuments dating back nearly 5,500 years, to about the time when the Great Pyramids were being constructed in Egypt. And evidence from several areas in the Central Andes shows that people were using early forms of cultigens by at least 8,000 B.P. By 4,500 B.P., the Andes and the Amazon Basin had well-established agricultural traditions. The Central Andes were especially noted for their political organization, public works, and intensive maize farming. Several massive and elaborate ceremonial centers arose in the highlands and on the coast of Peru around 5,000 B.P., forming the basis for the first great civilizations in South America.

These early South American civilizations developed without the benefit of writing or wheeled transport. Yet they produced exquisite textiles, painted ceramics, the finest metal technology in the pre-Hispanic New World, and engineering systems that tamed the rugged Andean landscape. South American civilization reached its height in the Inca Empire, an efficient and highly organized political entity administered from the ancient city of Cuzco. The Inca was the last great prehistoric civilization in South America. As in North America and the Old World, these great civilizations had their roots in the early adaptations of hunters and gatherers in a wide variety of regional environments stretching from the Andes to the mouth of the Amazon.

Unlike the eastern and western indigenous cultures of North America, which developed in near isolation, the pre-Colombian cultures of South America were linked along an east-west axis. Like all the major enduring cultures of the world, these cultures drew upon the resources and the genius of two contrasting but complementary regional populations. One of these populations was that of the Andes—a world of different peoples and cultures living in high mountain valleys and coastal plains linked by rivers and valleys. The other population was that of the tropical world of the eastern lowlands, a region potentially capable of carrying dense populations based on intensive agriculture. By successfully encompassing these two regional populations, South American culture has added a dimension to itself: the further reserves of historical and practical knowledge that have allowed the complex whole to survive since the Ice Age.

HISTORIES WITHOUT PLACES AND
PEOPLE WITHOUT HISTORIES

The peopling of the Americas has recently become politically important as a matter of national pride. Now that we believe that the first Americans might not have had their roots solely in northeast Asia, the question of who first discovered America is stirring passionate debate not only among archaeologists, linguists, geneticists, and geologists but also among pundits, journalists, and politicians. The countries now interested in being the homeland of the first Americans include Russia, Spain, France, Denmark, Japan, China, and Korea. All around the Pacific Rim (and recently in Europe) are people who would love to demonstrate that the first Americans were not only Asians but Japanese Asians, or not only Europeans but Danes.[6]

Scholars who have written about European colonial domination of Native American populations sometimes see these hopeful expressions of national pride as an effort to reconquer or recolonize the earliest human history of the Americas. This early history may be easier to manipulate because here at the precipice of deep time there is no written record to help us sort out the facts. No one can speak authoritatively for people without histories, for histories without places.

What about these people's descendants? What role do the first Americans play in the construction of Native American national identities? Are present-day Native Americans even representative of those 10,000 to 20,000 years ago? How do groups and nations envision their relation to a culturally and geographically distant and diversified past?

To ask these questions is not to deny the legitimacy of these voices. Traditional leaders of some North American groups state that no matter what the archaeologists may think, their stories and myths tell them that their people have always been in North America after having emerged from the underworld. Many South American groups, on the other hand, see their ancestors as having come from the west, across the Pacific Ocean. It is necessary to understand in what sense these and other accounts are true. But this understanding does not lie in the simple project of equating emergence with migration or of seeing one as a transformation of the other. Rather, to understand such accounts is to understand the cultural importance and historical contexts of these different narratives. They are no less true or less significant than the Bible. As Naranjo, of the Santa Clara Pueblo, writes, we live not in a universe but a multiverse world where "there are many levels of simultaneous existence and these understandings pre-date time."[7]

Human evolution has been a continuous cycle of dispersals and migrations. Over millions of years, groups continually branched off, some moving on while others settled. The existence of many different cultures in the world today is witness to this history of human migration. Of the many dispersal patterns taken by our early ancestors, those of prehistoric Americans represent one of the most ambitious. They were the first humans to successfully adapt to the Arctic zone, cross the Bering land bridge, and disperse and settle in various parts of the American continents. We now know that the first Americans were far more culturally complex and sophisticated than just simple big-game hunters. In the future we may discover that the Americas of the late Pleistocene were one of the world's first real ethnic melting pot and multicultural society. The diversity of the early archaeological, genetic, linguistic, and skeletal records suggests a shared American identity rooted in multiple migrations and, to state it in contemporary terms, no true categories of race or ethnicity. The multiple scientific disciplines and others studying the first Americans will continue to teach us about who the first people to reach the New World were, where they came from, and when and why they arrived. I believe the picture that emerges will show us one of the most intricate, thrilling, and inspiring episodes of the human adventure on Earth.

APPENDIX

Radiocarbon Dates for Major Sites Discussed in the Text

When available, laboratory numbers, type of material dated, and references are provided. All radiocarbon dates are uncalibrated.

Site	Excavation Provenience	Material Dated	Sample	Years B.P.	Source
Colombia					
El Abra II	Feature 3	charcoal	BETA-5710	9,025±90	(Correal Urrego 1986:125)
	Feature 8	charcoal	GrN-5746	9,325±100	(Correal Urrego 1986:125)
	Subunit C4	charcoal	BETA-2134	9,340±90	(Correal Urrego 1986:125)
				10,720±400	(Correal Urrego 1986:125)
				11,210±90	(Correal Urrego 1986:125)
	Subunit C3	charcoal mixed with soil	GrN-5556	12,400±160	(Correal Urrego 1986:125)
El Abra III	(1.90–1.91m)	charcoal	BETA-2133	8,810±430	(Correal Urrego 1986:125)
El Abra IV	(0.94 m)	charcoal	I-6363	9,050±470	(Correal Urrego 1986:125)
Palestina 2	CX-90 N20-30cm	charcoal	BETA-40854	10,230±80	(López Castellano, 1991)
	CX-90 N30-40cm	charcoal	BETA-40855	10,400±90	(López Castellano, 1991)
Peña Roja		charred seeds	GX-17395	9,125±250	(Gnecco and Mora 1997:686)
		charcoal	BETA-52963	9,160±90	(Gnecco and Mora 1997:686)
		charcoal	BETA-52694	9,250±140	(Gnecco and Mora 1997:686)
Pubenza	Layer 4	gasteropod	GrN-20101	13,280±110	(Herrera et al. 1992)
	Layer 8	calcareous seed	GrN-20102	15,050±100	(Herrera et al. 1992)
	Layer 10	gasteropod	GrN-197	16,010±70	(Herrera et al. 1992)
	Layer 12	humic clay	GrN-20106	17,790±120	(Herrera et al. 1992)
Puerto Nare	Unit T-46	charcoal	BETA-70040	10,350±60	(Herrera et al. 1992)

Site	Unit/Level	Material	Lab number	Date	Reference
Tibito	Unit 3A (1.10m)	mastodon and horse bones	GrN-9375	11,740±110	(Correal Urrego 1986:119)
Tequendama I	M+L	charcoal	GrN-7115	9,740±135	(Urrego and Van der Hammer 1977)
	E-III	charcoal	GrN-6730	9,990±100	(Urrego and Van der Hammer 1977)
	J-I	charcoal	GrN-6210	10,626±95	(Urrego and Van der Hammer 1977)
	F-I	charcoal	GrN-6732	10,130±150	(Urrego and Van der Hammer 1977)
	L-4	charcoal	GrN-7113	10,140±100	(Urrego and Van der Hammer 1977)
	F-I	charcoal	GrN-7114	10,150±50	(Urrego and Van der Hammer 1977)
	L-6B	charcoal	GrN-6731	10,460±130	(Urrego and Van der Hammer 1977)
	M(-L)-5	charcoal	GrN-6505	10,590±90	(Urrego and Van der Hammer 1977)
	M(-L)-6A	charcoal	GrN-6207	10,730±105	(Urrego and Van der Hammer 1977)
	LM-8	charcoal	GrN-6539	10,920±260	(Urrego and Van der Hammer 1977)
	D	charcoal	GrN-6579	22,250±470	(Urrego and Van der Hammer 1977)
	JII	charcoal	GrN-6538	28,890±840	(Urrego and Van der Hammer 1977)
San Isidro		charcoal	BETA-65877	9,530±100	(Gnecco and Mora 1997:686)
		charcoal	BETA-93275AMS	10,030±60	(Gnecco and Mora 1997:686)
		charcoal	BETA-65878	10,050±100	(Gnecco and Mora 1997:686)
San Juan Bedout	Level 0.35–0.40	charcoal	BETA-40852	10,350±60	(Herrera et al. 1992)
Sauzalito	Level 0.35–0.40	charcoal	BETA-23476	9,300±100	(Herrera et al. 1992)
	Tr. III. n. 7	charcoal	BETA-18441	9,670±150	(Herrera et al. 1992)
	Tr. III. n. 5	charcoal	BETA-23475	9,550±110	(Herrera et al. 1992)

(continues)

Site	Excavation Provenience	Material Dated	Sample	Years B.P.	Source
Sueva	Unit 3	charcoal	GrN-8111	10,090±90	(Correal U. 1986:125)
				11,740±110	(Correal U. 1981:42)
Ecuador					
Chobshi		charcoal	TX-1132	10,010±430	(Lynch and Pollock 1980:21)
Cubilán		charcoal	TX-1133	8,480±200	(Temme 1982)
El Inga		charcoal	R 1070/2	9,033±144	(Mayer-Oakes 1986)
Site OGSE-80D-E 110		charcoal	TX-3770	10,840±410	(Stothert 1985)
(Las Vegas)	B-D 112-113	charcoal	TX-4706	10,300±240	(Stothert 1985)
	CH 111-112	shell	TX-4461	10,100±130	(Stothert 1985)
San José				11,248	(Mayer-Oakes 1982)
				9,321	(Mayer-Oakes 1982)
Talará		shell carbonate		11,200±115	(Richardson 1978)
Venezuela					
Taima-Taima		masticated twigs	SI-3316	12,980±85	(Bryan and Ghrun 1979:56)
			Birm-802	13,000±200	(Bryan and Ghrun 1979:56)
			USGS-247	13,860±120	(Bryan and Ghrun 1979:56)

(continues)

Perú

Site	Subunit	Material	Lab No.	Date	Reference
Ascope			GIF-4912	9,670±170	(Rick 1980:65)
Complejo Paiján				10,584±280	(Bryan 1978)
				12,845±280	(Ossa 1978)
El Palto[1]		charcoal		11,650±180	(Dillehay 1992)
Guitarrero	Complex I				
	Unit 63	charcoal	SI-1497	9,140±90	(Lynch 1980)
		charcoal	GX-1779	9,790±240	(Lynch 1980)
		charcoal	SI-1498	9,660±150	(Lynch 1980)
		charcoal	SI-1496	9,475±130	(Lynch 1980)
		charcoal	GX-1859	12,560±360	(Lynch 1980)
	Complex II	charcoal	GX-1778	10,535±290	(Lynch 1980)
	Unit 22	charcoal	SI-1499	9,580±135	(Lynch 1980)
	Unit 159	charcoal	GX-1780	10,475±300	(Lynch 1980)
		charcoal	SI-1502	10,240±110	(Lynch 1980)
Huaro Cave		bone collagen		13,160±700	(Sandweiss et al. 1989)
Huaro Cave		bone collagen		13,510±700	(Cardich 1978)
La Cumbre		mastodon bone	GX-2019	10,535±280	(Ossa 1978:293)
		mastadon bone	GX-2494	12,360±700	(Ossa 1978:293)
Las Conchas				9,680±160	(Llagostera 1979)
Lauricocha		charcoal and burned bone		9,525±250	(Cardich 1978:96)

Site	Excavation Provenience	Material Dated	Sample	Years B.P.	Source
Pachamachay		charcoal		11,800±130	(Rick 1980:65)
			UCLA-2118A	11,800±930	(Rick 1980:65)
Pampa de los Fósiles			GIF-3781	10,200±180	(Chauchat 1987)
			GIF-4161	9,810±180	(Chauchat 1987)
			GIF-5162	9,600±170	(Chauchat 1987)
			GIF-4914	9,490±170	(Chauchat 1987)
			GIF-4915	9,300±160	(Chauchat 1987)
			GIF-5161	9,360±170	(Chauchat 1987)
Cerro Chivateros			UCLA-683	10,430±160	
Pikimachay	Zone J		UCLA-1653A	17,650±3000	(McNeish et al. 1980)
		sloth bones	I-5851A	20,200±1050	(McNeish et al. 1980)
	Zone I		UCLA-1653B	14,150±180	(McNeish et al. 1980)
		collagen	UCLA-1653C	12,750±1400	(McNeish et al. 1980)
	Zone H1 and H		UCLA-1964	12,200±180	(McNeish et al. 1980)
Quebrada Jaguay	*Sector I*				
	1-2-D, Level 3b	charcoal	BGS-1943	10,274±125	(Sandweiss et al. 1998:1830)
	1970, Layer 4	charcoal		10,200±140	(Sandweiss et al. 1998:1830)
	1-2-B, Level 4c	charcoal	BGS-2024	11,080±220	(Sandweiss et al. 1998:1830)
	1-2-D, Level 4c	charcoal	BGS-1942	11,105±260	(Sandweiss et al. 1998:1830)

		material	lab number	date	reference
Sector II					
	II-1-D, Level 2c3	charcoal	BGS-1937	10,725±175	(Sandweiss et al. 1998:1830)
	1992, Level 3	charcoal	BGS-1702	10,770±130	(Sandweiss et al. 1998:1830)
Quebrada Tacahuay	3A-8	charcoal	BETA-108860C	10,530±140	(Keefer et al. 1998:1834)
	1-8	charcoal	BETA-108692A	10,750±80	(Keefer et al. 1998:1834)
	1-8	charcoal	BETA-95869C	10,770±150	(Keefer et al. 1998:1834)
Quirihuac		bone	GX-2493	9,930±820	(Ossa 1978:293)
		wood		10,005±320	(Ossa 1978:293)
		wood		12,745±350	(Ossa 1978:293)
		wood		12,400±750	(Ossa 1978:293)
Ring Site		shell carbonate		10,575±105	(Sandweiss et al. 1989)
Telarmachay	Layer VII C6	charcoal	Pucp-1825	12,040±120	(Lavallee et al. 1995:45)
Toquepala				8,750±480	(Ravines 1972)
				9,340±128	(Ravines 1972)
Tres Ventanas				10,300±170	(Rick 1980:65)
South Andes (Northwest Argentina and North-Central Chile)					
Agua de la Cueva				9,840±90	(Durán 1991)
				10,350±299	(Durán 1991)

(continues)

Site	Excavation Provenience	Material Dated	Sample	Years B.P.	Source
Agua de la Cueva 45				9,840±90	(Nuñez 1983)
Agua de la Cueva 46				10,350±220	(Nuñez 1983)
Cueva Sofia 1			PITT-0684	11,570±60	(Nuñez 1983)
Cuyín Manzano			KN-1432	9,920±85	(Nuñez 1983)
Englefield			Sa-20-c	9,326±150	(Nuñez 1983)
Gruta del Indio			GRN-5558	10,350±350	(Semper and Lagiglia 1966)
Huachichocana Cave			GAK-5447	10,200±480	(Fernández 1988)
				9,620±130	(Fernández 1988)
Inca Cueva 4	Level 2		LP-137	10,620±140	(Aschero 1984)
				10,350±299	(Aschero 1984)
				9,840±90	(Aschero 1984)
Marazzi	Inferior Level		GIF-1034	9,595±210	(Nuñez 1983)
Monte Verde	Upper Layer of MV-5 (Noncultural Deposits)	wood and charcoal	TX-4436	10,860±130	(Dillehay 1997)
		wood and charcoal	TX-3210	11,760±470	(Dillehay 1997)
		wood silver	TX-3472	11,600±120	(Dillehay 1997)
Lower Layer of MV-5		unburned wood	BETA-59081	10,330±160	(Dillehay 1997)
		unburned wood	BETA-52015	11,640±90	(Dillehay 1997)

(continues)

Middle Layer of MV-7	unburned wood	BETA-68996	12,000±110	(Dillehay 1997)
	unburned wood	BETA-68997	11,800±80	(Dillehay 1997)
	peat ball	BETA-35193	23,660±320	(Dillehay 1997)
	peat ball	BETA-41983	27,860±2010	(Dillehay 1997)
Upper Layer of MV-8	unburned wood	BETA-52011	>42,100	(Dillehay 1997)
Monte Verde (Cultural Deposits) MV-II Layer	bone	TX-3760	11,990±200	(Dillehay 1997)
	wood artifact	BETA-6755	12,230±140	(Dillehay 1997)
	charcoal	TX-3208	13,565±250	(Dillehay 1997)
	amino acids from collagen in ivory artifact	OXA-105	12,000±250	(Dillehay 1997)
	carbonized wood	TX-5374	11,790±200	(Dillehay 1997)
	charred wood	TX-5376	11,929±120	(Dillehay 1997)
	wood artifact	OXA-381	12,450±150	(Dillehay 1997)
Upper Layer of SCH-4 (MV-7) (ancient creek bank)	wood artifact	TX-4437	12,650±130	(Dillehay 1997)
	wood artifact	TX-5375	12,740±440	(Dillehay 1997)
	burned artifact	BETA-59082	12,780±240	(Dillehay 1997)
	burned wood	BETA-65842	12,420±130	(Dillehay 1997)
Lower Layer of SCH-4 (base of MV-7)	charred wood	BETA-6754	33,370±530	(Dillehay 1997)
	carbonized wood	BETA-7825	33,020>	(Dillehay 1997)

Site	Excavation Provenience	Material Dated	Sample	Years B.P.	Source
Nague	Base		BETA-39081	10,120±80	(Núñez 1983)
Río Bueno[2]		charcoal		10,400±90	(Dillehay and Gordon 1989)
Quereo	I	wood		11,600±190	(Núñez 1989:17)
				11,400±145	(Núñez 1989:17)
	II			10,925±85	(Núñez et al. 1987:172)
				11,100±150	(Núñez et al. 1987:172)
San Lorenzo 1			N-3423	10,400±130	(Núñez 1989)
			HU-299	10,280±120	(Núñez 1989)
			N-3424	9,960±125	(Núñez 1989)
San Pedro Viejo Pichasca			IVIC-728	9,890±80	(Santoro 1989)
Tagua-Tagua-1				10,380±320	(Núñez et al. 1994)
				11,000±170	(Núñez et al. 1994)
				11,380±320	(Núñez et al. 1994)
				11,320±300	(Núñez et al. 1994)
Tagua-Tagua-2		mastadon bone	BETA-45520	10,120±130	(Núñez et al. 1994)
		carbon concentration	BETA-45519	9,900±100	(Núñez et al. 1994)
		carbon concentration	BETA-45518	9,700±90	(Núñez et al. 1994)
Tiliviche	Level 1-E		SI-3116	9,760±365	(Santoro 1989)
Toconce			NR	9,590±90	(Santoro 1989)

(continues)

Traful	Level 21	GX-1711G	9,285±105	(Núñez 1983)
	Level 18	Ingeis 2676	9,430±230	(Núñez 1983)
	Level 13	LP-62	9,285±313	(Núñez 1983)
Tuina 1			9,080±130	
Brazil				
Bahia				
Abrigo Pilão		BETA-10017	9,390±90	(Bryan 1993)
		BETA-10015	9,610±90	(Bryan 1993)
BA-RC-28		SI-6748	9,110±100	(Kipnis 1998)
Morro Furado		SI-5565	8,860±115	(Kipnis 1998)
		SI-7160	9,110±100	(Kipnis 1998)
		SI-6750	21,090±420	(Kipnis 1998)
		SI-6751	18,570±130	(Kipnis 1998)
		SI-6752	16,200±290	(Kipnis 1998)
Goiás				
GO-JA-01	Cut I, Layer 12	SI-2347	8,740± 90	(Schmitz 1987:25)
	18 I, Layer G	SI-3696	8,805±100	(Schmitz 1987:25)
	18 I, Layer F	SI-3695	8,915±115	(Schmitz 1987:25)
	12 H, Layer H	SI-3697	9,020±70	(Schmitz 1987:25)
	12 H, Layer J	SI-3698	9,060±65	(Schmitz 1987:25)
	12 H, Layer Q	SI-3700	9,510±60	(Schmitz 1987:25)

Site	Excavation Provenience	Material Dated	Sample	Years B.P.	Source
			N-2348	10,400±130	(Schmitz 1987:25)
			SI-3699	10,580±115	(Schmitz 1987:25)
			SI-3699	10,580±115	(Schmitz 1987:25)
			N-2348	10,740±90	(Schmitz 1987:25)
GO-JA-02	Cut I, Layer 18		SI-3107	9,195±75	(Schmitz 1987:25)
	Cut I, Layer 26		SI-3108	10,120±180	(Schmitz 1987:25)
GO-JA-03	Cut IV, Layer 22		SI-3110	9,765±75	(Schmitz 1987:25)
GO-JA-14	Cut II, Layer 11		SI-3111	10,740 ±85	(Schmitz 1987:25)
GO-JA-26			SI-5562	8,370±75	(Schmitz 1987:25)
			SI-5563	8,880±90	(Schmitz 1987:25)
GO-NI-49			SI-2769	10,750±300	(Schmitz 1987:25)
Mato Grosso					
Abrigo de Sol			SI-3479	9,370±70	(Miller 1983)
			BETA-10017	9,390±90	(Miller 1983)
			BETA-10605	9,495±90	(Miller 1983)
			SI-3476	10,405±100	(Miller 1983)
			SI-3477	12,300±95	(Miller 1983)
Santa Elina			GIF-9367	9,460±90	(Kipnis 1998)
			GIF-8954	10,120±120	(Kipnis 1998)

Mato Grosso do Sul

MS-PA-02		BETA-22634	10,090±70	(Kipnis 1998)
		BETA-22645	10,340±110	(Kipnis 1998)

Minas Gerais

Lapa Vermelha	charcoal	GIF-3726	11,680±500	(Guidón and Delibrias 1985:403)
	bone	BETA-84439	9,330±60	(Prous 1986:176–177)
	bone	GIF-3208	9,580±200	(Laming-Emperaire et al. 1975:145)
	human bone	BETA-84439	9,930±60	(W. Neves, personal communication 1998)
Santana do Riacho		GIF-5089	11,960±250	(Prous 1986:292–295)
		GIF-5087	8,150±150	(Prous 1986:292–295)
		CDTN-1039	8,185±110	(Prous 1986:292–295)
		GIF-5088	8,230±280	(Chausson and Delibrias 1991/1993)
		CDTN-1044	8,381±280	(Prous 1986:292–295)
		CDTN-1002	8,400±300	(Prous 1986:292–295)
		CTDN-1001	8,500±500	(Prous 1986:292–295)
		CTDN-1069	8,840±130	(Prous 1986:292–295)
		GIF-4511	8,990±150	(Chausson and Delibrias 1991/1993)

(continues)

Site	Excavation Provenience	Material Dated	Sample	Years B.P.	Source
			GIF-4110	9,460±110	(Chausson and Delibrias 1991/1993)
			GIF-5089	11,960±250	(Prous 1986:292–295)
		human bone	BETA-104292	7,840±60	(W. Neves, personal communication 1998)
		human bone	BETA-96760	5,740±70	(W. Neves, personal communication 1998)
		human bone	BETA-96758	5,340±60	(W. Neves, personal communication 1998)
		human bone	BETA-104291	2,270±50	(W. Neves, personal communication 1998)
MG-VG-11			SI-5509	8,865±110	(Kipnis 1998)
			SI-5508	9,135±105	(Kipnis 1998)
MG-VG-19			SI-5511	8,845±90	(Kipnis 1998)
Cerca Grande, Abrigo 6			P-519	9,028±120	(Stuckenrath 1963:96–97)
			P-521	9,720±128	(Stuckenrath 1963:96–97)
		human bone	BETA-84442	6,420±60	(W. Neves, personal communication 1998)
Cerca Grande, Abrigo 7			BETA-84446	9,130±60	(Kipnis 1998)
Gruta do Gentio II			SI-2373	8,215±120	(Prous 1986:289–291)
			SI-3210	8,620±110	(Prous 1986:289–291)
			SI-6837	10,190±120	(Prous 1986:289–291)

Site	Material	Lab ID	Date	Reference
Lapa do Boquete		BETA-98573	9,350± 80	(Prous 1986:289–291)
		CDTN-1077	9,870±260	(Prous 1986:289–291)
		CDTN-3011	9,870±485	(Prous 1986:289–291)
		CDTN-1004	10,000±232	(Prous 1986:289–291)
		CDTN-3015	10,250±345	(Prous 1986:289–291)
		CDTN-3114	10,910±140	(Prous 1986:289–291)
		CDTN-1080	11,440±240	(Prous 1986:289–291)
		CDTN-3009	11,440±475	(Prous 1986:289–291)
		CDTN-1084	12,000±300	(Prous 1986:289–291)
		CDTN-2264	12,000±500	(Prous 1986:289–291)
		CDTN-2403	12,070±170	(Prous 1986:289–291)
Lapa do Dragao		CTDN-1008	10,000±255	(Kipnis 1998)
		CTDN-1007	11,000±300	(Kipnis 1998)
Lapa dos Bichos		BETA-100392	8,640±90	(Kipnis 1998)
		BETA-89592	8,890±90	(Kipnis 1998)
		BETA-100391	9,140±90	(Kipnis 1998)
		BETA-100396	9,390±160	(Kipnis 1998)
		BETA-100397	10,450±79	(Kipnis 1998)
Lapa Pequena		Birm-868	8,240±160	(Kipnis 1998)
Lagoa Santa Region	human bones	BETA-108186	7,270±60	(W. Neves, personal communication 1998)
	human bones	BETA-108187	6,800±50	(W. Neves, personal communication 1998)

(continues)

Site	Excavation Provenience		Material Dated	Sample	Years B.P.	Source
Lapa Mortuaria			human bones	GIF-4304	5,380±1450	(W. Neves, personal communication 1998)
Gruta das Onças			human bones	UCR-3187/ CAMS-10909	4,380±70	(W. Neves, personal communication 1998)
Pará						
Caverna da Pedra Pintada	Unit 2 (Initial Period)		charred wood	B76952CAMS	10,450±60	(Roosevelt et al. 1996)
			carbonized seed	B76953CAMS	10,560±60	(Roosevelt et al. 1996)
			carbonized seed	GX17407	10,905±60	(Roosevelt et al. 1996)
			carbonized seed	GX17406	11,110±310	(Roosevelt et al. 1996)
	Unit 5 (Initial Period)		carbonized seed	GX17400CAMS	10,392±78	(Roosevelt et al. 1996)
			carbonized seed	GX17414	10,875±295	(Roosevelt et al. 1996)
			carbonized seed	GX17413	11,145±135	(Roosevelt et al. 1996)
	Unit 6 (Initial Period)		carbonized seed	GX17421	10,275±275	(Roosevelt et al. 1996)
			carbonized seed	GX17420	10,655±285	(Roosevelt et al. 1996)
			carbonized seed	GX17422	10,305±275	(Roosevelt et al. 1996)
	Unit 7 (Late Period)		carbonized seed	B75001CAMS	10,230±60	(Roosevelt et al. 1996)
	Unit 7 (Initial Period)		carbonized seed	B75002CAMS	10,260±60	(Roosevelt et al. 1996)
			charred wood	B75007CAMS	10,290±80	(Roosevelt et al. 1996)
			charred wood	B75004CAMS	10,300±60	(Roosevelt et al. 1996)
			carbonized seed	B75006CAMS	10,320±70	(Roosevelt et al. 1996)
			carbonized seed	B75003CAMS	10,390±70	(Roosevelt et al. 1996)
			charred wood	B75005CAMS	10,450±60	(Roosevelt et al. 1996)

(continues)

Unit 9 (Early Period)	carbonized seed	B75008CAMS	10,280±70	(Roosevelt et al. 1996)
	carbonized seed	B75009CAMS	10,330±60	(Roosevelt et al. 1996)
	charred wood	GX19525CAMS	10,370±70	(Roosevelt et al. 1996)
	humate from same	GX19525CAMS	10,330±70	(Roosevelt et al. 1996)
	carbonized seed	GX19524CAMS	10,380±60	(Roosevelt et al. 1996)
	humate from same	GX19524CAMS	10,510±60	(Roosevelt et al. 1996)
	charred wood	GX19526CAMS	10,480±70	(Roosevelt et al. 1996)
	humate from same	GX19525CAMS	10,570±70	(Roosevelt et al. 1996)
	charred wood	GX19530CAMS	10,260±70	(Roosevelt et al. 1996)
	humate from same	GX19530CAMS	10,210±60	(Roosevelt et al. 1996)
	carbonized seed	GX19529CAMS	10,420±70	(Roosevelt et al. 1996)
	humate from same	GX19529CAMS	10,250±70	(Roosevelt et al. 1996)
	carbonized seed	GX19531CAMS	10,370±60	(Roosevelt et al. 1996)
	humate from same	GX19531CAMS	10,180±60	(Roosevelt et al. 1996)
Unit 10 (Early Period)	carbonized seed	GX19532CAMS	10,110±60	(Roosevelt et al. 1996)
	humate from same	GX19532CAMS	10,190±60	(Roosevelt et al. 1996)

Site	Excavation Provenience	Material Dated	Sample	Years B.P.	Source
		humate from seed	GX19534CAMS	10,190±50	(Roosevelt et al. 1996)
		carbonized seed	GX19527CAMS	10,290±70	(Roosevelt et al. 1996)
		humate from same	GX19527CAMS	10,330±70	(Roosevelt et al. 1996)
		carbonized seed	GX19528CAMS	10,290±70	(Roosevelt et al. 1996)
		humate from same	GX19528CAMS	10,120±70	(Roosevelt et al. 1996)
		charred wood	GX19535CAMS	10,310±70	(Roosevelt et al. 1996)
		humate from same	GX19535CAMS	10,210±70	(Roosevelt et al. 1996)
		charred wood	GX19533CAMS	10,360±60	(Roosevelt et al. 1996)
		humate from same	GX1953325CAMS	10,220±60	(Roosevelt et al. 1996)
	Unit 10 (Initial Period)	carbonized seed	GX19537CAMS	10,250±70	(Roosevelt et al. 1996)
		humate from same	GX19537CAMS	10,470±70	(Roosevelt et al. 1996)
		humate from carb. seed	GX19536CAMS	10,350±70	(Roosevelt et al. 1996)
		carbonized seed	GX19538CAMS	10,410±60	(Roosevelt et al. 1996)
		humate from same	GX19538CAMS	10,390±70	(Roosevelt et al. 1996)
	Unit 11 (Late Period)	carbonized seed	B76955CAMS	10,210±60	(Roosevelt et al. 1996)
		carbonized wood	B76954CAMS	10,360±50	(Roosevelt et al. 1996)

Unit 11 (Early Period)	carbonized seed	GX19523CAMS	10,450±60	(Roosevelt et al. 1996)
	humate from same	GX19523CAMS	10,000±60	(Roosevelt et al. 1996)
	charred wood	GX19540CAMS	10,390±60	(Roosevelt et al. 1996)
	humate from same	GX19540CAMS	10,230±60	(Roosevelt et al. 1996)
	charred wood	GX19539CAMS	10,470±70	(Roosevelt et al. 1996)
	humate from same	GX19539CAMS	10,000±60	(Roosevelt et al. 1996)
	humate from seed	GX19541CAMS	10,490±80	(Roosevelt et al. 1996)
Pernambuco				
Brejo de Madre de Deus 3		SI-6296	8,495±75	(Kipnis 1998)
		SI-6298	11,060±90	(Kipnis 1998)
Cha do Caboclo		MC-1042	8,100±135	(Kipnis 1998)
		MC-1056	9,250±160	(Kipnis 1998)
		MC-1046	11,000±250	(Kipnis 1998)
Pedra do Caboclo		MC-1003	8,400±200	(Kipnis 1998)
Piaui				
Baixao do Perna I		GIF-5414	9,540±170	(Parenti 1996)
Alice Böer			14,200±1150	(Bryan and Beltrão 1978)

(continues)

313

Site	Excavation Provenience	Material Dated	Sample	Years B.P.	Source
Caldeirao de Rodriguez			GIF-5650	9,480±170	(Guidón 1986:168)
			GIF-5406	17,000±400	(Guidón 1986:168)
Sitio de Meio			BETA-47494	8,800±60	(Kipnis 1998)
			BETA-47493	8,960±70	(Kipnis 1998)
			BETA-65856	9,200±60	(Kipnis 1998)
			GIF-4628	12,200±600	(Kipnis 1998)
			GIF-5406	18,600±600	(Kipnis 1998)
Toca da Baixa do Cipu			GIF-6957	8,700±90	(Kipnis 1998)
Toca da Barra Antoniao			GIF-8712	9,670±140	(Kipnis 1998)
Toca da Boa Vista I			GIF-5864	9,160±160	(Kipnis 1998)
			BETA-32972	9,650±100	(Kipnis 1998)
			GIF-4629	9,730±140	(Kipnis 1998)
			BETA-32971	10,530±110	(Kipnis 1998)
			MC-2481	9,700±120	(Kipnis 1998)
Toca da Boa Vista II			MC-2513	9,850±120	(Kipnis 1998)
Toca de Cima do Pilão			BETA-27345	10,390±80	(Kipnis 1998)
Toca do Bojo I			GIF-4626	8,050±170	(Kipnis 1998)
			GIF-170	8,080±170	(Kipnis 1998)
			GIF-4925	9,080±170	(Kipnis 1998)
			GIF-4624	9,700±120	(Kipnis 1998)
			GIF-4627	9,700±200	(Kipnis 1998)

(continues)

Site	Sample	Date	Reference
Toca do Paraguaio	MC-2510	8,600±100	(Kipnis 1998)
	MC-2480	8,670±120	(Kipnis 1998)
	MC-2511	8,780±120	(Kipnis 1998)
Pedra Furada ST-I-East	GIF-8108	6,150±60	(Parenti 1996)
ST-V-West 78	GIF-5863	26,160±130	(Parenti 1996)
ST 2-I-East	GIF-8390	27,220±80	(Parenti 1996)
ST 2-III-West 82	GIF-7242	7,230±80	(Parenti 1996)
ST 2-X-West 78	GIF-4928	7,640±160	(Parenti 1996)
ST 2-II-West 82	GIF-6161	7,750±80	(Parenti 1996)
ST 1-XII-West 78	GIF-4625	8,050±170	(Parenti 1996)
	GIF-6157	8,080±120	(Parenti 1996)
	GIF-6436	8,170±80	(Parenti 1996)
ST 1-VII-West 82	GIF-6162	8,450±80	(Parenti 1996)
ST 1-2(1)-East	GIF-8350	8,600±60	(Parenti 1996)
ST 1-VII-West 82	FZ 436	9,506±135-132	(Parenti 1996)
ST 1-4(1-2)-East	GIF-8351	9,800±60	(Parenti 1996)
ST 1-VII-West 82	GIF-8983	10,040±80	(Parenti 1996)
ST 1-4(3)-East	GIF-8352	10,050±80	(Parenti 1996)
ST 1-Test 2 (80)	GIF-5862	10,400±180	(Parenti 1996)
	FZ 430	10,454±114	(Parenti 1996)
	BETA-22859	10,540±350	(Parenti 1996)
PF 3-XVIII-West82	GIF-6159	14,300±210	(Parenti 1996)
PF 3-178-192-West80	GIF-5397	17,000±400	(Parenti 1996)
PF 3—1-West 87	BETA-22086	18,310±190	(Parenti 1996)

Site	Excavation Provenience	Material Dated	Sample	Years B.P.	Source
	PF 3-5(3)-East		GIF-8125	19,300±200	(Parenti 1996)
	PF 3-XVII-West 82		GIF-6160	21,400±400	(Parenti 1996)
	PF 2-203-210-West 80		GIF-5398	25,000	(Parenti 1996)
	PF 2-192-203-West 80		GIF-5648	25,000	(Parenti 1996)
	PF 2-XX-West 82		GIF-6147	25,200±320	(Parenti 1996)
	PF 2-5(3)-East		GIF-8353	25,600±450	(Parenti 1996)
	PF 2-XIX-West 82		GIF-5963	26,300±600	(Parenti 1996)
	PF 2-XIX-West 83		GIF-6309	26,300±800	(Parenti 1996)
	PF 2-XIX-West 82		GIF-5962	26,400±500	(Parenti 1996)
	PF 2-XIX-West 83		GIF-6308	27,000±800	(Parenti 1996)
	PF 2-7(8)-East		GIF-8354	29,740±650	(Parenti 1996)
	PF 2-XIX(II)-West 84		GIF-6651	29,860±650	(Parenti 1996)
	PF 2-XIX-West 82		GIF-6041	31,500±950	(Parenti 1996)
	PF 2-XXI-West 84		GIF-6652	31,700±830	(Parenti 1996)
	PF 2-—2-West 87		BETA-22085	31,860±560	(Parenti 1996)
	PF 2-XXIII(I)-West 84		GIF-6653	32,160±1000	(Parenti 1996)
	PF 1-13(4)-West 88		GIF-9018	35,000	(Parenti 1996)
	PF 1-—3-West 87		BETA-22858	39,200>	(Parenti 1996)
	PF 1-14(2)-West		GIF-A 80357	39,500± 1600	(Parenti 1996)
	PF 1-—3-West 87		GIF-7619	40,800±4420-1850	(Parenti 1996)
	PF 1-13(2)-East		GIF-8355	41,000±3000-2200	(Parenti 1996)
	PF 1-—4-West 87		GIF-7681	41,500±4200-3100	(Parenti 1996)
	PF 1-14(1)-West		GIF-A 889097	42,400± 2600	(Parenti 1996)
	PF 1-13(1)-East		GIF-A 89354	42,600>	(Parenti 1996)

	PF 1-13(1)-East		GIF-9020	44,800±1400	(Parenti 1996)
	PF 1-13(1)-East		GIF-9021	45,000	(Parenti 1996)
	PF 1-9(8)-Tr.6		GIF-A 89098	47,000>	(Parenti 1996)
	PF 1-14(1)-total East		GIF-A 89265	48,000>	(Parenti 1996)
	PF 1-13(1)-East		GIF-9019	50,000	(Parenti 1996)
Toca Sitio do Meio			GIF-5403	12,330±230	(Guidon 1986:168)
			GIF-4628	12,200±60	(Guidon 1986:168)
			GIF-4927	13,900±300	(Guidon 1986:168)
Toca da Esperanza	Layer I	carbonate crust	GIF-7575	22,000±500	(Kipnis 1998)
	Layer II	breccia		27,0000	(Kipnis 1998)
	Layer IV	breccia		30,0000	(Kipnis 1998)
			GIF-86.1	295,000±780	(Beltrao et al. 1987:29)
			GIF-86.2	270,000±130	(Beltrao et al. 1987:29)
			LA-87.20	258,000±84	(Beltrao et al. 1987:29)
			MP-87-140.20	291,000±84	(Beltrao et al. 1987:29)
			LA-87.36	218,000±61	(Beltrao et al. 1987:29)
			MP-87-141.36	204,000±34	(Beltrao et al. 1987:29)
Rio Grande do Sul					
RS-I-50			SI-801	12,770±220	(Miller 1987:41)
RS-Q-2			SI-2351	12,690±100	(Miller 1987:41)
RS-I-68			SI3750	11,555±230	(Miller 1987:41)
RS-I-69			SI-2630	10,985±100	(Miller 1987:41)
RS-I-69			N-2523	10,800±150	(Miller 1987:41)
RS-I-69			N-2521	10,400±110	(Miller 1987:41)

(continues)

Site	Excavation Provenience	Material Dated	Sample	Years B.P.	Source
RS-I-66			SI-2622	10,810±275	(Miller 1987:41)
RS-I-98			SI-3752	10,810±275	(Miller 1987:41)
RS-IJ-67			SI-2637	9,595±175	(Miller 1987:41)
RS-I-72			SI-2634	9,450±115	(Miller 1987:41)
RS-I-70			SI-2632	9,120±340	(Miller 1987:41)
RS-IJ-67			SI-2636	8,585±115	(Miller 1987:41)
Pampa Patagonia					
Argentina					
Arroyo Feo	Level 11		CSIC-514	9,410±70	(Gradin et al. 1979)
			CSIC-396	9,330±80	(Gradin et al. 1979)
Arroyo Seco Sitio 2	Inferior Component Unit Y	Toxodon platesnis	AA-7965AMS	11,590±90	(Politis 1996:164)
		Equus amerhippus	AA-7964AMS	11,250±100	(Politis 1996:164)
		Glossoterium robustus	AA-9049AMS	10,500±90	(Politis 1996:164)
		Equus amerhippus	TO-1504AMS	8,890±90	(Politis 1996:164)
		Megatherium americanun	LP-53	8,390±240	(Politis 1996:164)
		Megatherium americanun	TO-1506AMS	7,320±50	(Politis 1996:164)
Cerro Casa de Piedra 7				8,300±115	
				9,730±110	
Cerro El Sombrero			AA-4765	10,725±90	(Flegenheimer and Zárate 1997)

Site	Component	Lab No.	Date	Reference
Cerro La China		AA-4766	10,270±85	(Flegenheimer and Zárate 1997)
		AA-4767	10,675±110	(Flegenheimer and Zárate 1997)
		AA-5220	10,480±70	(Flegenheimer and Zárate 1997)
		I-12741	10,730±150	(Flegenheimer and Zárate 1997)
		AA-1327	10,790±120	(Flegenheimer and Zárate 1997)
		AA-8952	10,745±75	(Flegenheimer and Zárate 1997)
		AA-8953	10,804±75	(Flegenheimer and Zárate 1997)
		AA-8954	10,525±75	(Flegenheimer and Zárate 1997)
Cerro La China		AA-8955	11,150±135	(Flegenheimer and Zárate 1997)
		AA-8956	10,560±75	(Flegenheimer and Zárate 1997)
Cerro La China		AA-1328	10,610±180	(Flegenheimer and Zárate 1997)
La Moderna	Lower Component	BETA-7824	6,550±160	(Politis 1996:160)
	Doedicurus clavicaudatus	TO-1507AMS	12,350±370	(Politis 1996:160)
		TO-1507-1AMS	7,010±100	(Politis 1996:160)
		TO-1507-2AMS	7,510±370	(Politis 1996:160)
		TO-2610AMS	7,460±80	(Politis 1996:160)
Cerro Tres Tetas			11,560±140	
Cueva de las Manos	AF 1 Layer 11	CSIC-514	9,410±70	(Gradin et al. 1987:120)
	ARP 1 Layer 6	CSIC-396	9,930±80	(Gradin et al. 1987:120)
		CSIC-138	9,320±90	(Gradin et al. 1987:120)
		CSIC-385	9,300±90	(Gradin et al. 1987:120)

(continues)

319

Site	Excavation Provenience	Material Dated	Sample	Years B.P.	Source
Cueva Tixi		charcoal	AA-12130	10,375±90	(Mazzanti 1997:58)
		charcoal	AA-12131	10,045±95	(Mazzanti 1997:58)
Cueva Tres Arroyos		camelid bones		11,880±250	(Massone et al. 1998)
		hearth sediment	BETA-101023AMS	10,600±90	(Massone et al. 1998)
		hearth sediment	BETA-113171AMS	10,580±50	(Massone et al. 1998)
		mammal bones		10,280±110	(Massone et al. 1998)
Epullán Grande		charcoal	LP-213	9,970±100	(Crivelli Montero et al. 1996)
Los Toldos	Layer 11B	charcoal	(FRA-98)	12,600±600	(Cardich 1978:296)
Paso Otero		bone	AA-19291	10,190±120	(Martínez 1997)
Piedra Museo				9,710±105	(Miotti 1992)
		charcoal	AA-20125	12,890±90	(Miotti and Cattáneo 1997)
Tres Arroyos				10,420±100	(Massone 1983)
				10,280±110	(Massone 1983)
				11,880±250	
Southern Chile					
Cueva del Medio		charcoal		9,595±115	(Nami 1987:41)
				10,310±70	(Nami 1987:41)
				10,550±120	(Nami 1987:41)
				12,390±180	(Nami 1987:41)

Cueva Lago Sofía 1				11,570±60	
Fell's Cave	Layer 18		I-5146	10,080±160	(Bird 1938, 1946)
	Layer 19		W-915	10,720±300	(Bird 1938, 1946)
	First occup.		I-3988	11,000±170	(Bird 1938, 1946)
	Level 17		I-5145	9,030±230	(Bird 1938, 1946)
Uruguay					
El Tigre		charcoal		11,240±60	(Hilbert 1991)

GLOSSARY

ARCHAEOLOGICAL CULTURE: The largest grouping of all artifact categories assumed to represent the total of human activities carried out by an ancient culture.

ARCHAIC PERIOD: A New World chronological period characterized by permanent to semipermanent settlements and the transition from a hunting and gathering to an agricultural economy.

ARTIFACT: A discrete and portable object whose physical features result totally or in part from human activity; artifacts are ceramics, projectile points, scrapers, and other tools.

ASSEMBLAGE: All of the artifacts from a given site.

ASSOCIATION: Occurrence of an item of archaeological data adjacent to another item and in one or the same geological layer or context.

ATTRIBUTE: The minimum trait used as a criterion for grouping artifacts into classes; includes stylistic, form, and technological attributes.

BERINGIA: Land connection between Siberia and Alaska created by drops in sea level during the most recent glacial period.

BIFACE: A flat stone tool made by chipping both sides of a core until there is a sharp edge produced along one or more sides.

BLADE: A long, thin, and parallel-sided flake usually made from a cylindrical core (see Lithic).

BURIN: A chisel-edge implement used for working bone, wood, and other materials.

CARBON 14 DATING: A method of chronometric dating based on the decay of carbon 14.

CHIPPED STONE ARTIFACTS: A class of stone artifacts produced by fracturing flakes from a core.

CLOVIS SPEARPOINT: The characteristic fluted point found in North America. The point is made by chipping both sides of a long blade to form a sharp point. Most Clovis points range between 6 and 20 centimeters in length.

COARSE-SCALED: Major environmental differences such as savannas, forests, and deserts.

COMPLEX SOCIETIES: Populations that developed a lifeway more advanced than hunters and gatherers, such as sedentary agricultural societies and urban state societies.

CONVERGENCE: A phenomenon wherein two cultural traits independently developed similar features. These features are usually stylistically similar but functionally different.

CORE: A stone tool artifact from which flakes are removed; it is used as a tool or a blank from which other tools are made. All tools are derived from cores. Once a core has been reduced in size and suitable flakes can no longer be removed, it is discarded.

CULTURE: A particular way humans discover, invent, and develop in order to survive. Culture is the human strategy of adaptation. A specific lifeway may be defined by diagnostic traits found in a defined territory such as the Clovis and other cultures.

CULTURAL ADAPTATION: The total adjustments of a human society to its social and natural environments.

CULTURAL DRIFT: Gradual cultural change due to the imperfect transmission of information between generations.

CULTURAL ECOLOGY: The study of the dynamic interaction between human society and its environment, viewing culture as the primary adaptive mechanism to the relationship.

CULTURAL EVOLUTION: The theory that human societies change via a process analogous to the evolution of biological species.

CULTURAL INVENTION: The origin of new cultural forms within a society, by either accident or design.

CULTURAL TRADITION: The most dominate cultural manifestation of a region, often characterized by the presence of a particular type of projectile point or unifacial tool.

CURATED TECHNOLOGY: Stone tools that are resharpened and kept in the tool inventory because they are specially made or made of an imported high quality raw material. Usually not discarded until they have been completely reused and expended.

DEBITAGE: The debris resulting from the manufacturing of chipped stone artifacts that provides evidence for the reconstruction of late Pleistocene manufacturing behavior.

DEPOSITION OR DISPOSAL: The last stage of human behavior, in which artifacts are discarded or thrown away.

DEPOSITS: The geological stratum, level, or layer containing archeological materials in a site.

DIAGNOSTIC TRAIT: A specific trait or feature characteristic of a single tool type or culture, such as the fluted channel on the Clovis points.

DIFFUSION: Transmission of ideas from one culture to another.

DIRECT PERCUSSION: A technique used for the manufacture of chipped stone artifacts in which flakes are produced by striking a core with a hammerstone or striking a core against a fixed stone or anvil.

DOMESTICATION: Adaptations made by animal and plant species to the cultural environment as a result of human interference in reproductive or other behavior; it is often detectable as specific physical changes in faunal or floral organisms.

ECOLOGICAL NICHE: The specific microhabitat in which a particular population lives and the way the population exploits that microhabitat.

ETHNOARCHAEOLOGY: Ethnographic studies designed to aid archaeological interpretation, such as the description of behavioral processes, especially the ways material items enter the archaeological record after disposal.

ETHNOGRAPHY: The study of historical and present-day indigenous peoples.

EXOTIC: Not native to the region where an artifact is found.

EXPEDIENT TECHNOLOGY: An all-purpose tool—a sort of Swiss Army knife, so to speak. This type of technology usually is a uniface and usually, once used, it is thrown away.

FEATURE: A nonportable artifact, not recoverable from its layer without destroying its integrity.

FINE-SCALED: Minor environmental differences such as the location and quantity of food resources in such particular habitats as deserts, forests, and coastlines.

FLAKE: A smaller chip of stone knocked from a larger stone core. A stone artifact detached from a core, either as debitage or as a tool. Flakes range between 2 and 25 centimeters or more depending on the size of the core from which they were struck.

FLOTATION: This technique agitates buried cultural deposits in water to separate, float, and collect small plant debris not normally seen by excavators.

FLUTING: The fluted trait applies to any longitudinally-oriented flake scar or channel in the base of a spearpoint.

FORAGING: Subsisting by hunting, gathering, and fishing.

FOUNDING POPULATION: The first (usually small) population colonizing a new territory and subsequently increasing in numbers and expanding into new areas.

FUNCTION: The purpose or use of a component or artifact of a culture. Used to reconstruct activities of past societies.

GENE FLOW: The movement of genes from one population to another, or from one part of a population to another, as a result of interbreeding.

GENETIC VARIATION: Physical differences between individuals that result from inheriting different genes from their parents.

GRINDING AND PECKING TECHNOLOGY: Making an artifact by tapping or pecking the surface to loosen the raw material and then grinding it to a desired shape, for instance, a grinding stone for preparing plant food.

GROUND SURVEY: A surface survey technique using direct observation to gather archaeological data present on the ground surface, specifically mapping and surface collection.

HOLOCENE PERIOD: The geological period after the Pleistocene period when the ice sheets had melted and more modern climates were established. Dates from about 14,000 to 11,000 years ago to the present day.

HOMO SAPIENS: The species that appeared 200,000 to 300,000 years ago; includes Neanderthals and anatomically modern humans.

ICE AGE: See the Pleistocene period.

IMBRICATION: Overlapping cultural or environmental zones.

INDUSTRY: A gross artifact category defined by shared material and technology, such as chipped stone industry.

LANCEOLATE: A long, usually symmetrically-shaped blade or spearpoint chipped on both sides.

LAW OF SUPERPOSITION: Geological layers are deposited sequentially with the oldest laid down first. If a stratigraphic cut in a site is intact, the youngest to oldest layers will be represented from the top to the bottom, respectively.

LIMACE: These are elongated, unifacial blades with steeply worked edges. The limace is made of parallel-sided blades from a prepared core, a specialized development of the unidirectional type of core. One good core of this kind, once prepared, can yield many parallel-sided blades with little or no preparation. In this respect, it is an advance in technology—an advance of core technology aimed at obtaining one flake of a predetermined size.

LITHIC: Artifacts made from stone, including chipped stone and pecked and ground stone.

LIVING FLOOR: The level or layer in an archaeological site that represents what was once the surface of the land. All bones and artifacts remain in the position in which they were either placed or dropped.

LUNATES: Scrapers and other tools shaped like a half-moon.

MATRIX: The physical or geological medium that surrounds, holds, or supports archaeological material.

MIDDEN: An accumulation of debris, resulting from human disposal of material; it may be the result of one-time refuse disposal or long-term disposal resulting in stratification.

MIGRATION: Movement of human populations from one area to another, usually resulting in cultural contact.

MODEL: A theoretical scheme constructed to understand a specific set of data or phenomena; descriptive models deal with the form and structure of phenomena, whereas explanatory models seek underlying causes for phenomena.

MOLECULAR CLOCK: The idea that genetic change takes place at a constant rate and thus can be employed to measure the time that has passed since two species departed from a common ancestor.

PARADIGM: A conceptual or theoretical framework for a scientific discipline; a strategy for interpreting a research method, body of data, and goals.

PEBBLE TOOL: Any stone tool artifact made from a river or beach pebble. These tools are smaller than cobble stone tools and may range between 5 and 15 centimeters in size.

PERIOD: A broad and general chronological unit defined for a site or region, based on combined data such as defined complexes.

PHASE: An arbitrary chronological unit defined for data categories such as artifact industries and used in cultural historical interpretation.

PLEISTOCENE PERIOD: A geological period characterized by successive glacial advances and retreats; the period begins around 1.9 million years ago and ends around 13,000 to 11,500 years ago. Also known as the Ice Age.

PRESSURE FLAKING: A technique for manufacturing chipped stone artifacts, in which flakes or blades are produced by applying pressure against a core with a punch usually made of wood or bone.

PRIMARY CONTEXT: The condition where provenience, association, and matrix have not been disturbed since the original deposition of archaeological data.

PROJECTILE POINTS: A special kind of elongated and pointed biface usually thought to be utilized as spearpoints mounted on lances or as arrows to hunt animals. Projectile points may take several different forms—for example, a bipointed laurel leaf; a triangular form with a stem for hafting to a lance or arrow; or a lanceolate form with a flat or slightly concave base.

PROTO-ARCHAIC STAGE: A cultural stage that began at the end of the Pleistocene, characterized by the development of a generalized hunting and gathering economy exploiting a wide range of resources, including big game, in multiple environments. This stage is the predecessor to the broader and more diversified subsistence strategy of the later Holocene period.

PROVENIENCE: The three-dimensional location of archaeological data within or on the matrix at the time of discovery.

RADIOCARBON DATING: Dating of organic material based on the constant rate of decay of radioactive isotopes.

REGION: A geographically defined area containing a series of interrelated human communities sharing a single cultural and ecological system.

ROCKSHELTERS: Sites protected by an overhang of rock.

SAMPLE: A set of units selected from a population.

SAMPLE SIZE: The total number of sample units drawn from a sampling frame.

SAMPLING BIAS: A sample unit that represents only a portion of the total sampling frame but is used to characterize the entire frame.

SECONDARY CONTEXT: The condition where provenience, association, and matrix have been wholly or partially altered by transformational processes after original deposition of archaeological data.

SETTLEMENT PATTERN: The distribution of features and sites across the landscape.

SITE: A spatial clustering of archaeological data, comprising artifacts and features in any combinations. A location where artifacts are found.

SOCIAL SYSTEM: One of the three basic components of culture; the means by which human societies organize themselves and their interactions with other societies.

SOLUTREAN: An Upper Paleolithic cultural tradition that flourished only between 24,000 and 18,000 B.P. in southwest France and Spain. It is characterized by its laurel-leaf blades.

STRATA: The definable layers of archaeological matrix or features revealed by excavation.

STRATIFICATION: Multiple strata whose order of deposition reflects the law of superposition.

STRATIGRAPHY: The archaeological evaluation of the significance of stratification to determine the temporal sequence of data within stratified deposits by using both the law of superposition and context evaluation.

STYLISTIC ATTRIBUTES: Attributes defined by the surface characteristics of artifacts—color, texture, decoration, and so forth—leading to stylistic classification.

STYLISTIC TYPES: Artifact classes based on stylistic attributes.

SURFACE COLLECTION: The systematic gathering of exposed artifacts; one of two basic ground survey methods used in the surface survey of archaeological sites, the other being mapping.

SURFACE SURVEY: A method of data acquisition in which data are gathered and evaluated from the surface of archaeological sites, usually by

the mapping of features and the surface collection of artifacts and features.

SYSTEM: An organization that functions through the interdependence of its parts.

TAPHONOMY: The study of the transformational processes of faunal and floral materials after the death of the original organisms.

TECHNOLOGICAL ATTRIBUTES: Attributes composed of raw material characteristics and those resulting from manufacturing methods; these attributes lead to technological classifications.

TECHNOLOGICAL TYPES: Artifact classes based on technological attributes.

TOOL: An artifact that appears to have been created for a specific purpose.

TOOLKIT: An collection of artifacts utilized to accomplish a specific task, such as a knives, scrapers, and drills to process the meat and hide of a slayed animal.

TRADITION: Cultural continuity through time.

TRANSFORMATIONAL PROCESSES: Conditions and events that affect archaeological data from the time of deposition to the time of recovery in a site.

TRANSHUMANCE: Seasonal movement of hunters and gatherers between different environmental zones. This pattern is usually associated with groups residing in mountainous areas.

TYPE: A class of data defined by a consistent clustering of attributes.

YARDANG: Older geological surfaces that have not been eroded by water and wind. They form mesa-like features on the present-day landscape.

NOTES

Preface

1. T. D. Dillehay, *Monte Verde: A Late Pleistocene Settlement in Chile*, vol. 1, *The Paleoenvironmental Context* (Washington, D.C.: Smithsonian Institution Press, 1989); *Monte Verde: A Late Pleistocene Settlement in Chile*, vol. 2, *The Archaeological Context* (Washington, D.C.: Smithsonian Institution Press, 1997).

Chapter 1

1. B. Fagan, *The Great Journey: The Peopling of Ancient America* (New York: Thames and Hudson, 1989); eds. T. D. Dillehay and D. Meltzer, *The First Americans: Search and Research* (Boca Raton, Fla.: CRS Press, 1991).

2. J. Adovasio and D. R. Pedler, "Monte Verde and the Antiquity of Humankind in the Americas," *Antiquity* 71 (1997):573–580; D. Meltzer, "Monte Verde and the Pleistocene Peopling of the Americas," *Science* 276 (1997):754–755; D. Meltzer, D. K. Grayson, G. Ardila, A. W. Barker, D. F. Dincauze, C. V. Haynes, F. Mena, L. Núñez, and D. J. Stanford, "On the Pleistocene Antiquity of Monte Verde, Chile," *American Antiquity* 62(1997):659–663.

3. R. Owen, "The Americas: The Case Against Ice-Age Human Population," in *The Origins of Modern Humans*, ed. F. H. Smith and F. Spencer (New York: Alan R. Liss, 1984), pp. 517–563.

4. C. V. Haynes, "The Earliest Americans," *Science* 166 (1969):709–715.

5. J. Nichols, *Linguistic Diversity and the Peopling of the Americas* (Berkeley: University of California Press, 1995).

6. N. O. Bianchi, G. Baillet, and C. M. Bravi, "Peopling of the Americas As Inferred Through the Analysis of Mitochondrial DNA," *Brazilian Journal of*

Genetics 18, no. 4 (1995):661–668; S. Callegari-Jacques, F. Salzano, T. A. Weimer, M. H. Hutz, F. L. Black, S. E. Santos, J. F. Guerrero, M. A. Mestriner, and J. P. Pandey, "Further Blood Genetic Studies on Amazonian Diversity-Data from Four Indian Groups," *Annals of Human Biology* 21 (1994):465–481; R. L. Cann, "MtDNA and Native Americans: A Southern Perspective," *American Journal of Human Genetics* 55 (1994):256–258; A. Torroni, T. Shurr, M. Cabell, M. Brown, J. Neel, M. Larsen, D. Smith, C. Vullo, and C. Wallace, "Asian Affinities and Continental Radiations of Four Founding Native America mtDNAs," *American Journal of Human Genetics* 53 (1993):563–590.

7. T. D. Dillehay, G. Ardila, G. Politis, and M. C. Beltrão, "Earliest Hunters and Gatherers of South America," *Journal of World Prehistory* 6 (1992):145–204.

8. Ibid.

9. D. Meltzer and T. D. Dillehay, "The Search for the Earliest Americans," *Archaeology* 52, no. 1 (1999):60–61; T. D. Dillehay, "The Late Pleistocene Cultures of South America," *Evolutionary Anthropology* 7 (1999):206–217.

10. Dillehay et al., "Earliest Hunters and Gatherers of South America."

11. R. Lewin, *The Origin of Modern Humans* (New York: Scientific American Library, 1998); P. S. Martin, "The Discovery of America," *Science* 179 (1973):969–974.

12. B. Fagan, *People of the Earth: An Introduction to World Prehistory* (New York: Longman, 1998).

13. R. Klein, *Ice-Age Hunters of the Ukraine* (Chicago: University of Chicago Press, 1973).

Chapter 2

1. D. F. Dincauze, "An Archaeological Evaluation of the Case for Pre-Clovis Occupations," *Advances in World Archaeology* 3 (1984):275–323; B. Fagan, *The Great Journey: The Peopling of Ancient America* (New York: Thames and Hudson, 1989); D. Meltzer, *Search for the First Americans* (New York: St. Remy Press, 1993); "On 'Paradigms' and 'Paradigm Bias' in Controversies Over Human Antiquity in America," in *The First Americans: Search and Research*, ed. T. D. Dillehay and D. Meltzer (Boca Raton, Fla.: CRS Press, 1991), pp. 13–49.

2. A. L. Bryan, "The Fluted Point Tradition in the Americas—One of Several Adaptations to Late Pleistocene Environments," in *Clovis: Origins and*

Adaptations, ed. R. Bonnischen and K. Turnmire (Corvallis: Center for the Study of the First Americans, University of Maine, 1991), pp. 15–33; "An Overview of Paleo-American Prehistory from a Circum-Pacific Perspective," in *Early Man in America from a Circum-Pacific Perspective*, ed. A. L. Bryan (Edmonton: Department of Anthropology, University of Alberta, 1978), p. 1.

3. V. Holliday, *Paleoindian Geoarchaeology of the Southern High Plains* (Austin: University of Texas Press, 1997); M. R. Waters and D. D. Kuehn, "The Geoarchaeology of Place: The Effect of Geological Processes on the Preservation and Interpretation of the Archaeological Record," *American Antiquity* 61 (1996):483–498.

4. K. Gordon, "Man the Scavenger," in *Anthropology Explored: The Best of Smithsonian AnthroNews*, ed. R. Seling and M. London (Washington, D.C.: Smithsonian Institution Press, 1998), pp. 66–74.

5. T. F. Lynch, "The Paleo-Indians," in *Ancient South Americans*, ed. J. D. Jennings (New York: W. H. Freeman and Company, 1983), pp. 87–137.

6. B. G. Trigger, *A History of Archaeological Thought* (New York: Cambridge University Press, 1989).

7. J. Bird, "Antiquity and Migrations of the Early Inhabitants of Patagonia," *The Geographical Review* 1, no. 6 (1938):250–275.

8. A. Krieger, "Early Man in the New World," in *Prehistoric Man in the New World*, ed. J. Jennings and E. Norbeck (Chicago: University of Chicago Press, 1964), pp. 28–81.

9. D. Meltzer, *Search for the First Americans* (New York: St. Remy Press, 1993).

10. J. Hyslop, ed., *Travels and Archaeology in South Chile* (Iowa City: University of Iowa Press, 1988).

11. P. S. Martin, "Prehistoric Overkill," in *Pleistocene Extinctions: The Search for a Cause*, ed. P. S. Martin and H. E. Wright (New Haven: Yale University Press, 1967), pp. 75–120.

12. T. F. Lynch, "The Paleo-Indians," in *Ancient South Americans*, ed. J. D. Jennings (New York: W. H. Freeman and Company, 1983), pp. 87–137; "Glacial-Age Man in South America: A Critical Review," *American Antiquity* 55 (1990):12–36.

13. T. F. Lynch and K. Kennedy, "Early Human Cultural and Skeletal Remains from Guitarrero Cave, Northern Peru," *Science* 169 (1970):1307–1309.

14. G. S. Vescelius, "Early and/or Not-So-Early Man in Peru: The Case of Guitarrero Cave, Part I," *Quarterly Review of Archaeology* 2, no. 1–2

(1981):11–15; "Early and/or Not-So-Early Man in Peru: The Case of Guitarrero Cave, Part II," *Quarterly Review of Archaeology* 2, no. 1–2 (1981):18–19.

15. A. L. Bryan, ed., *Early Man in America from a Circum-Pacific Perspective* (Edmonton: Department of Anthropology, University of Alberta, 1978); Bryan, "An Overview of Paleo-American Prehistory from a Circum-Pacific Perspective."

16. D. Meltzer, "Monte Verde and the Pleistocene Peopling of the Americas," *Science* 276 (1997):754–755. D. Meltzer, D. K. Grayson, G. Ardila, A. W. Barker, D. F. Dincauze, C. V. Haynes, F. Mena, L. Núñez, and D. J. Stanford, "On the Pleistocene Antiquity of Monte Verde, Chile," *American Antiquity* 62 (1997):659–663.

Chapter 3

1. C. M. Clapperton, *Quaternary Geology and Geomorphology of South America* (Amsterdam: Elvesier, 1993).

2. J. C. Thouret, T. Van Der Hammen, B. Salomons, and E. Juvigne, "Paleoenvironmental Changes and Glacial Stages of the Last 50,000 Years in the Cordillera Central, Colombia," *Quaternary Research* 46 (1996):1–18; A. Ashworth and J. W. Hoganson, "The Magnitude and Rapidity of the Climate Change Marking the End of the Pleistocene in the Mid-Latitudes of South America," *Palaeogeography, Palaeoclimatology, and Palaeoecology* 101 (1993):263–270; L. G. Thompson, E. Mosley-Thompson, M. E. Davis, P. Lin, K. A. Henderson, J. Cole-Dai, J. F. Bolzan, K. Liu, "Late Glacial Stage and Holocene Tropical Ice Core Records from Huascaran, Perú," *Science* 269 (1995):46–48.

3. V. Rull, "Late Pleistocene and Holocene Climates of Venezuela," *Quaternary International* 31 (1996):85–94; T. Van der Hammen, "The Pleistocene Changes of Vegetation and Climate in Tropical South America," *Journal of Biogeography* 1 (1974):3–26; C. Ochsenius and R. Gruhn, *Taima-Taima: A Late Pleistocene Paleo-Indian Kill Site in Northernmost South America—Final Reports of 1976 Excavations* (Coro, Venezuela: Universidad de San Francisco de Miranda, 1979).

4. C. M. Clapperton, M. Hall, P. Mothes, M. Hole, J. W. Still, K. F. Helmens, P. Kuhry, and A. M. Gemmell, "A Younger Dryas Ice Cap in the Equatorial Andes," *Quaternary Research* 47 (1997):13–28; C. J. Heusser and N. J.

Shackleton, "Tropical Climate Variation on the Pacific Slopes of the Ecuadorian Andes Based on a 25,000-Year Pollen Record from Deep-Sea Sediment Core Tri 163–31b," *Quaternary Research* 42 (1984):222–225.

5. F. Sylvestre, M. Servant, S. Servant-Vildary, C. Causse, M. Fournier, and J. P. Ybert, "Lake-Level Chronology on the Southern Bolivian Altiplano (18°–23° S) During Late-Glacial Time and Early Holocene," *Quaternary Research* 51 (1999):54–66; M. Grosjen, M. A. Geyth, B. Messerli, and U. Schotterer, "Late-Glacial and Early Holocene Lake Sediments, Ground-Water Formation, and Climate in the Atacama Altiplano 22°–24° S," *Journal of Paleolimnology* 14 (1995):241–252.

6. C. J. Heusser, "Ice Age Vegetation and Climate of Subtropical Chile," *Palaeogeography, Palaeoclimatology, Palaeoecology* 80 (1990):107–127; J. H. Mercer, "Chilean Glacial Chronology 20,000 to 11,000 Carbon–14 Years Ago," *Science* 176 (1972):1118–1120; J. W. Hoganson and A. Ashworth, "Fossil Beetle Evidence for Climatic Change 18,000–10,000 Years B.P. in South-Central Chile," *Quaternary Research* 37 (1992):101–116; F. Lamy, D. Hebbein, and H. Wefer, "High-Resolution Marine Record of Climatic Change in Mid-Latitude Chile During the Last 28,000 Years Based on Terrigenous Sediment Parameters," *Quaternary Research* 51 (1999):83–93.

7. N. Hulton, D. Sugden, A. Payne, C. Clapperton, "Glacier Modeling and the Climate of Patagonia During the Last Glacial Maximum," *Quaternary Research* 42 (1994):1–19; A. R. Prieto, "Late Quaternary Vegetational and Climatic Changes in the Pampa Grassland of Argentina," *Quaternary Research* 45 (1996):73–88.

8. H. Behling, "Late Quaternary Vegetational and Climatic Changes in Brazil," *Review of Palaeobotany and Palynology* 99 (1998):143–156; E. M. Latrubesse and C. A. Rambonell, "A Climatic Model for Southeastern Amazonia in Late Glacial Times," *Quaternary International* 21 (1994):163–169; M. P. Ledru, "Late Quaternary Environmental and Climatic Changes in Central Brazil," *Quaternary Research* 39 (1993):90–98; M. P. Ledru, P. I. Soares, F. S. Braga, M. Fournier, L. Martin, K. Sugio, and B. Turcq, "The Last 50,000 Years in the Neotropics (Southern Brazil) Evolution of Vegetation and Climate," *Palaeogeography, Palaeoclimatology, Palaeoecology* 123 (1996):239–257; M. P. Ledru, P. Blanc, P. Charles-Dominique, M. Fournier, L. M. B. Riera, and C. Tardy, "Reconstitution palynologique de la foret guyanaise au cours des 3000 dernieres annes," *C. R. Academy of Sciences Paris* 324 (1997):469–476; J. Muller,

G. Irion, J. Núñez de Mello, and W. Junk, "Hydrological Changes of the Amazon During the Last Glacial-Interglacial Cycle in Central Amazonia (Brazil)," *Naturwissenchaften* 82 (1995):232–235; P. E. Oliveira, "A Palynological Record of Late Quaternary Vegetation and Climatic Change in Southeast Brazil" (Ph.D. diss., Ohio State University, 1992).

9. A. Ashworth and J. W. Hoganson, "The Magnitude and Rapidity of the Climate Change Marking the End of the Pleistocene in the Mid-Latitudes of South America," *Palaeogeography, Palaeoclimatology, and Palaeoecology* 101 (1993):263–270.

10. D. Hopkins, *American Beginnings: The Prehistory and Palaeoecology of Beringia* (Chicago: University of Chicago Press, 1996).

11. A. Oyuela-Calcedo, "Rock Versus Clay: Pottery Technology in San Jacinto-I, Colombia," in *The Emergence of Pottery: Technology and Innovation in Early Societies*, ed. W. Barnett and J. W. Hoopes (Washington, D.C.: Smithsonian Institution Press, 1995), pp. 132–144; A. Roosevelt, "Early Pottery in the Amazon: Twenty Years of Scholarly Obscurity," in *The Emergence of Pottery: Technology and Innovation in Early Societies*, ed. W. Barnett and J. W. Hoopes (Washington, D.C.: Smithsonian Institution Press, 1995), pp. 115–131.

12. T. F. Lynch, "The Paleo-Indians," in *Ancient South Americans*, ed. J. D. Jennings (New York: W. H. Freeman and Company, 1983), pp. 87–137.

13. C. Fairbanks, "A 17,000-Year Glacio-Eustatic Sea Level Record: Influence of Glacial Melting Rates on the Younger Dryas Event and Deep Ocean Circulation," *Nature* 347 (1989):637–647.

14. K. R. Fladmark, "Routes: Alternative Migration Corridors for Early Man in North America," *American Antiquity* 44, no. 1 (1979):183–194; R. Gruhn, "Linguistic Evidence in Support of the Coastal Route of Earliest Entry into the New World," *Man* 23 (1998):77–100; R. Gruhn, "Language Classification and Models of the Peopling of the Americas," in *Archaeology and Linguistics*, ed. P. McConvell and N. Evans (Melbourne: Oxford University Press, 1997), pp. 99–110.

15. P. S. Martin and H. E. Wright, eds., *Pleistocene Extinctions: The Search for a Cause* (New Haven: Yale University Press, 1967); P. Ward, *The Call of Distinct Mammoths* (New York: Basic Books, 1997).

16. V. Markgraf, "Paleoenvironmental Changes at the Northern Limit of the Subantarctic *Nothofagus* Forest, Lat. 37° S, Argentina," *Quaternary Research* 28 (1987):119–129.

17. L. Binford, "Willow Smoke and Dogs' Tails: Hunter-Gatherer Settlement Systems and Archaeological Site Formation," *American Antiquity* 45 (1980):1–17.

Chapter 4

1. T. F. Lynch, "The Paleo-Indians," in *Ancient South Americans*, ed. J. D. Jennings (New York: W. H. Freeman and Company, 1983), pp. 87–137; Juliet Morrow and Toby Morrow, "Geographic Variation in Fluted Projectile Points: A Hemisphere Perspective," *American Antiquity* 64:215–230.

2. A. L. Bryan, "Paleoenvironments and Cultural Diversity in Late Pleistocene South America," *Quaternary* 3 (1973):237–256; "An Overview of Paleo-American Prehistory from a Circum-Pacific Perspective," in *Early Man in America from a Circum-Pacific Perspective*, ed. A. L. Bryan (Edmonton: Department of Anthropology, University of Alberta, 1978), p. 1; "Paleoamerican Prehistory As Seen from South America," in *New Evidence for the Pleistocene Peopling of the Americas*, ed. A. L. Bryan (Orono: Center for the Study of Early Man, University of Maine, 1986), pp. 1–14.

3. T. D. Dillehay, "The Late Pleistocene Cultures of South America," *Evolutionary Anthropology* 7 (1999):206–217; T. D. Dillehay, G. Ardila, G. Politis, and M. C. Beltrão, "Earliest Hunters and Gatherers of South America," *Journal of World Prehistory* 6 (1992):145–204.

4. Bryan, "Paleoenvironments and Cultural Diversity in Late Pleistocene South America"; "An Overview of Paleo-American Prehistory from a Circum-Pacific Perspective"; "Paleoamerican Prehistory As Seen from South America."; R. Gruhn and A. L. Bryan, "A Reappraisal of the Edge-Trimmed Tool Tradition," in *Explorations in American Archaeology: Essays in Honor of Wesley R. Hurt*, ed. M. G. Plew (Lanham, Md.: University Press of America, 1998), pp. 37–53.

5. G. Politis, "Fishtail Projectile Points in the Southern Cone of South America," in *Clovis: Origins and Adaptations*, ed. R. Bonnischen and K. Turnmire (Corvallis: Center for the Study of the First Americans, University of Maine, 1991), pp. 287–302; L. Borrero and C. McEwan, "The Peopling of Patagonia: The First Human Occupation," in *Patagonia: Natural History, Prehistory, and Ethnography at the Uttermost End of the Earth*, ed. L. Borrero and C. McEwan (Princeton: Princeton University Press, 1997), pp. 32–45; G. Ardila

and G. Politis, "Nuevos datos para un viejo problema: Investigación y discusión en torno del poblamiento de América del Sur," *Revista del Museo del Oro* 23 (Bogotá, Colombia: 1989), 3–45; H. G. Nami, "Excavación arqueológica y hallazgo de una punta de proyectil 'Fell's I' en la Cueva del Medio, Seno de la Ultima Esperanza, Chile," *Anales del Instituto de la Patagonia* 16 (Punta Arenas, Chile: 1985–1986), 103–110; "Informe sobre la Segunda y Tercera Expedición a la Cueva del Medio: Perspectivas Arqueológicas para la Patagonia Austral," *Anales del Instituto de la Patagonia* 17 (Punta Arenas, Chile: 1987), 73–106; "New Dates for the Paleoindian Societies of South America," *Current Research in the Pleistocene* 6 (1989):18–19; personal communication.

6. Dillehay et al., "Earliest Hunters and Gatherers of South America."

7. J. Bird, "Antiquity and Migrations of the Early Inhabitants of Patagonia," *The Geographical Review* 1, no. 6 (1938):250–275.

8. Ardila and Politis, "Nuevos datos para un viejo problema"; Politis, "Fishtail Projectile Points in the Southern Cone of South America."

9. Lynch, "The Paleo-Indians."

10. W. J. Mayer-Oakes, "El Inga: A Paleo-Indian Site in the Sierra of Northern Ecuador," *Transactions of the American Philosophical Society* 76, no. 4 (1986):1–63; W. J. Mayer-Oakes, "Early Man Projectile Points and Lithic Technology in the Ecuadorian Sierra," in *New Evidence for the Pleistocene Peopling of the Americas,* ed. A. L. Bryan (Orono: Center for the Study of Early Man, University of Maine, 1986), pp. 133–156.

11. Politis, "Fishtail Projectile Points in the Southern Cone of South America"; see also, Lynch, "The Paleo-Indians."

12. A. Rex González, "Las Culturas Paleoindias o Paleolíticas Sudamericanas: resumen y problemática actual," *Actas y Memorias, 36° Congreso Internacional de Americanistas* 1 (1966):15–41.

13. A. L. Bryan, ed., *Early Man in America from a Circum-Pacific Perspective* (Edmonton: Department of Anthropology, University of Alberta, 1978); "Paleoamerican Prehistory As Seen from South America."

14. Bryan, *Early Man in America from a Circum-Pacific Perspective;* "Paleoamerican Prehistory As Seen from South America"; "Paleoenvironments and Cultural Diversity in Late Pleistocene South America"; Dillehay et al., "Earliest Hunters and Gatherers of South America"; Dillehay et al., "Earliest Hunters and Gatherers of South America"; Bryan, "Paleoamerican Prehistory As Seen from South America."

15. G. Willey, *An Introduction to American Archaeology*, vol. 2, *South America* (Englewood Cliffs, N.J.: Prentice Hall, 1971).

Chapter 5

1. G. Correal Urrego and T. Van der Hammen, *Investigaciones arqueológicas en los abrigos rocosos de Tequendama* (Biblioteca del Banco Popular, Premios de Arqueología, 1, 1977).

2. G. Correal Urrego, "Evidencias Culturales y Megafauna Pleistocénico en Colombia," in *Publicación de la Fundación de Investigaciones Arqueológicas Nacional 12* (Bogotá, Colombia: Banco de la República, 1981).

3. W. Hurt, T. van der Hammen, and G. Correal Urrego, "The El Abra Rockshelters, Sabana De Bogotá, Colombia," *Occasional Papers and Monographs of the Indiana University Museum* 2 (1977):21–23.

4. T. F. Lynch, "Glacial-Age Man in South America: A Critical Review," *American Antiquity* 55 (1990):12–36.

5. G. Correal Urrego, *Investigaciones Arqueológicas en Abrigos Rocosos de Nemocón y Sueva* (Bogotá, Colombia: Fundación de Investigaciones Arqueológicas Nacionales, 1979).

6. C. Gnecco, "Los árboles: un sitio en el valle de Popayán" (unpublished manuscript, Bogotá, Colombia: Fundación de Investigaciones Arqueológicas Nacionales, Banco de la República); H. Lleras and C. Gnecco, "Puntas de Proyectil en el Valle de Popayán," *Boletín del Museo del Oro* 17 (Bogotá, Colombia: 1986), 44–57.

7. G. Correal Urrego, "Apuntes sobre Medio Ambiente Pleistocénico y Hombre Prehistórico en Colombia," in *New Evidence for the Pleistocene Peopling of the Americas*, ed. A. L. Bryan (Orono: Center for the Study of Early Man, University of Maine, 1986), p. 115; "Exploraciones arqueológicas en la costa Atlántica y Valle del Magdalena: Sitios precerámicos y tipologías líticas," *Caldasia* 11 (Bogotá, Colombia: 1977), 33–129; G. Ardila and G. Politis, "Nuevos datos para un viejo problema: Investigación y discusión en torno del poblamiento de América del Sur," *Revista del Museo del Oro* 23 (Bogotá, Colombia: 1989), 3–45.

8. C. E. López Castellano, "Evidencias Paleoindias en el Valle Medio del Río Magdalena," *Boletín de Arqueología* 2 (1995):3–23 (Bogotá, Colombia: Fundación de Investigaciones Arqueológicas Nacionales).

9. C. Gnecco and S. Mora, "Late Pleistocene/Early Holocene Tropical Forest Occupations at San Isidro and Peña Roja, Colombia," *Antiquity* 71 (1997):683–690; Gnecco, "Los árboles: un sitio en el valle de Popayán."

10. G. Correal Urrego, "Evidencias de cazadores especializados en el sitio de la Bahía Gloria, Golfo de Uraba," *Revista de la Academia Colombiana de Ciencias Exactas, Físicas y Naturales* 15 (Bogotá, Colombia: 1983), 77–82.

11. J. Bird and R. Cooke, "The Occurrence in Panama of Two Types of Paleo-Indian Projectile Points," in *Early Man in America from a Circum-Pacific Perspective,* ed. A. L. Bryan (Edmonton: Department of Anthropology, University of Alberta, 1978), pp. 263–327.

12. J. M. Cruxent, "Stone and Bone Artifacts of Taima-Taima," in *Taima-Taima: A Late Pleistocene Paleo-Indian Kill Site in Northernmost South America. Final Report of 1976 Excavations,* ed. C. Ochsenius and R. Gruhn (Coro, Venezuela: Programa CIPICS, Monografías Científicas, Universidad Francisco de Miranda, 1979), pp. 77–89; see also Lynch, "Glacial-Age Man in South America."

13. A. L. Bryan and R. Gruhn, "The Radiocarbon Dates of Taima-Taima," in *Taima-Taima: A Late Pleistocene Paleo-Indian Kill Site in Northernmost South America. Final Report of 1976 Excavations,* ed. C. Ochsenius and R. Gruhn (Coro, Venezuela: Programa CIPICS, Monografías Científicas, Universidad Francisco de Miranda, 1979), pp. 53–58; C. Ochsenius, "Cuaternario en Venezuela," in *Introducción a la Paleoecología en el Norte de Sudamérica* (Coro, Venezuela: Cuadernos Falconianos, 1980); C. Ochsenius and R. Gruhn, eds., *Taima-Taima: A Late Pleistocene Paleo-Indian Kill Site in Northernmost South America. Final Reports of 1976 Excavations* (Coro, Venezuela: Programa CIPICS, Monografías Científicas, Universidad Francisco de Miranda, 1979).

14. R. Morlan, "Pre-Clovis People: Early Discoveries of America," in *Americans Before Columbus: Ice-Age Origins,* monograph no. 12, ed. R. C. Carlisle (Pittsburgh, Pa.: University of Pittsburgh, 1988).

15. D. Meltzer, *Search for the First Americans* (New York: St. Remy Press, 1993).

16. G. Ardila and G. Politis, "Nuevos datos para un viejo problema: Investigación y discusión en torno del poblamiento de América del Sur," *Revista del Museo del Oro,* 1989, 23:3–45. Bogotá, Colombia.

17. T. F. Lynch, "Glacial-Age Man in South America: A critical review," *American Antiquity,* 1990, 55:12–36.

18. Ardila and Politis, "Nuevos datos para un viejo problema."

19. Urrego, "Apuntes sobre Medio Ambiente Pleistocénico y Hombre Pre-histórico en Colombia"; G. Ardila and G. Politis, "Nuevos datos para un viejo problema."

20. W. J. Mayer-Oakes, "Early Man Projectile Points and Lithic Technology in the Ecuadorian Sierra," in *New Evidence for the Pleistocene Peopling of the Americas,* ed. A. L. Bryan (Orono: Center for the Study of Early Man, University of Maine, 1986), pp. 133–156; "El Inga: A Paleo-Indian Site in the Sierra of Northern Ecuador," *Transactions of the American Philosophical Society* 76, no. 4 (1986):1–63.

21. E. Salazar, "El Hombre Temprano en el Ecuador," in *Nueva Historia del Ecuador,* ed. E. Ayala (Quito, Ecuador: Editorial Grijalbo Ecuatoriana, 1988), pp. 73–128.

22. M. Temme, "Excavaciones en el sitio precerámico de Cubilán (Ecuador)," *Miscelánea Antropológica Ecuatoriana* 2 (Quito, Ecuador: 1982), 135–164.

23. T. F. Lynch and S. Pollock, "Chobshi Cave and Its Place in Andean and Ecuadorean Archaeology," *Anthropological Papers in Memory of Earl Swanson, Jr.* (Pocatello: Idaho Museum of Natural History, 1989).

24. K. Stothert, "The Preceramic Las Vegas Culture of Coastal Ecuador," *American Antiquity* 50 (1985):613–637; "Los cazadores y recolectores tempranos de la costa del Ecuador," paper presented at the 45° Congreso Internacional de Americanistas, Bogotá, Colombia, 1988.

25. J. B. Richardson III, "The Preceramic Sequence and the Pleistocene and Post-Pleistocene Climate of Northwest Perú," in *Variation in Anthropology,* ed. D. Lathrap and J. Douglas (Urbana: Illinois Archaeological Survey, 1973), pp. 199–211; "Early Man on the Peruvian North Coast, Early Maritime Exploitation, and the Pleistocene and Holocene Environment," in *Early Man in America from a Circum-Pacific Perspective,* ed. A. L. Bryan (Edmonton: Department of Anthropology, University of Alberta, 1978), pp. 274–289; "Modeling the Development of Sedentary Maritime Economies on the Coast of Perú: A Preliminary Statement," *Annals Carnegie Museum* 50 (1981):139–150.

26. T. D. Dillehay, J. Rossen, and P. Netherly, "The Nanchoc Tradition: The Beginnings of Andean Civilization," *American Scientist* 85 (1997):46–55; M. A. Malpass, "The Paiján Occupations of the Casma Valley, Perú," in *Investigations of Andean Past,* ed. D. Sandweiss (Ithaca: Cornell Latin American Studies Program, 1983), pp. 1–20.

27. E. Lanning, "Pleistocene Man in South America," *World Archaeology* 2 (1970):90–111.

28. C. Chauchat, "The Paiján Complex, Pampa de Cupisnique, Perú," *Nawpa Pacha* 17 (Perú: 1975), 143–146; "Replicating Ancient Artisan's Expertise," *Mammoth Trumpet* 10, no. 3 (1995):6–11; *Sitios Arqueológicos de la Zona de Cupisnique y Margen Derecha del Valle de Chicama* (Lima, Perú: Instituto Nacional de Cultura La Libertad-Instituto Francés de Estudios Andinos, 1998).

29. P. Ossa, "Paiján in Early Andean Prehistory: The Moche Valley, North Coast of Perú," in *Early Man in America from a Circum-Pacific Perspective*, ed. A. L. Bryan (Edmonton: Department of Anthropology, University of Alberta, 1978), pp. 290–295.

30. P. Ossa and M. Moseley, "La Cumbre: A Preliminary Report on Research into the Early Lithic Occupation of the Moche Valley, Perú," *Nawpa Pacha* (Perú: 1972), pp. 1–16.

31. C. Chauchat, "Replicating Ancient Artisan's Expertise," *Mammoth Trumpet* 10, no. 3 (1995):6–11.

32. J. Briceño Rosario, "La Tradición de Puntas de Proyectil 'Cola de Pescado' en Quebrada Santa María, y el Problema del Poblamiento Temprano en los Andes Centrales," *Revista Arqueológica "SIAN"* 4 (Trujillo, Perú: 1997), 2–6.

33. M. E. Moseley, *The Incas and Their Ancestors* (London: Thames and Hudson, 1992).

34. Lanning, "Pleistocene Man in South America."

35. D. H. Sandweiss, J. B. Richardson III, E. J. Hsu, and R. A. Feldman, "Early Maritime Adaptations in the Andes: Preliminary Studies at the Ring Site, Perú," in *Ecology, Settlement, and History in the Osmore Drainage, Perú*, pt. 1, BAR International Series, 545, ed. D. S. Rice, C. Stanish, and P. R. Scarr (London: 1989), pp. 35–84.

36. D. K. Keefer, S. D. deFrance, M. E. Moseley, J. B. Richardson III, D. R. Satterlee, and A. Day-Lewis, "Early Maritime Economy and El Niño Events at Quebrada Tacahuay, Perú," *Science* 281 (1998):1833–1835; D. H. Sandweiss, H. Melnis, R. L. Burger, A. Caño, B. Ojeda, R. Paredes, M. C. Sandweiss, and M. Glascock, "Quebrada Jaguay: Early South American Maritime Adaptations," *Science* 281 (1998):1830–1832.

37. A. Llagostera, "9,700 Years of Maritime Subsistence in the Pacific," *American Antiquity* 44 (1979):309–324; "Caza y Pesca Marítima (9.000 a 6.000 A.C.)," in *Culturas de Chile. Prehistoria: Desde los Orígenes Hasta los Albores de la*

Conquista, ed. J. Hidalgo, V. Schiappacasse, H. Niemeyer, C. Aldunate, and I. Solimano (Santiago, Chile: Editorial Andrés Bello, 1989), pp. 57–80.

38. L. Núñez, J. Varela, and R. Casamiquela, *Ocupación Paleoindio en Quereo: Reconstrucción Multidisciplinaria en el Territorio Semi-Arido de Chile (IV Región)* (Antofagasta, Chile: Imprenta Universitaria, Universidad del Norte, 1983).

39. J. Montané, "El Paleoindio en Chile," in *Actas del 41º Congreso Internacional de Americanistas,* Tomo III (México City, México: 1976), 492–503; L. Núñez, "Tágua-Tágua: Un sitio de matanza en el centro de Chile," paper presented at the First World Conference on Mongoloid Dispersion, University of Tokyo, Tokyo, Japan, 1994.

40. J. Montané, "El Paleoindio en Chile," in *Actas del 41º Congreso Internacional de Americanistas,* Tomo III (México City, México: 1976), 492–503; L. Núñez et al., "Cuenca de Tágua-Tágua en Chile: El Ambiente del Pleistoceno y ocupaciones humanas," *Revista Chilena de Historia Natural* 67, no. 4 (Santiago, Chile: 1994), 503–519.

41. Z. Seguel and O. Campaña, "Presencia de megafauna en la provincia de Osorno (Chile) y sus posibles relaciones con cazadores superiores," *Actas y Trabajos del I Congreso de Arqueología Argentina* (Rosario, Argentina: Museo Histórico Provincial, Dr. Julio Marcos, 1975), 242–273.

42. T. F. Lynch, "The Paleo-Indians," in *Ancient South Americans,* ed. J. D. Jennings (New York: W. H. Freeman and Company, 1983), pp. 87–137.

43. L. J. Jackson, "A Clovis Point from South Coastal Chile," *Current Research in the Pleistocene* 12 (1995):21–23.

44. T. D. Dillehay, *Monte Verde: A Late Pleistocene Settlement in Chile,* vol. 1, *Paleoenvironmental and Site Context* (Washington, D.C.: Smithsonian Institution Press, 1989).

45. T. D. Dillehay, *Monte Verde: A Late Pleistocene Settlement in Chile,* vol. 2, *The Archaeological Context* (Washington, D.C.: Smithsonian Institution Press, 1997).

46. G. Willey, *An Introduction to American Archaeology,* vol. 2, *South America* (Englewood Cliffs, N.J.: Prentice Hall, 1971).

47. T. F. Lynch, *Excavations at Quishqui Puncu in the Callejón de Huaylas, Perú,* Occasional Papers 26 (Pocatello: Idaho State University, 1970).

48. A. Cardich, "Recent Excavations at Lauricocha (Central Andes) and Los Toldos (Patagonia)," in *Early Man in America from a Circum-Pacific Perspective,* ed. A. L. Bryan (Edmonton: Department of Anthropology, University of Alberta, 1978), pp. 296–300.

49. T. F. Lynch, *Guitarrero Cave: Early Man in the Andes* (New York: Academic Press, 1980).

50. T. F. Lynch, "Chobshi Cave in Retrospect," *Andean Past* 2 (1998):1–32.

51. R. S. MacNeish, R. K. Vierra, A. Nelken-Turner, and C. J. Fagan, *Prehistory of the Ayacucho Basin, Perú*, vol. 3, *Nonceramic Artifacts* (Ann Arbor: University of Michigan Press, 1980).

52. T. D. Dillehay, "A Regional Perspective of Preceramic Times in the Central Andes," *Reviews in Anthropology* 12 (1985):193–205.

53. T. F. Lynch, "Preceramic Transhumance and the Process of Domestication," *American Antiquity* 36, no. 2 (1971):139–148.

54. J. W. Rick, *Prehistoric Hunters of the High Andes* (New York: Academic Press, 1980).

55. D. Lavalleé, M. Julien, J. Wheeler, and C. Karlin, *Telarmachay: Cazadores y Pastores de los Andes* (Lima, Perú: Instituto Francés de Estudios Andinos, 1995).

56. J. Wheller, E. Pires-Ferreira, and P. Kaulicke, "Preceramic Animal Utilization in the Central Peruvian Andes," *Science* 194 (1976):483–490.

57. R. Ravines, "Secuencia y cambios en los artefactos líticos del sur del Perú," *Revista del Museo Nacional* 38 (Lima, Perú: 1972), 133–184.

58. L. Núñez and C. Moragas, "Ocupación arcaica temprana en Tiliviche, norte de Chile (I Región)," *Boletín del Museo Arqueológico de La Serena* 16 (La Serena, Chile: 1977), 53–76.

59. A. Fernández Distel, *Las cuevas de Huachichocana, su posición dentro del Precerámico con agricultura incipiente del noroeste argentino* (Mainz, West Germany: Beitrage zur Allgemeinen und Vergleichenden Archaologie, Verlag Phillipp von Zabern, 1988).

60. C. Santoro, "Antiguos cazadores de la Puna (9.000 a 6.000 A.C.)," in *Culturas de Chile: Prehistoria: Desde sus Orígenes Hasta los Albores de la Conquista*, ed. J. Hidalgo (Santiago, Chile: Editorial Andrés Bello, 1989), pp. 33–55; L. Núñez, "Paleoindian and Archaic Cultural Periods in the Arid and Semi-arid Regions of Northern Chile," *Advances in World Archaeology* 2 (1983):161–203; L. Núñez, "Los Primeros Pobladores (20.000?–9.000 A.C.)," in *Culturas de Chile: Prehistoria: Desde los Orígenes Hasta los Albores de la Conquista*, ed. J. Hidalgo, V. Schiappacasse, H. Niemeyer, C. Aldunate, and I. Solimano (Santiago, Chile: Editorial Andrés Bello, 1989), pp. 13–32; L. Núñez, "Ocupación arcaica en la puna de Atacama: secuencia, movilidad y cambio," in *Prehistoria Sudamericana: Nuevas Per-*

spectivas, ed. B. Meggers (Washington, D.C.: Taraxacum, 1992), pp. 283–308; L. Núñez and T. D. Dillehay, *Movilidad giratoria, armonía social y desarrollo en los Andes meridionales* (Antofagasta, Chile: Universidad del Norte, Departamento de Arqueología, 1979); L. Núñez and C. Santoro, "Primeros poblamientos del cono sur de América (XII-IX Milenio A.P.)," *Revista Arqueología Americana* 1 (1990):92–139; L. Núñez, J. Varela, and R. Casamiquela, "Ocupación Paleoindia en el centro-norte de Chile: Adaptación circumlacustre en las tierras bajas," *Estudios Atacameños* 8 (Antofagasta, Chile: 1987), 142–185.

61. J. Arellano, "Primeras evidencias sobre el paleoindio en Bolivia," in *Investigaciones Paleoindias al Sur de la Línea Ecuatorial,* ed. L. Núñez and B. Meggers (Antofagasta, Chile: Estudios Atacameños, Número Especial, Universidad del Norte, 1987), pp. 186–197.

62. T. F. Lynch, "Harvest Time, Transhumance, and the Process of Domestication," *American Anthropologist* 75 (1973):254–259; R. S. MacNeish, T. C. Patterson, and D. L. Browman, *The Central Peruvian Prehistoric Interaction Sphere* (Andover, Mass.: Peabody Foundation of Anthropology, 1975).

63. D. Bovavia, *Los Camélidos Sudamericanos: Una Introducción a su Estudio* (Lima, Perú: Instituto Francés de Estudios Andinos, 1996).

Chapter 6

1. H. de Lumley, M. A. de Lumley, M. C. Beltrão, Y. Yokoyama, J. Labeyrie, J. Danon, G. Delibrias, C. Falguers, and J. Bischoff. "Decouverte d'outils taillès associes a des faunes du Pleistocene moyen dans la Toca da esperança, Etat de Bahía, Bresil." *C. R. Academe des Sciences de Paris* 306 (1988):307–317.

2. M. C. Beltrão, J.R.S. de Moura, W. S. Vasconcellos, and S.M.N. Neme, "Thermoluminescence Dating of Burnt Cherts from Alice Boër Site (Brazil)," in *New Evidence for the Pleistocene Peopling of the Americas,* ed. A. L. Bryan (Orono: Center for the Study of Early Man, University of Maine, 1986), pp. 203–214; N. Guidón, "Las Unidades Culturales de São Raimondo Nonato, Sudeste del Estado de Piaui, Brasil," in *New Evidence for the Pleistocene Peopling of the Americas,* ed. A. L. Bryan (Orono: Center for the Study of Early Man, University of Maine, 1986), p. 157; N. Guidón and G. Delibrias, "Carbon–14 Dates Point to Man in the Americas 32,000 Years Ago," *Nature* 321 (1986):769–771.

3. Guidón, "Las Unidades Culturales de São Raimondo Nonato, Sudeste del Estado de Piaui, Brasil."

4. R. Kipnis, "Early Hunter-Gatherers in the Americas: Perspectives from Central Brazil," *Antiquity* 72 (1998):581–592; P. I. Schmitz, "Prehistoric Hunters and Gatherers of Brazil," *Journal of World Prehistory* 1, no. 1 (1987):1–26.

5. A. C. Roosevelt, M. Lima da Costa, C. Machado, M. Michab, N. Mercier, H. Valldas, J. Feathers, W. Barnet, M. Imazio da Silveira, A. Henderson, J. Silva, B. Chernoff, D. Reese, J. Holman, N. Toth, and K. Shick, "Paleoindian Cave Dwellers in the Amazon: The Peopling of the Americas," *Science* 272 (1996):373–384.

6. Schmitz, "Prehistoric Hunters and Gatherers of Brazil"; P. I. Schmitz, "Caçadores antigos no sudoeste de Goiás, Brasil," in *Investigaciones Paleoindias al Sur de la Línea Ecuatorial*, ed. L. Núñez and B. Meggers (Antofagasta, Chile: Estudios Atacameños, Número Especial, Universidad del Norte, 1987), pp. 16–36.

7. Schmitz, "Prehistoric Hunters and Gatherers of Brazil"; A. Prous, "L'Archéologie au Brésil: 300 siècles d'occupation humaine," *L'Anthropologie* 90 (1996):257–306; A. Prous, "Os Mais Antigos Vestigios Arqueológicos no Brasil Central (Estados de Minas Gerais, Goiás and Bahía)," in *New Evidence for the Pleistocene Peopling of the Americas*, ed. A. L. Bryan (Orono: Center for the Study of Early Man, University of Maine, 1986), pp. 173–181; A. Prous, *Arqueologia Brasileira* (Brasilia, Brasil: Editorial UNB, 1991); A. Prous, "Santana do Riacho, Tomo II," *Archivos do Museu de Historia Natural* 13–14 (Belo Horizonte, Brazil: 1993), 3–440.

8. Schmitz, "Prehistoric Hunters and Gatherers of Brazil."

9. Prous, "L'Archéologie au Brésil: 300 siècles d'occupation humaine."

10. M. C. Beltrão et al., "Thermoluminescence Dating of Burnt Cherts from Alice Boër Site (Brazil)."

11. E. T. Miller, "Resultados preliminares das pesquisas arqueológicas paleo-indígenas no Río Grande do Sul, Brasil," *Actas del XLI Congreso Internacional de Americanistas* 3 (México City, México: 1976), 484–491; E. T. Miller, "Pesquisas Arqueológicas Paleoindígenas no Brasil Occidental," in *Investigaciones Paleoindias al Sur de la Línea Ecuatorial*, ed. L. Núñez and B. Meggers (Antofagasta, Chile: Estudios Atacameños, Número Especial, Universidad del Norte, 1987), pp. 37–61.

12. A. L. Bryan, "An Overview of Paleo-American Prehistory from a Circum-Pacific Perspective," in *Early Man in America from a Circum-Pacific Perspective*, ed.

A. L. Bryan (Edmonton: Department of Anthropology, University of Alberta, 1978), p. 1; "Paleoamerican Prehistory As Seen from South America," in *New Evidence for the Pleistocene Peopling of the Americas*, ed. A. L. Bryan (Orono: Center for the Study of Early Man, University of Maine, 1986), pp. 1–14.

13. M. Bombín and A. L. Bryan, "New Perspectives on Early Man in Southwestern Río Grande do Sul, Brazil," in *Early Man in America from a Circum-Pacific Perspective*, ed. A. L. Bryan (Edmonton: Department of Anthropology, University of Alberta, 1978), pp. 301–302; R. Gruhn and A. L. Bryan, "A Reappraisal of the Edge-Trimmed Tool Tradition," in *Explorations in American Archaeology: Essays in Honor of Wesley R. Hurt,* ed. M. G. Plew (Lanham, Md.: University Press of America, 1998), pp. 37–53.

14. A. V. Vialou and D. Vialou, "Les Premiers Peuplements Préhistoriques du Mato Grosso," *Bulletin de la Société Prehistorique Francaise* 91 (1994):257–261.

15. W. Hurt, "Recent Radiocarbon Dates for Central and Southern Brazil," *American Antiquity* 30, no. 1 (1964):25–33.

16. F. Fidalgo, L. M. Guzmán, G. Politis, M. Salemme, and E. Tonni, "Investigaciones arqueológicas en el Sitio 2 de Arroyo Seco (Pdo. de Tres Arroyos-Pcia. Buenos Aires-Argentina)," in *New Evidence for the Pleistocene Peopling of the Americas*, ed. A. L. Bryan (Orono: Center for the Study of Early Man, University of Maine, 1986), pp. 148–149; G. Politis, "¿Quien mató al Megaterio?," *Ciencia Hoy* 2 (Buenos Aires, Argentina: 1989), 26–35; "Revisão dos Sitios Pleistocenicos do Territorio Argentino," *Revista da Fundação Museu do Homem Americano* 1, no. 1 (São Paulo, Brazil: 1996), 1–64.

17. G. Politis, "Arqueología del Area Interserrana Bonaerense" (Ph.D. diss., Facultad de Ciencias Naturales y Museo, Universidad Nacional de la Plata, Buenos Aires, Argentina, 1984).

18. G. A. Martínez, "A Preliminary Report on Paso Otero 5, A Late-Pleistocene Site in the Pampean Region of Argentina," *Current Research in the Pleistocene* 14 (1997):53–54.

19. N. Flegenheimer, "Excavaciones en el sitio 3 de la localidad de Cerro La China (Provincia de Buenos Aires)," *Revista de la Sociedad Argentina de Antropología* 17, no. 1 (Buenos Aires, Argentina), 28–45; "Recent Research at Localities Cerro La China and Cerro El Sombrero, Argentina," *Current Research in the Pleistocene* 4 (1987):148–149; N. Flegenheimer and M. Zárate, "Considerations of Radiocarbon and Calibrated Dates from Cerro La China

and Cerro El Sombrero, Argentina," *Current Research in the Pleistocene* 14 (1997):27–28.

20. D. L. Mazzanti, "An Archaeological Sequence of Hunter-Gatherers in the Tandilia Range: Cueva Tixí, Buenos Aires, Argentina," *Antiquity* 70 (1996):450–452; D. L. Mazzanti, "Excavaciones Arqueologicas en el Sitio Cueva Tixí, Buenos Aires, Argentina," *Latin American Antiquity* 8, no. 1 (1997):55–62.

21. E. A. Crivelli, D. Curzio, and M. J. Silveira, "La estratigrafía de la Cueva de Trafúl 1 (Pcia. de Neuquén)," *Prehistoria* 1 (1993):9–160.

22. R. Ceballos, "El Sitio Cuyín Manzano," *Series y Documentos* 9 (Viedma, Argentina: Centro de Investigaciones Científicas de Río Negro, 1982), 1–66.

23. E. A. Crivelli, U. Pardinias, M. M. Fernandez, and M. Lezcano. "Cueva Epullán Grande (Pcia. del Neuquén). Informe de Avance," *Prehistorias* 2 (1996): 185–265.

24. J. Bird, "Antiquity and Migrations of the Early Inhabitants of Patagonia," *Geographical Review* 1, no. 6 (1938):250–275; "A Comparison of South Chilean and Ecuadorian 'Fishtail' Projectile Points," *Kroeber Anthropological Society Papers* 40 (1969):52–71; J. Hyslop, ed., *Travels and Archaeology in South Chile* (Iowa City: University of Iowa Press, 1988).

25. A. Cardich, "Las culturas Pleistocénicas y post-Pleistocénicas de los Toldos (Santa Cruz, Argentina)," in *Tomo Centenario del Museo de la Plata* (La Plata, Argentina: Museo Nacional de Historia Natural, 1977); "Arqueología de Los Toldos y El Ceibo (Provincia de Santa Cruz, Argentina)," in *Investigaciones Paleoindias al Sur de la Línea Ecuatorial,* ed. L. Núñez and B. Meggers (Antofagasta, Chile: Estudios Atacameños, Número Especial, Universidad del Norte, 1987), pp. 118–141; A. Cardich and A. Hajduk, "Secuencia arqueológica y cronología radiocarbónica de la cueva 3 de Los Toldos (Santa Cruz, Argentina)," *Relaciones de la Sociedad Argentina de Antropología* 7 (Buenos Aires, Argentina: 1973), 85–123; A. Cardich and N. Flegenheimer, "Descripción y tipología de las industria líticas más antiguas de Los Toldos," *Revista de la Sociedad Argentina de Antropología* 12 (Buenos Aires, Argentina: 1978), 225–242; A. Cardich, E. Mansur, M. Giesso, and V. Duran, "Arqueología de las Cuevas de 'El Ceibo,' Provincia de Santa Cruz, Argentina," *Relaciones de la Sociedad Argentina de Antropología* 14, no. 2 (Buenos Aires, Argentina: 1982), 173–209; A. Cardich and L. Miotti, "Recursos Faunísticos en la Economía de los Cazadores-Recolectores de Los Toldos (Provincia de Santa Cruz, Argentina),"

Relaciones de la Sociedad Argentina de Antropología 15 (Buenos Aires, Argentina: 1983), 145–157.

26. L. Miotti, "Paleoindian Occupation at Piedra Museo Locality, Santa Cruz Province, Argentina," *Current Research in the Pleistocene* 9 (1992), 27–30; L. Miotti and R. Cattaneo, "Bifacial/Unifacial Technology c. 13.000 Years Ago in Southern Patagonia," *Current Research in the Pleistocene* 14 (1997), 60–61; L. Miotti and M. Salemme, "Biodiversity, Taxonomic Richness and Specialists-Generalists During Late Pleistocene/Early Holocene Times in Pampa and Patagonia (Argentina, Southern South America)," *Quaternary International* 53/54 (1999):53–68.

27. M. Massone, "El poblamiento humano aborígen de Tierra del Fuego," in *Culturas Indígenas de la Patagonia* (Madrid, Spain: Biblioteca del V Centenario, Ediciones Cultura Hispánica, 1989), pp. 131–144; M. Massone et al., "Los Cazadores Tempranos y sus Fogatas: Una Nueva Historia para la Cueva de Tres Arroyos 1, Tierra del Fuego," *Boletín de la Sociedad Chilena de Arqueología* 26 (Santiago, Chile: 1997), 11–18; M. Massone, "Hombre Temprano y Paleoambiente en la Región de Magallanes: Evaluación Crítica y Perspectivas," *Anales del Instituto de la Patagonia* 24 (Punta Arenas, Chile: 1995), 81–98.

28. H. Nami, "Cueva del Medio: A Significant Paleoindian Site in Southern South America," *Current Research in the Pleistocene* 4 (1987):157–159; "Informe sobre la segunda y tercera expedición a la Cueva del Medio: Perspectivas arqueológicas para la Patagonia Austral," in *Anales del Instituto de la Patagonia* 17 (Punta Arenas, Chile: 1987), 71–105.

29. L. A. Borrero, "Problemas con la definición arqueológica de sistemas adaptativos," in *Arqueología de las Américas, 45º Congreso Internacional de Americanistas* (Bogotá, Colombia: Fondo de Promoción de la Cultura, Banco Popular, 1988), pp. 247–262.

30. G. M. Mengoni, "Patagonian Prehistory: Early Exploitation of Faunal Resources (13,500–8,500 B.P.)," in *New Evidence for the Pleistocene Peopling of the Americas*, ed. A. L. Bryan (Orono: Center for the Study of Early Man, University of Maine, 1986), pp. 271–280; G. M. Mengoni, "Extinción, colonización y estrategias adaptativas paleoindias en el extremo austral de Fuego-Patagonia," in *Precirculados de las ponencias científicas presentadas a los simposios del IX Congreso Nacional de Arqueología Argentina* (Buenos Aires, Argentina: 1988), pp. 119–129.

31. A. R. Prieto, "Late Quaternary Vegetational and Climatic Changes in the Pampa Grasslands of Argentina," *Quaternary Research* 45 (1996):73–88.

Chapter 7

1. T. D. Dillehay, G. Ardila, G. Politis, and M. C. Beltrão, "Earliest Hunters and Gatherers of South America," *Journal of World Prehistory* 6 (1992):145–204.

Chapter 8

1. T. D. Dillehay, "¿Donde están los restos óseos humanos del período pleistocénico tardío? Problemas y perspectivas en la búsqueda de los primeros Americanos," *Boletín de Arqueología de la PUCP* 1 (Lima, Perú: 1997), 55–64.

2. Terms such as Mongoloids and non-Mongoloids often have racial meanings, which is not the case here. Instead they are used to denote a particular school of thought about the migration of people from the Old to the New World.

3. R. E. Taylor, L. A. Payen, C. A. Prior, P. J. Stota Jr., R. Gillespie, J. A. Gowlett, R. E. Hedges, A. J. Hull, T. H. Zabel, D. J. Donahue, and R. Berger, "Major Revision in the Pleistocene Age Assignments for North American Human Skeletons by C–14 Accelerator Mass Spectometry: None Older than 11,000 C–14 Years Ago," *American Antiquity* 50 (1985):138–145.

4. T. D. Dillehay, "Introduction: Andean Mortuary Practices," in *Tombs for the Living: Andean Mortuary Practices*, ed. T. D. Dillehay (Washington, D.C.: Dumbarton Oakes Research Library and Collection, 1995), pp. 1–26.

5. J. F. O'Connell and J. Allen, "When Did Humans First Arrive in Greater Australia and Why It Is Important to Know?" *Evolutionary Anthropology* 6 (1998):132–146.

6. R. L. Kelly and L. C. Todd, "Coming into the Country: Early Paleoindian Hunting and Mobility," *American Antiquity* 53 (1988):231–244.

7. C. G. Turner II, "Relating Eurasian and Native American Populations Through Dental Morphology," in *Method and Theory for Investigating the Peopling of the Americas*, ed. R. Bonnichsen, G. Steele, and D. Gentry (Corvallis: Oregon State University, 1994), pp. 131–140.

8. R. Haydenbilt, "Dental Variation Among Four Prehispanic Mexican Populations," *American Journal of Physical Anthropology* 100 (1996):225–246; J. F. Powell, "Paleobiology of the First Americans," *Evolutionary Anthropology* 2 (1993):138–146; J. G. Lorenz and D. G. Smith, "Distributions of Four Founding mtDNA Haplogropus Among Native North Americans," *American Journal of Physical Anthropology* 101 (1996):307–324; D. A. Merriwhether, F. Roth-

hammer, and R. Ferrel, "Genetic Variation in the New World: Ancient Teeth, Bone, and Tissues As Sources of DNA," *Experientia* 50 (1994):592–601; D. A. Merriwhether, W. W. Hall, A. Vahine, and R. E. Ferrelf, "MtDNA Variation Indicates Mongolia May Have Been the Source of the Founding Population of the New World," *American Journal of Human Genetics* 59 (1996):204–212.

9. D. Munford, M. C. Zanini, and W. A. Neves, "Human Cranial Variation in South America: Implications for the Settlement of the New World," *Brazilian Journal of Genetics* 18 (1995):673–688; W. A. Neves, H. M. Puccarelli, and D. Meyer, "The Contribution of the Morphology of the Early South and North American Skeletal Remains to the Understanding of the Peopling of the Americas," *American Journal of Physical Anthropology* 16 (1993):150–151; W. A. Neves, Danusa Munford, and Maria do Carmo Zanini, "Cranial Morphological Variation and the Colonization of the New World: Towards a Four Migration Model," paper presented at the 65th annual meeting of the American Association of Physical Anthropologists, Durham, North Carolina, April 9–11, 1996; M. M. Lahr, *The Evolution of Modern Human Diversity: A Study of Cranial Variation* (London: Cambridge University Press, 1995).

10. C. L. Brace, "Biocultural Interaction and the Mechanism of Mosaic Evolution in the Emergence of 'Modern' Morphology," *American Anthropologist* 97, no. 4 (1995):7–11.

11. G. Steele and J. F. Powell, "Peopling of the Americas: Paleobiological Evidence," *Human Biology* 64 (1995):303–336; D. G. Steele and J. F. Powell, "Historical Review of the Skeletal Evidence for the Peopling of the Americas," paper presented at the Society for American Archaeology Conference, Seattle, Washington, 1998.

12. C. Chauchat, "Early Hunter-Gatherers on the Peruvian Coast," in *Peruvian Prehistory,* ed. R. Keatinge (Cambridge: Cambridge University Press, 1988), pp. 41–68.

13. T. A. Cockburn, "Infectious Disease in Ancient Populations," *Current Anthropology* 12 (1971):45–62.

14. J. M. Greenberg, C. G. Turner III, and S. L. Segura, "The Settlement of the Americas: Comparison of the Linguistic, Dental, and Genetic Evidence," *Current Anthropology* 27 (1986):477–497; R. L. Cann, "MtDNA and Native Americans: A Southern Perspective," *American Journal of Human Genetics* 55 (1994):256–258; S. D. Peña, "The Human Genome Diversity Project and the Peopling of the Americas," *Brazilian Journal of Genetics* 18, no. 4 (1995):641–643;

F. M. Salzano, "DNA, Proteins, and Human Diversity," *Brazilian Journal of Genetics* 18 (1995):661–668.

15. D. A. Merriwhether, F. Rothhammer, and R. Ferrel, "Genetic Variation in the New World: Ancient Teeth, Bone, and Tissues As Sources of DNA," *Experientia* 50 (1994):592–601; Merriwhether et al., "MtDNA Variation Indicates Mongolia May Have Been the Source of the Founding Population of the New World."

16. A. C. Stone and M. Stoneking, "mtDNA Analysis of a Prehistoric Oneota Population: Implications for the Peopling of the New World," *American Journal of Human Genetics* 62 (1998):1153–1170.

17. A. Torroni, J. V. Neel, R. Barrantes, T. G. Shurr, and D. C. Wallace, "Mitochondrial DNA 'Clock' for the Amerinds and Its Implications for Timing of Entry in North America," *Proceedings of the National Academy of Sciences* 91 (1994):1158–1162; A. Torroni, T. Shurr, M. Cabell, M. Brown, J. Neel, M. Larsen, D. Smith, C. Vullo, and C. Wallace, "Asian Affinities and Continental Radiations of Four Founding Native America mtDNAs," *American Journal of Human Genetics* 53 (1993):563–590.

18. C. Wallace, K. Garrison, and W. Knowler, "Dramatic Founder Effects in Amerindian Mitochondrial DNAs," *American Journal of Physical Anthropology* 68 (1985):149–155.

19. T. G. Schurr, S. W. Ballinger, Y. Y. Gan, J. A. Godge, D. A. Merriwhether, D. N. Lawrence, and W. C. Knowler, "Amerindian Mitochondrial DNAs Have Rare Asian Mutations at High Frequencies, Suggesting They Derived from Four Primary Maternal Lineages," *American Journal of Human Genetics* 55(1993):613–623; Torroni et al., "Asian Affinities and Continental Radiations of Four Founding Native America mtDNAs"; Torroni et al., "Mitochondrial DNA 'Clock' for the Amerinds and Its Implications for Timing of Entry in North America"; A. Torroni, R. I. Sukerik, T. G. Schurr, Y. B. Starikovskaya, M. F. Cabell, M. H. Crawford, A. G. Comuzzie, and D. C. Wallace, "mtDNA Variation of Aboriginal Siberians Reveals Distinct Genetic Affinities with Native Americans," *American Journal of Human Genetics* 53 (1993):591–608.

20. H. Ward, "Extensive Mitochondrial Diversity with a Single Amerindian Tribe," *Proceedings of the National Academy of Sciences* 88 (1991):8720–8724; R. H. Ward et al., "Genetic and Linguistic Variation in the Americas," *Proceedings of the National Academy of Sciences* 90 (1993):10,663–10,667.

21. Bianchi et al., "Peopling of the Americas As Inferred Through the Analysis of Mitochondrial DNA"; F. L. Black, "Reasons for Failure of Genetic

Classifications of South Amerinds Populations," *Human Biology* 63 (1991):763–774; S. Callegari-Jacques, F. Salzano, T. A. Weimer, M. H. Hutz, F. L. Black, S. E. Santos, J. F. Guerrero, M. A. Mestriner, and J. P. Pandey, "Further Blood Genetic Studies on Amazonian Diversity-Data from Four Indian Groups," *Annals of Human Biology* 21 (1994):465–481.

22. E. J. Szathmary, "mtDNA and Native Americans: A Southern Perspective," *American Journal of Genetics* 53 (1993):793–799.

23. F. Rothhammer, C. Silva, S. M. Callegari-Jacques, E. Llop, and F. M. Salzano, "Gradients of HLA Diversity in South American Indians," *Annals of Human Biology* 24, no. 3 (1997):197–208; M. P. Belich, F. Rothhammer, and N. O. Bianchi, "Origin and Distribution of B MtDNA Lineage in South America," *American Journal of Human Genetics* 56 (1995):1247–1248; F. Rothhammer and C. Silva, "Gene Geography of South America: Testing Models of Population Displacement Based on Archaeological Evidence," *American Journal of Physical Anthropology* 89 (1992):441–446.

24. E. A. Trachtenberg, H. A. Erlich, O. Rickards, G. F. DeStefano, and W. Klitz, "HLA Class II Linkage Disequilibrium and Haplotype Evolution in the Cayapa Indians of Ecuador," *American Journal of Human Genetics* 57 (1995):415–424.

25. W. H. Hildebrand, J. Zemour, R. C. Williams, R. Lux, M. L. Petzi Erier, and P. Parham, "Unusual HLA-B Alleles in Two Tribes of Brazilian Indians," *Nature* 357 (1992):326–328. F. E. Leon-S, Amparo Ariza-DeLeon, Adriana Ariza-DeLeon, "HLA, Trans-Pacific Contacts, and Retrovirus," *Human Immunology* 42 (1995):348; D. I. Watkins, S. MacAdams, X. Liu, C. Strang, E. Milford, D. Levine, T. Garber, A. Dogon, C. Lord, S. Ghim, G. Troup, A. Hughes, and N. Letvin, "New Recombinant HLA-B Alleles in a Tribe of South American Amerindians Indicate Rapid Evolution of MHC Class Loci," *Science* 357 (1992):329–333; M. A. Zago, E. J. Melo Santos, J. B. Clegg, J. F. Guerreiro, J. J. Martinson, J. Norwich, and M. S. Figuereido, "-Globin Gene Haplotypes in South American Indians," *Human Biology* 67 (1995):535–546.

26. K. Wright, "First Americans," *Discover* 20 (1998):52–63.

27. Szathmary, "mtDNA and Native Americans: A Southern Perspective."

28. Nichols, *Linguistic Diversity and the Peopling of the Americas.*

29. R. Gruhn, "The Pacific Coastal Route of Initial Entry: An Overview," in *Abstracts of the First World Summit Conference in the Peopling of the Americas*, ed. J. Tomenchuk and R. Bonnichsen (Corvallis: Center for the Study of the

First Americans, University of Maine, 1989), pp. 6–7; R. Gruhn, "The South American Context of the Pedra Pintada Site in Brazil," *Current Research in the Pleistocene* 14 (1997):29–30.

Chapter 9

1. L. A. Borrero, "Distribuciones Discontinuas de Puntas de Proyectil en Sudámerica," paper presented at the eleventh International Congress of Anthropological and Ethnological Sciences, Vancouver, Canada, 1983.

2. R. L. Kelly and L. C. Todd, "Coming Into the Country: Early Paleoindian Hunting and Mobility," *American Antiquity* 53 (1988):231–244.

3. D. Anderson, "Models of Paleoindian and Early Archaic Settlement," in *The Paleo-Indian and Early Archaic Southeast,* ed. D. Anderson and K. Sassaman (Tuscaloosa: University of Alabama Press, 1996), pp. 29–57.

4. J. Beaton, "Colonizing Continents: Some Problems from Australia and the Americas," in *The First Americans: Search and Research,* ed. T. D. Dillehay and D. Meltzer (Boca Raton, Florida: CRC Press, 1991), pp. 209–230.

5. C. Gamble, *The Palaeolithic Settlement of Europe* (New York: Cambridge University Press, 1986).

6. D. Pearsall, "Domestication and Agriculture in the New World Tropics," in *Last Hunters, First Farmers,* ed. D. Price and B. Gebauer (Santa Fe: School of American Research, 1995), pp. 157–192; J. Quilter, "Late Preceramic Perú," *Journal of World Prehistory* 5, no. 4 (1991):387–435.

Chapter 10

1. J. Speth, "Early Hominid Subsistence Strategies in Seasonal Habitats," *Journal of Archaeological Science* 14 (1987):13–29.

2. C. Gamble, *The Palaeolithic Settlement of Europe* (New York: Cambridge University Press, 1986).

3. R. Whallon, "Elements of Cultural Change in the Later Palaeolithic," in *The Human Revolution: Behavioral and Biological Perspectives on the Origins of Modern Humans,* ed. P. Mellars and C. Stringen (Princeton: Princeton University Press, 1989), pp. 433–454, esp. p. 439.

4. S. Mithen, *Thoughtful Foragers: A Study of Prehistoric Decision-Making* (Cambridge: Cambridge University Press, 1990); "Simulating Mammoth

Hunting Extinction: Implications for the Late Pleistocene of the Central Russian Plain," in *Hunting and Animal Exploitation in the Later Palaeolithic and Mesolithic Eurasia,* ed. G. L. Peterkin, H. M. Bricker, and P. Mellars, pp. 162–178 (Washington, D.C.: Anthropological Papers of the American Anthropological Association, no. 4, 1993).

Chapter 11

1. D. Meltzer, " Why Don't We Know When the First People Came to the New World?," *American Antiquity* 54 (1989):471–490.

2. Juliet Morrow and Toby Morrow, "Geographic Variation in Fluted Projectile Points: A Hemisphere Perspective," *American Antiquity* 64 (1999): 215–230.

3. K. Tankersley, "Variation in the Early Paleoindian Economies of Late Pleistocene Eastern North America," *American Antiquity* 63 (1998):7–20.

4. B. Fagan, *People of the Earth* (Boston: Little Brown and Co., 1992).

5. D. Pearsall, "Domestication and Agriculture in the New World Tropics," in *Last Hunters, First Farmers,* ed. D. Price and B. Gebauer (Santa Fe: School of American Research, 1995), pp. 157–192; J. Quilter, "Late Preceramic Perú," *Journal of World Prehistory* 5, no. 4 (1991):387–438.

6. C. Petit, "Rediscovering America," *U.S. News and World Report* 125, no. 14 (1998):56–64; K. Wright, "First Americans," *Discover* 20:52–63.

7. Tessie Naranjo, "Thoughts on Migration by Santa Clara Pueblo," *Journal of Anthropological Archaeology* 14 (1995):247–250.

Appendix

1. T. Dillehay, "Informe Técnico de la Campaña de 1992 en el Valle de Zaña, Perú" (Lima, Perú: Instituto Nacional de Cultura, 1992).

2. T. Dillehay and A. Gordon, "Investigación Arqueológica en el valle del Río Bueno, Chile" (Valdivia: Manuscript on file in the Universidad Austral de Chile, 1989).

INDEX